China's Rise
and the Two Koreas

China's Rise
and the
Two Koreas

Politics, Economics, Security

Scott Snyder

LYNNE
RIENNER
PUBLISHERS

BOULDER
LONDON

Published in the United States of America in 2009 by
Lynne Rienner Publishers, Inc.
1800 30th Street, Boulder, Colorado 80301
www.rienner.com

and in the United Kingdom by
Lynne Rienner Publishers, Inc.
3 Henrietta Street, Covent Garden, London WC2E 8LU

Library of Congress Cataloging-in-Publication Data
Snyder, Scott, 1964–
  China's rise and the two Koreas : politics, economics, security / Scott
Snyder.
    p. cm.
  Includes bibliographical references and index.
  ISBN 978-1-58826-618-7 (hardcover : alk. paper)
  ISBN 978-1-58826-622-4 (pbk. : alk. paper)
  1. China—Foreign relations—Korea (South) 2. Korea (South)—Foreign
relations—China. 3. China—Foreign relations—Korea (North) 4. Korea
(North)—Foreign relations—China. 5. China—Foreign relations—1949–
I. Title.
  DS740.5.K6S63 2009
  327.510519—dc22
                                        2008033733

British Cataloguing in Publication Data
A Cataloguing in Publication record for this book
is available from the British Library.

Printed and bound in the United States of America

   The paper used in this publication meets the requirements
of the American National Standard for Permanence of
Paper for Printed Library Materials Z39.48-1992.

5   4   3   2   1

Contents

List of Tables and Figures   vii

Preface   ix

1 Introduction   1

2 China's Shift to a Two-Koreas Policy   23

3 The Transformation of Sino–South Korean
Economic Relations   47

4 Emerging Political Challenges in the Sino–
South Korean Relationship   83

5 China's Evolving Economic and Political Relations
with North Korea   109

6 China's Strategic Policy Dilemmas and the Future
of North Korea   137

7 The China–South Korea–United States Security Triangle   163

8 The Korean Peninsula and Sino-Japanese Rivalry   183

9 The New Sino-Korean Economic Relationship:
Implications for Northeast Asian Security   199

Appendix A: China–North Korea High-Level Bureaucratic
Meetings, 1992–2006 — 215
Appendix B: China–South Korea High-Level Bureaucratic
Meetings, 1992–2006 — 219

Bibliography — 225
Index — 229
About the Book — 241

Tables and Figures

Tables

2.1 China's Trade with North and South Korea, 1981–2005   41
3.1 Sino–South Korean Trade, 1991–2006   49
3.2 South Korea's Foreign Direct Investment in China, 1992–2006   50
3.3 South Korea's Investment in China, 1992–2006   52
3.4 United States–South Korea, United States–China, and
     South Korea–China Trade Balances, 1988–2000   53
3.5 China's Foreign Direct Investment in South Korea, 1988–2007   60
5.1 North Korea's Gross National Product, 1995–2006   111
5.2 China's Trade with North Korea vs. Inter-Korean Trade,
     1993–2006   112
5.3 China's Petroleum and Grain Exports to North Korea,
     1990–2005   115

Figures

4.1 North and South Korean High-Level Interactions with China,
     1992–2005   87
5.1 China–North Korea High-Level Visits and Exports,
     1992–2005   131

Preface

This project began while I was a program officer at the US Institute of Peace. A 1997 research trip to China's northeastern provinces to investigate reports of the crisis that accompanied North Korea's famine intensified my interest in the complicated nature of China's diplomatic and political interactions with North Korea. The following year, the Asia Pacific Center for Security Studies hosted a conference on the future of the Korean peninsula that included many of the people I met during that trip.

During that conference, a South Korean participant asserted that if South Korea were to develop a stronger economic and trade relationship with China than with the United States there would be spillover effects on South Korea's political relations. Thus, the growth of the Sino–South Korean economic relationship would inevitably have political and security ramifications for South Korea that could lead to the end of the US–South Korean alliance. Likewise, the assertion implied that China should have no trouble working its will in Pyongyang, despite North Korea's apparent defiance of Chinese crisis-management efforts. That response stuck with me and informed the central hypothesis of this study. When China became South Korea's leading trade and investment partner in 2004 and 2006, respectively, I recalled the 1998 conference and determined to investigate more deeply the interrelationship of economic interdependence and political leverage.

My interest in the development and implications of Sino-Korean relations has also been enhanced through several professional opportunities. First, the Pacific Forum Center for Strategic and International

Studies (CSIS) invited me to write a quarterly analysis of developments in Sino-Korean relations for the e-journal *Comparative Connections,* a task I have been performing for almost a decade, which has forced me to remain current on developments in the relationship.

Second, during my time as the Asia Foundation's Korea representative based in Seoul, I was able to support exchange and training projects involving North Korean legal specialists, which were held in China. During this time I traveled through Beijing and maintained contact with Chinese specialists on North Korea. I also had the good fortune to visit Yanji and Rajin-Sonbong at least once a year, where I gained a firsthand appreciation of local views of the interaction across the Sino–North Korean border.

Third, following my return to Washington, DC, in 2004, I benefited from participation in a collaboration between the US Institute of Peace and CSIS to further analyze Chinese views of developments in North Korea and the implications for enhanced cooperation between the United States and China.

Each of these professional opportunities provided invaluable preparation for undertaking this research effort, which would not have been possible without the generous support and encouragement of Al Song and Marin Strmecki at the Smith Richardson Foundation. I owe a further debt of gratitude to my colleagues at the Asia Foundation—Doug Bereuter, Barnett Baron, Nancy Yuan, John Brandon, Gordon Hein, and others—who enabled me to focus on this project full-time and allowed me to fully honor the spirit and letter of my commitment to this study.

Shin Gi-wook was gracious in offering me both an intellectually stimulating and a quiet environment in which to develop the ideas and structure for the key chapters and concepts of the book as a Pantech Fellow at Stanford University's Shorenstein Asia-Pacific Research Center during 2005 to 2006. My stay at Stanford coincided with the visiting appointments of Daniel Sneider and David C. Kang, who provided a great deal of moral and intellectual support for the development of the book.

I have benefited from the willingness of many professional colleagues to take the time to provide critical evaluations of various chapters, including Alan D. Romberg, Katy Oh, Ralph Hassig, Joe Winder, L. Gordon Flake, Peter Beck, Abraham Kim, Leif-Eric Easley, Brad Glosserman, Bonnie Glaser, Toby Dalton, and David C. Kang. In addition, I had the opportunity to present individual chapters and main concepts that informed the study to several roundtables hosted by the Asia Foundation in Washington, DC, as well as presentations hosted by the

Shorenstein Asia-Pacific Research Center at Stanford University and by the Korea office of the Asia Foundation in Seoul.

I owe Ed Reed, Moon Chunsang, Lee Kyungsook, Lee Hyunjung, Lim Eunyoung, and Cho Soyoung in the Asia Foundation's Korea office special thanks for being such excellent colleagues and for allowing me to call on them from time to time after I returned to Washington, DC. I greatly appreciate their help. Claire Bai provided invaluable research assistance for interviews in Beijing, and John Stinner's painstaking efforts produced the tables contained in the book. I also want to acknowledge Nancy Yuan, John Brandon, Hope Stewart, Yvonne Day, See-Won Byun, and Lee Lefkowitz in the Asia Foundation's office in Washington, DC, for their support and assistance.

The professional staff at Lynne Rienner Publishers has been encouraging and easy to work with. I thank Marilyn Grobschmidt, Jason Cook, Shena Redmond, and Lynne Rienner, as well as two anonymous reviewers, for their efforts and constructive criticisms at various points along the way.

Finally, my parents, Buck and Carol Snyder, and my in-laws, Sangseol Lee and Kye-hak Pyo, have provided constant encouragement to me. But my wife, SoRhym, had to live with the project. On September 20, 2008, we welcomed our daughter, Elliana Soleil. It is to them that this book is dedicated.

—*Scott Snyder*

1
Introduction

China's unprecedented economic growth is paving the way for an expansion of political influence with its neighbors in East Asia, so much so that China's economic rise has potentially profound implications for the balance of power on the Korean peninsula and in Northeast Asia. With the end of the Cold War, economic interdependence replaced ideology as a defining factor in East Asian relations, facilitating China's expanded economic relations throughout Asia and opening new economic and political opportunities between South Korea and China. These opportunities came at the expense of North Korea, as Chinese leaders gradually found that mutual economic interests with South Korea outweighed long-standing ideological and personal ties with North Korea.

South Korea's strong-state, export-led development experience successfully propelled a process of industrialization and modernization surpassed only by the pace of economic and social transformation of China's modernization, for which South Korea's own development path provided an early model. Potential benefits from economic cooperation between China and South Korea became irresistible while China's ties with North Korea stagnated, leading eventually to Sino–South Korean diplomatic normalization in 1992 despite objections from North Korea's top leaders, who saw normalization with South Korea as a betrayal. The normalization of China–South Korea relations laid the foundation for the realization of an economic and political relationship that has grown beyond anyone's wildest expectations, creating new opportunities, challenges, and dilemmas for China in its management of relations with the two Koreas.

While the Sino–South Korean relationship has flourished, China has continued to maintain ties with North Korea, although North Korea's simultaneous dependence on and defiance of China is increasingly viewed in Beijing more as a burden than as a benefit. North Korea and China had once been bound together by strong ideological, personal, social, and psychological bonds, but now have little in common except geography. North Korean leaders have viewed China's adoption of economic reforms and growing ties with South Korea as a betrayal of socialist ideals and of the traditional Sino–North Korean relationship. Therefore, North Korea has become simultaneously alienated from China even as it becomes increasingly dependent on China to meet its most critical economic needs. The unprecedented growth of Sino–South Korean economic relations, combined with the economic dependency on China of an economically failed but nuclear-capable North Korea, raises challenging questions about possible changes in the dynamics of East Asian political and security relations. These changes might also have important implications for the future of South Korea's alliance with the United States.

In the late 1980s, China's economic influence on South Korea was negligible. South Koreans were highly wary of China's long-standing political relationship with North Korea. However, the level of bilateral trade has grown significantly between the two countries, from US$6.4 billion at the time of Sino–South Korean diplomatic normalization in 1992 to over US$145 billion in 2007, an increase of more than twentyfold.[1] Both countries are projecting that the bilateral trade volume will surpass US$200 billion by 2010. Since 2004, China has been South Korea's largest trading partner and the largest destination for South Korean foreign direct investment and tourism. In 2006, over 3.9 million South Korean tourists (nearly 10 percent of South Korea's total population) visited China, and almost 1 million Chinese visitors came to South Korea. The 57,000 South Korean students in China during 2006 were the largest group of foreign students attending Chinese universities at that time, representing one-third of all foreign students in China.[2] China has been an attractive tourist destination for South Koreans and a place that may seem oddly recognizable and yet new to many of them, both from the perspective of shared culture and, for South Korean businesspeople, as an environment in which prior experience with government-business relations under strong-state authoritarianism may be familiar. Many South Koreans believe their economic future depends on the development of the Sino–South Korean relationship.

The rise of China as an economic partner has coincided with the emergence of a debate in South Korea over implications of China's rise for the US–South Korean security alliance. This debate, buoyed by

South Korean nationalist sentiment, has centered on whether South Korea can shed its security dependence on the United States in order to assert itself as an autonomous actor capable of laying the foundations for regional cooperation among the great powers in Northeast Asia.[3] Critics of this position assert that, despite South Korea's growth as an economic power, it is still geographically surrounded by larger powers, a position that will inevitably require it to tilt toward a strong ally versus neutrality, and that South Korea's best option is to assert its own interests on the basis of a strong alliance with a global power that is geographically distant from the peninsula.[4]

As China's development proceeds, economic factors have the potential to influence political and security relations in ways that may reshape the regional security environment. The influence of China's economic rise on regional political and security relations has already affected regional views of third-party roles in the event of a cross-strait conflict: Australia, a close ally of the United States, is sufficiently tied to China economically that top leaders have distanced themselves from more aggressive US public statements regarding how Australia would respond to rising cross-strait tensions, despite strong US-Australian security ties.[5] Likewise, one of the key issues of debate in the US–South Korean alliance is the question of "strategic flexibility," which for South Koreans has revolved primarily around the question of whether a US intervention in the event of a military conflict involving Taiwan would bring with it political or economic costs for South Korea.[6]

Developments connected to China's rise are clearly influencing US security policy in Asia. Much attention has been given to US "hedging" against China's rise,[7] including the strengthening of the US-Japanese alliance, the significance of the US "defense transformation" as a vehicle to counter the possible rise of China as a "peer competitor" of the United States,[8] the development of a new strategic relationship between the United States and India, and US attempts to strengthen security ties with countries such as Singapore, the Philippines, Malaysia, Indonesia, and Vietnam.[9] China is responding to these developments not only by strengthening its military capacity, but also, and more importantly for this study, by attempting to utilize the newfound economic and financial instruments now at its disposal to underwrite a stable regional order favorable to Chinese interests. One result is that Asians now trade with each other more than they trade with the rest of the world, a factor that appears to promote regional stability and that may illustrate China's growing political influence in East Asia.[10] But to what extent is it possible for a state to utilize economic tools as leverage to achieve political or strategic aims in the development of new political relations or to shape its own political and security environment? Is it possible for China to utilize South Korea's economic dependency as a tool for influencing the latter's political choices? Is South Korea politically constrained by its economic relationship with China in ways that in turn constrain alliance cooperation? Does the United States have tools to counter such a situation if indeed it were to develop?

In this book I examine the development and management of China's political and economic relations with both North and South Korea over the course of the period since China's normalization with Seoul in August 1992, with special reference to the interplay between economic interdependence and political influence. My primary argument is that China's attempts to utilize economic instruments as political leverage to induce specific desired outcomes in its relations with the two Koreas have generally not been successful; neither has the increasing economic dependency of North or South Korea on China been "transformative" in changing the nature or strategic preferences of either Korea more to China's liking. The transformation of the Sino–South Korean economic relationship has contributed to improved bilateral political relations, while North Korea has simultaneously become both economically dependent on and politically alienated from China. South Korea's foreign policy has been influenced by closer economic relations with China, but not to the extent that Seoul is likely to pursue strategic realignment with Beijing or willingly forego the security benefits of the alliance with the United States. However, the United States should be cognizant of the fact that China's economic rise has boosted China's influence on the Korean peninsula in ways that promote incipient competition to shape the future foreign policy orientation of the peninsula.

From "Security Externalities" to "Economic Interdependence"

An understanding of the influence of increased economic interdependence on the extent of political influence between states should assist in understanding a significant feature of international relations in the post–Cold War era. During the Cold War, economic and security benefits flowed in the same direction within political blocs, and trade between adversaries was low. A theoretical literature developed during the Cold War around the premise that preferences in political relations and "security externalities" are likely to shape and reinforce trade relationships among allies while dampening trade relationships with potential adversaries.[11] But trade and investment patterns since the end of the Cold War have developed with few political constraints, enabling broadened economic opportunities for doing business with former enemies. As a result, new and mutually beneficial economic relationships developed with little consideration for security implications or pursuit of relative gains.

Joanne Gowa and Edward Mansfield argue that "free trade is more likely within, rather than across, political-military alliances, and alliances are more likely to evolve into free-trade coalitions if they are embedded in bipolar systems than in multi-polar systems."[12] China's emergence as South Korea's leading trade partner (surpassing the United States) reinforces questions about the durability of the US–South Korean alliance, a question that is also reinforced by theoretical findings from alliance theory. For instance, a study by Brett Ashley Leeds and Burcu Savun finds that alliances are usually terminated "when one or more members experience changes that affect the value of the alliance, for instance a change in international power, a change in domestic political institutions, or the formation of a new outside alliance."[13] Given the centripetal pull of China's economic growth, some scholars predict that the formation of a new outside alliance between China and South Korea is only a matter of time.[14] According to this argument, high levels of economic interdependence might be seen as either a prior condition or a rationale for pursuing a security alliance with another state, or it could be an effect derived from the preexisting condition of alliance relations built around political and security concerns.

There are few examples of countries that have successfully maintained a security alliance with one party (i.e., South Korea's alliance with the United States) while relying on a third party (whether or not the third party is deemed a potential adversary, i.e., China) for economic prosperity. Since the end of the Cold War, the previous tight relationship between security and economic partnerships has broken down as global economic integration has developed without special regard for security partnerships, and with little thought for the possibility that today's trading partner could be tomorrow's enemy. The situation today is the opposite of the situation that existed during the Cold War, when South Korea depended on the United States for both security benefits and market access as a precondition for export-led industrialization. South Korea's increasing dependence on China for trade while relying on security guarantees from the United States has had little apparent effect to date, but it is not clear whether such a situation is sustainable or whether there may be future circumstances that would eventually require South Korea to make a choice between the economic benefits that flow from China and the security benefits that flow from the United States.

Traditionally, the orientation of the Korean peninsula has been a matter of importance in the context of historical rivalries among Asian powers; North and South Korea's strategic choices may be an important indicator of how East Asian relations may reorder themselves in the context of China's current economic and political rise. At the end of the nineteenth century, China, Japan, and Russia all sought a foothold on the Korean peninsula as the vehicle for pursuing their broader regional security interests. Prior to the end of the nineteenth century, the Korean peninsula was firmly tied to Beijing as part of a political order in which China's leadership exercised tremendous influence on the conduct of security and foreign affairs related to Korea, in return for Korean obeisance to China's leadership. This state of affairs was reflected in the regular tribute missions that Korea's king sent to the Chinese emperor, a form of obeisance that reflected China's dominant political, cultural, and socioeconomic role vis-à-vis the Korean kingdom. By the late nineteenth century, this traditional China-centered order began to break down in the context of the weakening of Qing China, the slow decline of the Korean Chosun dynasty, and the rise of Japanese influence on the Korean peninsula in the context of the Meiji Restoration.

Since dynastic Korea was weak and vulnerable, the Korean peninsula became a battleground among contending major powers during the Sino-Japanese war (1894–1895) and the Russo-Japanese war (1904–1905), the settlement of which left Korea at the mercy of Japan through the Treaty of Portsmouth and the Taft-Katsura Memorandum. Given the resurgence of conflict between China and Japan in a distinctly postcolonial era, a more economically powerful South Korea logically should have some diplomatic tools at its disposal to reduce the likelihood that the Korean peninsula could be caught up in renewed Sino-Japanese rivalry. But how South Korea might use those tools and whether or not South Korean diplomats are able to put together a successful diplomatic strategy to avert being caught up in renewed regional tensions remain to be seen. Thus it is reasonable to consider the impact of Korea's increasing economic interdependence with China on the future of regional relations in Asia.

China's Economic Reforms, Globalization, and Impact on Foreign Policy

China's integration with the global economy has stimulated new perspectives on international relations among Chinese specialists, derived from their own experience with almost three decades of economic development. China's ability to utilize interdependence and globalization to support economic development has become the basis for maintaining its prosperity and growth. China's expanded trade and investment ties with its neighbors may also carry strategic benefits, to the extent that its near neighbors become economically dependent on China as an engine for continued economic growth as the best way to ensure their own prosperity.

Chinese officials and scholars alike appear to hold to views that economic interdependence—or inducing economic dependency—is an important strategic tool that China can use to its advantage in pursuit of its national interests. One of China's foremost strategic thinkers, Renmin University scholar Shi Yinhong, observes that, "in the basic trends of the world in the 21st century, what is the most important is, of course, globalization that has led to the rapid growth of China's national strength; what is the second most important is world multipolarization which the rapid growth of China's national strength has promoted."[15]

Many in China presume that one result of its rise is that enhanced economic interdependence will serve as a centripetal force, drawing regional actors into a relationship of greater dependence on China. Globalization, if effectively manipulated to China's own strategic ends, will not only be useful in preserving peace on China's periphery, but will also be an important factor in drawing those states into a relationship of economic and political dependence on China, limiting the alternatives of China's near neighbors and raising the price of cooperation with forces that may be perceived as hostile to China's interests. China's expanding economic relations with neighboring countries—both through trade patterns with developing states and through development assistance to forestall instability in weak or failing states—may provide important new leverage for enhancing China's security, for expanding its role as an indispensable regional power, and for shaping the regional environment in ways that reduce the possibility of threats from hostile states or other rising powers. The Asian financial crisis of the late 1990s apparently marked a key turning point in China's perspective on globalization—and by extension marked a dramatic shift in China's willingness to participate in and promote multilateral cooperation on economic as well as political and security issues. China has consciously decided to embrace globalization as a force that can be utilized to its benefit in order to harness political and security benefits derived from its enhanced economic interdependence with its neighbors.

China's view of globalization—amplified by the dramatic changes derived from its own rapid economic development—has been in line with the classic liberal view that economic interdependence can reduce the likelihood of conflict and great power confrontation. As stated by Wang Guangya, China's ambassador to the United Nations: "As mankind ushers in the 21st century, rapid economic globalization and political multi-polarization have increased the interdependence of countries to an unprecedented degree. In this new era, peace will make winners of us all and conflicts will make all of us losers. The traditional pattern of clashes triggered by the rise of a large power is bound to give way to peaceful coexistence. In its push for development, China will not and cannot retread that 'zero-sum' path traditionally taken by powers on the rise. Our only option is peaceful development in which all countries are winners."[16] These views represent the core assumptions behind the theory of China's "peaceful rise."[17]

China's thinking on globalization seeks to effectively take advantage of perceived new realities resulting from enhanced economic interdependence to achieve its own political and strategic ends. Thus, China's dominantly liberal views of the consequences of economic interdependence also have a realist component: economic globalization and economic interdependence could be used as strategic tools for constraining a US superpower in a web of multilateral ties. China has consciously attempted to exploit globalization as a way of enhancing its stature and regional posture, as a vehicle by which to dampen fears associated with its rapid economic growth, and as a vehicle for "democratizing" US hegemony by promoting multipolarization and by pursuing its own "new security concept" through active participation in a wide range of multilateral forums as well as through its role in establishing the Shanghai Cooperation Organization. As stated by Shen Jiru of the Chinese Academy of Social Sciences, "the advance of economic globalization means that the interests of different countries are interwoven ever more closely, and this has become a powerful material force constraining U.S. hegemonism."[18] According to Yong Deng and Thomas Moore, "China's new foreign policy choice highlights the potential role of globalization in transforming great-power politics from the unmitigated struggle for supremacy of earlier eras to a more cooperative form of interstate competition that increases prospects for China's peaceful rise."[19]

China's acceptance of economic interdependence naturally makes regional stability a prerequisite for the pursuit of economic development. This preoccupation means that China must also take steps to ensure that its border areas remain stable. To the extent that this has led China to resolve myriad border disputes with its neighbors, its expanded focus on regional stability has been a positive development for East Asia, but the necessity of regional stability also calls into question the hallmark principles that China has traditionally elevated as guideposts of its foreign policy: the importance of peaceful coexistence, nonintervention, and mutual respect for national sovereignty.

For instance, China's natural resource needs along with its extensive capital reserves have made it possible for Beijing to pursue an overseas development strategy that utilizes capital investment to secure supply relationships. The availability of these economic tools also provides China with a greater ability to shape its own security environment—for instance, by forestalling the instability that might derive from the consequences of economic failure of weak states on China's periphery. China has done this through increased overseas assistance to Myanmar, Laos, and, most importantly for the purposes of this study, North Korea.[20]

Despite a transition in China's characterization of its relationship with North Korea from "special" to "normal," the latter's strategic location as a neighboring state on China's border ensures that it will continue to receive Chinese "strategic" economic assistance. China, previously a recipient of international assistance, emerged in 2005 as the world's third largest food donor, behind the United States and the European Union.[21] The largest share of that assistance went to North Korea to prevent a renewed food crisis that would have direct ramifications for stability in China's northeast. Such assistance dampens the possibility of renewed refugee flows similar to those that occurred at the height of the North Korean famine of the mid-1990s. Although the precise value of Beijing's overseas development assistance has been classified as a state secret, anecdotal evidence from Chinese scholars suggests that China's support to North Korea has risen in recent years from one-third to two-fifths of China's development budget at a time when China's overall spending on overseas development assistance is surely expanding to support its overseas interests and commitments in Africa and Latin America.[22]

The Debate over Economic Interdependence and the Political Impact of China's Rise

Various international relations theories provide partial insights into the relationship between economic interdependence and political influence in Sino-Korean relations, but an in-depth examination shows that such theories are inadequate to fully explain the nuances of these relations.

Realist scholars have warned of the destabilizing effects that might accompany a power transition in Asia, emphasizing that China's neighbors will balance against China's rise. According to this view, economic interdependence is likely to increase prospects for military conflict as each state pursues relationships on the basis of its desire to expand its own power at the expense of the other's. The fundamental consideration for states is the political question of how to survive and strengthen state power, and economic policy is simply an instrument for achieving the objective of enhancing state power. John Mearsheimer argues that "states that depend on others for critical economic supplies will fear cutoff or blackmail in a time of crisis or war."[23] Trade dependence is a critical concern, since the party that is less dependent on trade for its own economic growth or political standing would presumably be more willing to sacrifice the economic relationship and pursue military means by which to expand its power. On this basis, Richard Betts asks, "Should we want China to get rich or not? For realists, the answer should be no, since a rich China would overturn any balance of power."[24] According to this logic, South Korea should impose measures to restrain growth in bilateral trade and limit investment in China for fear of the strategic consequences of becoming subordinate to China's growing economic power.

On the other hand, neoliberal institutionalists argue that open markets and heightened economic exchanges will decrease the likelihood of interstate conflict. Enhanced economic interdependence through increasing trade and investment ties will mitigate the likelihood that political conflicts will result in war, because the cost of conflict would be too high compared to the "win-win" benefits of economic interdependence.[25] Additional literature from international political economy emphasizes the development of cross-border markets, and the accompanying development of "internationalist" political constituencies that stand to benefit from economic interdependence as forces that will create a mutually reinforcing economic dependence. The benefits derived from such interactions will strengthen internally based reform constituencies that will be able to win the domestic political debate over nationalist or other aggressive forces that are inclined to pursue conflict as a means by which to settle disputes.[26]

A liberal approach in the context of Sino–South Korean relations emphasizes the idea that increasing economic interdependence between China and South Korea will lessen the likelihood of Sino–South Korean conflict, ostensibly depriving the US–South Korean security alliance of a broader raison d'être beyond deterrence of North Korea in the event that peace is achieved on the Korean peninsula. Instead, China-centered economic interdependence would be sufficient to keep the peace in Asia and would undergird multilateral security and political cooperation, obviating the need for bilateral alliances in Asia. The US military would be obliged to leave the Korean peninsula, providing greater scope for China to expand its political as well as economic influence there. A growing number of proponents of this view in both China and South Korea are focused on how to put into place the architecture for multilateral security cooperation.[27] When fully developed, such cooperation could arguably obviate the need for an alliance with the United States. From this perspective, the US alliance system artificially and unnecessarily serves to exaggerate the regional role and influence of the United States, and inhibits forms of cooperation and community building that would otherwise come naturally on the Korean peninsula and in Northeast Asia.

Dale Copeland's "theory of trade expectations" provides insights consistent with the developments in China's relations with the two Koreas thus far. Copeland analyzes that perceived prospects for future trade as expanding or diminishing constitute a critical variable in understanding the impact of economic interdependence on the likelihood of political conflict or cooperation. Copeland's argument is that high economic interdependence will promote peaceful cooperation as long as states maintain positive expectations for future trade, but that if states have negative expectations for future trade, a highly dependent state may see conflict as a viable alternative to a peaceful situation where the benefits derived from trade continue to diminish.[28]

But Brian Pollins's work affirms that trade relations are stronger between countries that have good political relations with each other, in other words that "trade follows the flag."[29] This finding would tend to support a realist view of the relationship between trade and conflict, in opposition to a view that trade would be the determining factor in shaping political relations among states. However, mutual expectations for economic gains led to Sino–South Korean diplomatic normalization and have played an important role in deepening the political relationship during the first decade following normalization. If Pollins's theory that "trade follows the flag" is applied to the Sino–South Korean relationship, the natural conclusion would be that rapidly increasing Sino–South Korean economic interdependence is a result of some overriding political imperative or attraction between China and South Korea. If political forces have already resulted in Sino–South Korean economic interdependence, then the growth of Sino–South Korean economic ties foreshadows the inevitable obsolescence of the US–South Korean security alliance as South Korea is inevitably drawn into China's political as well as economic orbit.

David Kang has argued that "China's reemergence as the gravitational center of East Asia is natural" based on the historical precedents of Asian international relations. According to this view, Korea and other states bordering China will accept economic dependence and political constraints in order to join a peaceful—if hierarchical—China-centered system.[30] But many South Koreans are not satisfied with the notion of subordination to China, and a whole series of complicated political issues loom on the horizon as potential flashpoints for Sino-Korean relations in the future. Neither do North Koreans appear to be satisfied with their economic dependency on China or willing to sacrifice their political independence for the sake of a more harmonious relationship with China (or for that matter, with the international community). South Korea's management of its relationship with China, especially the strategic and political implications of economic interdependence with China, appears to be far more complex and nuanced than the options anticipated by the major schools of international relations theory.

Miles Kahler and Scott Kastner consider the political effectiveness of Korean, Taiwanese, and Chinese economic engagement strategies in order to analyze the promotion of economic engagement as a strategy for achieving political gains. Kahler and Kastner conclude that conditional economic engagement strategies involving quid pro quos have a low likelihood of success, but that "transformative engagement" strategies designed to change the very nature and economic structure of the target state may have some possibility of success if the target state is a democracy or if there is a broad consensus backing the strategy in the *initiating* country.[31]

China's closest neighbors, including South Korea, have primarily perceived China's economic rise as an opportunity to be embraced rather than as a threat against which to balance. Only since 2006, as China has become more competitive in third-country markets, have the economic implications of its rise given pause to South Koreans; but even as anxieties about the strategic implications of China's rise have grown, concerns about China have not stopped growth in bilateral trade and investment between China and South Korea. Neither did North Korea's extreme economic dependency on Beijing prevent the leadership in Pyongyang from testing a nuclear device in October 2006 despite Chinese objections. To the extent that increasing economic interdependence has been accompanied by economic dependency on China, or to the extent China has attempted to utilize economic interdependence as a vehicle for attaining political leverage by demanding quid pro quos, both Koreas have sought to preserve their independence from Chinese political influence through forms of balancing behavior (for South Korea, seeking to negotiate a free trade agreement with the United States; for North Korea, seeking a strategic relationship with the United States through diplomatic normalization), in the process blocking the possibility that China could utilize its growing economic influence on the Korean peninsula as political leverage.

Neither has unconditional engagement between China and the two Koreas been "transformative": China's economic policies toward North Korea are in tune with South Korean engagement policies pursued under Kim Dae Jung and Roh Moo Hyun for a decade, but the North Korean economy—instead of transforming—has become a bigger burden, demanding more and more subsidies to ensure its regime survival. Likewise, China's economic engagement of South Korea has not resulted in a South Korean transformation; although China has enhanced its economic and political influence in South Korea, it is unlikely that economic benefits alone will be sufficient to overcome the perpetuation of South Korea's security alliance with the United States, emerging political challenges in the Sino–South Korean relationship, and the emergence of South Korean strategic concerns about overdependence on China. These factors continue to constrain possibilities for "transformation" of the Sino–South Korean political relationship.

Economic Interdependence and China's Relations with the Korean Peninsula

China's rise and increasing economic interdependence with the Korean peninsula have several potential implications for political and security relations between China and the two Koreas. First, it raises the question of whether China can utilize greater economic interdependence with both North and South Korea as a tool for preserving regional stability and contributing to peace on the Korean peninsula. China has already utilized humanitarian assistance to promote North Korea's economic stability and to stem the flow of North Korean refugees to northeastern China, at the height of North Korea's famine during the mid-1990s. Likewise, China's ongoing provision of energy and food supplies constitutes a necessary economic "transfusion" that helps prevent North Korea's collapsed economy from resulting in greater political instability. China's economic rise has had an influence on North Korea, but the dividends of increased economic integration do not yet appear to have delivered political and security benefits in terms of increased Chinese leverage on the preferred policy direction of North Korea's leadership. Instead, rising economic integration appears to have caused China to share in economic and political risks deriving from North Korea's crisis escalation tactics and desire to prove itself impermeable to Chinese efforts to curb North Korea's challenge to regional and international stability.

Second, China's increasing economic interdependence with the two Koreas raises questions about whether North Korea's economic dependency on China might provide the latter with new political leverage to achieve its own strategic objectives toward the Korean peninsula. The expansion of China's economic ties with North Korea, in combination with a decline in Japanese–North Korean economic ties, has made China the largest and most important economic partner for North Korea in recent years. But there is little evidence that China's economic assistance to or trade with North Korea has provided Beijing with essential leverage to influence North Korea's political course. The limits of China's economic assistance as a factor in constraining North Korean policies is nowhere more evident than in North Korea's decision to test a nuclear device in October 2006, following several years of calculated efforts on the part of China to increase economic assistance to North Korea as a vehicle for opening high-level political influence. China has also devised economic assistance plans that attempt to induce North Korea to pursue economic reforms on a Chinese model. China's efforts to provide "demonstration lessons" to Kim Il Sung and Kim Jong Il through repeated tours highlighting the benefits of Chinese reform and opening have continuously raised hopes that North Korea will follow China's reform path, but there has been little action in that direction.[32]

Likewise, China has been cautious not to utilize North Korea's economic dependency as a stick to constrain or punish its neighbor. This course of action is virtually universally rejected out of fear that such a stick might either induce instability in North Korea, a development not in China's interest, or result in China's diminished influence with North Korea, but with no practical gains resulting from the withdrawal of economic benefits to North Korea. Although China experimented briefly with a symbolic "cutoff" of oil supplies to North Korea for a few days in 2003, blamed on technical factors, and took more active steps to restrict North Korean access to China's banking system in the aftermath of North Korea's nuclear test in 2006, Chinese policymakers have consistently rejected sanction approaches that have sought to squeeze its neighbor. Instead, it appears that China's preferred and most effective approach has been to offer the promise of additional benefits, but to withhold implementation until appropriate adjustments have been made inside North Korea as a prerequisite for gaining the promised economic assistance. In other words, China has followed a policy of soft coercion toward North Korea.

Third, the rise of China and increased dependency on China for economic growth prospects may constrain South Korean perceived political and security choices in ways that might have implications for economic, political, and security cooperation with other parties, including the United States. China's burgeoning economic ties with South Korea have catalyzed rapid improvements in the political relationship between Beijing and Seoul, and have enabled opportunities for closer cooperation and partnership in a wide range of areas, but increasing economic interdependence has also spawned fears of economic dependency in Seoul as China begins to catch up with and even surpass South Korea in global competitiveness in many sectors that South Korea had previously dominated. South Korean fears of economic dependency on China may have the effect of limiting political cooperation to the extent that Seoul fears the implications of being overly dependent on Beijing. Thus far there has been no case in which China has attempted to utilize economic leverage vis-à-vis South Korea to pursue political objectives, but South Korean concerns about economic dependency on China appear to be motivated primarily by such concerns. For instance, South Koreans themselves have begun to worry about the implications of economic dependency on China and have sought to diversify trade and investment ties, including through the negotiation of a Korean-US free trade agreement.

In the event of a downturn in the US-Chinese relationship, or if China's aggregate power continues to grow, South Korea may be forced to come to terms with this fundamental contradiction between its economic dependence on China and its security dependence on the United States. Given China's rising influence on the Korean peninsula, it is natural to ask about the conditions under which South Korea might pursue a strategic realignment, attenuating or even severing security ties with the United States and pursuing a closer security relationship with China so as to bring its political and security interests into greater alignment with its stake in economic relations with China.[33] One purpose of this review of developments in the Sino–South Korean economic, political, and security relationship is to consider precisely this question.

Structure of the Study

In the chapters that follow, I explore these themes as factors that may assist in understanding the significance and implications of the dramatic changes that have taken place in the Sino-Korean relationship over the course of the past two decades. Chapter 2 reviews the political and economic factors surrounding China's strategic decision to normalize its relations with South Korea, and also analyzes how China's choice to pursue diplomatic normalization with South Korea can be understood through an evaluation of the expectations for future trade and economic gains and losses that accompanied the decision to normalize relations. Driven by expectations of economic gains to be accrued through diplomatic normalization with South Korea, China adjusted its policy from one focused on its traditional alliance with North Korea to a two-Koreas policy in which China managed a strained relationship with its erstwhile socialist partners in Pyongyang while developing a vibrant economic relationship with South Korean counterparts. As the Sino–South Korean economic relationship exploded while the economic relationship with North Korea floundered, the relative economic success of South Korea and the failure of North Korea had direct effects on China's perception of the balance of power on the Korean peninsula.

Chapter 3 considers major issues in the development of the Sino–South Korean economic relationship, with special reference to the impact of the developing economic relationship on political and security issues. It reviews the "China fever" that took hold in South Korea in the 1990s following diplomatic normalization, the impact of the Asian financial crisis on Sino-Korean economic relations, the galvanizing effects of China's entry into the World Trade Organization, and the emergence of concerns about Korean competitiveness with Chinese products in global and local markets. This chapter pays special attention to the extent to which South Korea has become dependent on China for its own domestic economic growth, and the influence of economic factors on China's political and security approach to the Korean peninsula. The chapter also examines strategic challenges at the firm level posed by the rising importance of China's domestic market versus a focus on China as a production base for South Korean companies to export to third countries, and explores whether South Korea's perceived economic dependency on China provides the latter with political leverage in its relations with the former.

Chapter 4 examines the emerging political and security challenges in the Sino–South Korean relationship. It evaluates whether efforts to address those challenges may lead to deepening institutional cooperation or competition between South Korea and China, and the extent to which a decade of Chinese economic engagement with South Korea has or has not yielded greater cooperation on these critical issues. The chapter analyzes various political challenges in the Sino–South Korean relationship, including diverging perceptions of North Korea; management of refugees; handling of historical issues, including the origins of the Koguryo kingdom; the role of the United States on the Korean peninsula; and management of cross-strait relations. The chapter examines whether political and security frictions might serve as a brake on economic cooperation, and under what circumstances Sino–South Korean political or security conflicts might impinge on the robust economic relationship.

In Chapter 5, I review developments in the Sino–North Korean relationship from the early 1990s to the present. It assesses the tensions in Sino–North Korean relations that accompanied and were reflected by a decline in bilateral economic interactions, assesses China's handling of the North Korean leadership transition and food crisis of the mid-1990s and its implications, traces the evolution of Chinese policy toward the two Koreas—from a focus on equidistance to a focus on stability—as a key policy adjustment that enabled a shift in the direction of China's policy closer to South Korea at the expense of North Korea, and analyzes Chinese views of the North Korean economy and perceptions of China's own choices in utilizing economic tools as part of managing its relationship with North Korea.

Chapter 6 examines the evolution and parameters of the current debate among Chinese analysts over how to deal with North Korea. As Chinese analysts have considered how to ensure political and social stability in North Korea as a means to maintain regional stability, they have increasingly faced fundamental policy dilemmas that have only been sharpened by North Korea's increasingly uncooperative behavior. Some of these dilemmas are of particular interest as one considers the political implications of China's rise. For instance, China had long stood behind the "five principles of peaceful coexistence" and recognition of national sovereignty as a cornerstone of its foreign policy, but as China has taken on a more active role to promote regional stability, it has also used economic tools in its policies toward North Korea that are designed to enhance its influence and tame North Korean brinkmanship and crisis escalation. North Korean leaders have responded uneasily and even sharply to Chinese pressure, going out of their way to embarrass the Chinese or deny the influence of pressure by biting the hand that feeds them. China is caught between US exhortations that it use its economic leverage to bring North Korea into line, and North Korean efforts to prove that Chinese pressure has no effect and that China is employing its "leverage" and economic assistance to meet its own national security interests, not out of largesse toward North Korea.

Chapter 7 examines the emerging triangular interaction among China, South Korea, and the United States as each party addresses the North Korean nuclear issue, with special attention to the implications of this interaction for long-term regional stability in Northeast Asia. This chapter analyzes the likelihood and implications of possible changes in the current structure of the strategic triangle. It also examines the significance for regional relations of possible changes in the strategic triangle, and implications for managing the North Korean nuclear issue.

Chapter 8 examines major power relations in Asia and contending responses in South Korea as they relate to the prospect of renewed rivalry between China and Japan. It reviews the rise in tensions between China and Japan, and South Korea's responses to renewed tensions thus far. The range of South Korean responses under consideration provides useful background for considering the options that affected third parties might have for mitigating the negative effects of emerging security dilemmas among major powers. The chapter also takes a closer look at how changes on the Korean peninsula might stimulate or mitigate Sino-Japanese rivalry.

Chapter 9 considers the future of the Sino-Korean relationship and its implications for US security interests, including the sustainability of the US–South Korean security alliance. It assesses the range of prospective options and strategies likely to be pursued by China, South Korea, North Korea, and the United States, and their implications for East Asian regional security, and also forecasts possible scenarios for relationships among China, the United States, and South Korea. Special attention is given to recommending how the United States should manage its relationships in and policy toward Northeast Asia given the increased economic interdependence in Asia overall.

Notes

1. Trade numbers are drawn from the website of the Korean International Trade Association, http://www.kita.org.

2. Scott Snyder, "Teenage Angst: Fifteenth Anniversary of Sino-ROK Diplomatic Normalization," in Brad Glosserman and Carl Baker Jr., eds.,

Comparative Connections 9, no. 3, October 15, 2007, accessed at http://www. csis.org/media/csis/pubs/0703qchina_korea.pdf on November 26, 2007.

3. See Lee Chul-kee, "Strategic Flexibility of U.S. Forces in Korea," *Nautilus Policy Forum Online* no. 06-19A, March 9, 2006, accessed at http://www.nautilus.org/fora/security/0619lee.html on November 26, 2007.

4. See Victor D. Cha, "South Korea: Anchored or Adrift," in Richard J. Ellings and Aaron L. Friedberg, eds., *Strategic Asia 2003–2004: Fragility and Crisis* (Seattle: National Bureau of Asian Research, 2003), pp. 109–130.

5. Cam Simpson, "U.S. Partners in the Pacific Don't Share America's Stance on China," *Chicago Tribune,* March 16, 2006.

6. "Accord on Rapid Mobility," *Korea Herald,* January 23, 2006; John Feffer, "People Power Versus Military Power in East Asia," *Foreign Policy in Focus,* February 13, 2007, accessed at http://www.fpif.org/fpiftxt/3990 on June 11, 2008.

7. Evan Medeiros, "Strategic Hedging and the Future of Asia-Pacific Stability," *Washington Quarterly* 29, no. 1 (Winter 2006): 145–167.

8. *Quadrennial Defense Review Report* (Washington, DC: US Department of Defense, February 6, 2006), accessed at http://www.defenselink. mil/qdr/report/report20060203.pdf on November 6, 2007.

9. "New Power Dynamics in Southeast Asia: Issues for U.S. Policymakers," presentation at the Stanley Foundation's forty-seventh "Strategy for Peace" conference, October 2006, accessed at http://www.stanleyfdn. org/publications/pdb/spcpdb06.pdf on November 26, 2007; "Contending Perspectives: Southeast Asia and American Views on a Rising China," Strategic Studies Institute colloquium brief (Singapore: US Army War College, August 22–24, 2005; Washington, DC: US Army War College, December 3, 2005), accessed at http://www.strategicstudiesinstitute.army.mil/pdffiles/pub717.pdf on November 26, 2007.

10. See Ellen L. Frost, *Asia's New Regionalism* (Boulder: Lynne Rienner, 2007), pp. 163–165; Edward J. Lincoln, *East Asian Economic Regionalism* (Washington, DC: Brookings Institution, 2004), pp. 43–71.

11. Joanne Gowa, "Bipolarity, Multipolarity, and Free Trade," *American Political Science Review* 83, no. 4 (December 1989): 1245–1256.

12. Joanne Gowa and Edward D. Mansfield, "Power Politics and International Trade," *American Political Science Review* 87, no. 2 (June 1993): 408. The development of the Sino–South Korean trade relationship also corresponds with the end of Cold War bipolarity and the establishment of a more multipolar international system, so it is unclear how Gowa and Mansfield's hypothesis should apply to the development of Sino–South Korean economic relations.

13. Brett Ashley Leeds and Burcu Savun, "Terminating Alliances: Why Do States Abrogate Agreements?" *Journal of Politics* 69, no. 4 (2007): 1118.

14. Nicholas Eberstadt, Aaron L. Friedberg, and Geun Lee, "Introduction: What If? A World Without the U.S.-ROK Alliance," *Asia Policy* no. 5 (January 2008): 2–5.

15. "The Bottlenecks and Overall Strategy on the Road to a Powerful

State: An Interview with Shi Yinhong, a Renowned Scholar in International Relations," *Nanfeng Chuang* (Guangzhou), in Chinese, February 1, 2006, accessed at http://www.opensource.gov, doc. no. CPP20060216050009.

16. Wang Guangya, "Viewpoint: A Peaceful Role Player in World Affairs," *Beijing Review,* May 19, 2006, accessed at http://www.opensource.gov, doc. no. CPP20060519515028.

17. Zheng Bijian, "China's 'Peaceful Rise' to Great-Power Status," *Foreign Affairs* (September–October 2005): 18.

18. Shen Jiru, "Will the World Pattern Change?" *Renmin Ribao,* April 3, 2003, p. 13, accessed at http://www.opensource.gov, doc. no. CPP20030403000067, as cited in Yong Deng and Thomas G. Moore, "China Views Globalization: Toward a New Great-Power Politics?" *Washington Quarterly* 27, no. 3 (2004): 123.

19. Deng and Moore, "China Views Globalization," p. 118.

20. Joshua Kurlantzik, *Charm Offensive: How China's Soft Power Is Transforming the World* (New Haven: Yale University Press, 2007), pp. 56–60.

21. "China Provided Half of North Korea's Food Aid in 2005," *Kyodo News Service,* July 20, 2006, accessed at http://www.opensource.gov, doc. no. JPP20060720969024.

22. Author interviews in Beijing, June 2007.

23. John J. Mearsheimer, "Back to the Future: Instability in Europe After the Cold War," *International Security* 15, no. 1 (Summer 1990): 45.

24. Richard Betts, "Wealth, Power, and Instability: East Asia and the United States After the Cold War," *International Security* 18, no. 3 (Winter 1993): 55.

25. Albert O. Hirschman, *National Power and the Structure of Foreign Trade* (Berkeley: University of California Press, 1945); Richard Rosecrance, *The Rise of the Trading State: Commerce and Conquest in the Modern World* (New York: Basic, 1986).

26. See Etel Solingen, *Regional Orders at Century's Dawn: Global and Domestic Influences on Grand Strategy* (Princeton: Princeton University Press, 1998); Paul A. Papayaonou, "Economic Interdependence and the Balance of Power," *International Studies Quarterly* 41, no. 1 (March 1997): 113–140.

27. For instance, South Korea's Presidential Committee on Northeast Asian Cooperation Initiative is focused on this objective. See http://www.nabh.go.kr/english/policy/culture.html, accessed on November 29, 2007.

28. See Dale C. Copeland, "Economic Interdependence and War: A Theory of Trade Expectations," *International Security* 20, no. 4 (Spring 1996): 5–41.

29. Brian M. Pollins, "Does Trade Still Follow the Flag?" *American Political Science Review* 83, no. 2 (June 1989): 465–480; Omar M. G. Keshk, Brian M. Pollins, and Rafael Reuveny, "Trade Still Follows the Flag: The Primacy of Politics in a Simultaneous Model of Interdependence and Armed Conflict," undated manuscript, accessed at http://polisci.osu.edu/faculty/bpollins/papers/tradefollows.pdf on November 29, 2007.

30. David C. Kang, *China Rising: Peace, Power, and Order in East Asia* (New York: Columbia University Press, 2007), p. 4.

31. See Miles Kahler and Scott L. Kastner, "Strategic Uses of Economic Interdependence: Engagement Policies on the Korean Peninsula and Across the Taiwan Strait," *Journal of Peace Research* 43, no. 5 (2006): 523–541.

32. Mika Marumoto, "North Korea and the China Model: The Switch from Hostility to Acquiescence," in *Academic Paper Series on Korea, 2008*, vol. 1 (Washington, DC: Korea Economic Institute of America, 2008), pp. 98–117.

33. See Chung Jae Ho, "China's Ascendancy and the Korean Peninsula: From Interest Reevaluation to Strategic Realignment?" in David Shambaugh, ed., *Power Shift: China and Asia's New Dynamics* (Berkeley: University of California Press, 2005), pp. 151–169.

2
China's Shift to a
Two-Koreas Policy

The pride of place that North Korea has occupied in Beijing since the establishment of the People's Republic of China (PRC) in 1949 is nowhere more evident than in the location of its embassy at the heart of the Chaoyang diplomatic district. On October 7, 1949, six days after the modern founding of the People's Republic of China, it and the Democratic People's Republic of Korea (DPRK; North Korea) established diplomatic relations with each other. In the early days of the People's Republic of China, North Korea's embassy clearly marked the country as one of Beijing's closest allies. The compound where the embassy resided was a self-contained fortress with residential apartments, office buildings, entertainment facilities, and spacious grounds behind an expansive main building. Occupying an entire block of prime real estate across the street from a large public park in Beijing's diplomatic quarter, the North Korean embassy was one of the most spacious diplomatic compounds in Beijing. The three large apartment buildings in the compound provided accommodation to almost all North Koreans who passed through Beijing on diplomatic and quasi-diplomatic tasks, and the embassy was a home-away-from-home and diplomatic reception venue for North Korean leaders during their periodic official and secret visits to Beijing.

Although the compound has taken on a somewhat shabby appearance in recent decades, it remains as a testament to the long-standing ties between countries that share common experiences with liberation and revolution. Despite the socialist revolution, there still existed a clear hierarchy in the relationships of the newly established People's Republic of China with the outside world. Mao Zedong and Kim Il Sung, as contemporary communist revolutionaries who had successfully and simultaneously achieved national liberation, had much in common. They set similar agendas for themselves as fathers of their respective nations and as liberators determined to govern on the basis of socialist egalitarianism. Many of the tools that both leaders used in the early years of their rule borrowed from each other's experience. Model workers, model farms, land reforms, cults of personality, challenging relations with Moscow, central planning, revolutionary fervor, and even the common experience of fighting against US imperialists during the Korean War—all bound Mao and Kim together.

After Mao's death in 1976, however, Deng Xiaoping consolidated power and took China in a different direction, but Kim Il Sung continued to pursue socialist ideals under a system that in practice was more traditional than revolutionary. Hewing to the path of economic reform, China's economy grew at a breathtaking pace, following a development strategy that had previously been modeled by Japan and then the Republic of Korea (ROK; South Korea). As China's economic relationship with South Korea grew, South Korean economic and business influence in China gradually surpassed that of North Korea. Today in Beijing, the dim lights of the North Korean embassy seem to be overpowered and figuratively encircled by the lights from the large billboards advertising South Korean consumer products, from mobile telephones to automobiles to household goods. China's decision to normalize relations with South Korea at the cost of strained relations with traditional allies in North Korea is a powerful illustration of the role that expectations for future trade relations can have on the development—or decline—of bilateral relations between two countries.

China's One-Korea Policy During the Cold War

For decades following the Korean War, China and South Korea had virtually no bilateral economic relations and minimal political contact. South Korea's lack of contact with China was even more anomalous given China's historically dominant influence on the Korean peninsula. Korean kings during the Chosun dynasty had sent regular tribute missions to the Chinese emperor for centuries, and China sought to maintain predominance on the Korean peninsula at least in part as a strategic measure to enhance its own security.[1] Japan's defeat of China (1894–1895) and Russia (1904–1905) in two successive wars fought primarily on or near the peninsula marked a break in China's traditional dominant influence on the Korean peninsula. Japan controlled Korea throughout the Japanese colonial period (1910–1945). The Korean peninsula served as a strategic foothold for Japan's penetration of northeastern China. Following Japan's defeat in World War II, and throughout the Cold War, Washington became South Korea's primary economic and political focus.

In the early days following the Korean War, US economic assistance and political support provided critical economic transfusions that propped up South Korea, then a struggling economic basket case with an illiberal political leadership. During the early part of South Korea's economic takeoff, in the 1960s and 1970s, preferential access to US markets was an essential precondition that enabled South Korea's military dictator, Park Chung Hee, to pursue an export-led development strategy. The emergence of the United States as South Korea's leading trading partner in Cold War times was a natural byproduct of South Korea's security dependence. Despite China's geographical proximity to South Korea, there was virtually no trade between the two countries until the 1970s. Instead, Chinese leaders tried to depress bilateral trade relations in view of political considerations. Likewise, North Korea's closest political relationships with socialist comrades in the Soviet Union and China faced ups and downs as North Korean leaders sought to maximize their independence from Soviet and Chinese influence by playing them against each other, but economically North Korea remained dependent on Soviet and Chinese support to ensure its own survival. This pattern illustrates the way in which security and economic benefits throughout the Cold War tended to reflect the bipolar structure of US-Soviet confrontation.[2]

On the socialist side of the Asian Cold War divide, Mao's decision to enter the Korean War on the side of Kim Il Sung bound China and North Korea together in a special relationship, reinforcing ideological ties between the two socialist leaderships and cementing close personal ties.[3] Despite perceptions of Sino–North Korean "blood ties" forged by common war experience against US capitalist imperialists, the Sino–North Korean relationship was tumultuous and often strained by internal tensions. These tensions stemmed at least in part from Kim Il Sung's tactical efforts to play the Soviet Union and China against each other, and in part from Kim's innate suspicion of great power intentions toward Korea, derived from direct experience with Korea's loss of sovereignty at the hands of Japan.

One factor in North Korea's domestic politics that had an impact on its external relations in the 1950s and early 1960s was Kim Il Sung's tactical maneuvering to eliminate factions within the North Korean leadership that leaned toward the Soviet Union and China and that might provide opposition to Kim Il Sung's absolute rule. Having come into power with strong Soviet support and dependent on China's intervention to salvage North Korea during the Korean War, Kim Il Sung saw threats from potential rivals who had close ties to both of North Korea's great power patrons. He also needed to reaffirm his own legitimacy by disavowing challengers who might attack him for having been overly dependent on outside powers in the early years following the Korean War. Kim's dependence on China in the later stages of the Korean War was so complete that the United States negotiated the armistice primarily with Chinese counterparts. North Korea's army took a subordinate position during armistice negotiations. In the process of removing the Yenan faction (composed of Koreans who had returned from China), Kim minimized Chinese cultural influences in North Korean life by emphasizing "pure" Korean products and cultural practices. North Korea banished Chinese characters from its newspapers and attempted to minimize borrowed "Chinese" words. Much to China's consternation, North Korea de-emphasized the Chinese contribution to the Korean War, going so far as to virtually eliminate recognition of China's sacrifices in Korean museums that covered the history of the war period.[4]

China's autarkic economic policies eventually led to famine during the Great Leap Forward of the late 1950s, during which ethnic Koreans, many of whom had resettled in northeastern China during the Japanese colonial period, fled across the Yalu and Tumen rivers to beg for food from comparatively affluent North Korean relatives.[5] The experience of famine and hardship has ironically kept alive cross-border ties among Korean extended family members, since Chinese relatives were called upon to return the favor a generation later during North Korea's famine of the 1990s. A cross-border barter trade estimated at up to US$300 million per year has grown since the 1990s, in addition to local- and provincial-level economic support ties that had long existed between ethnic Korean inhabitants of China's northeastern provinces and their relatives inside North Korea.[6]

Through the shared experience of war, China and North Korea were bound together by ideology and personal ties among top leaders that grew out of a common revolutionary objective of fighting against Japanese colonial rule. These close personal ties were cemented during the Korean War. The two countries also held common fraternal ideological and revolutionary ties that were reinforced by the borrowing of common socialist organizational structures from the Soviet Union.[7] The first-generation revolutionary elite maintained personal ties that lasted well into the 1990s, but those ties have increasingly been forgotten or come under challenge from younger generations who do not share the same history or life experience. The respective political experiences of the two regimes showed many parallels until China took the path of economic reform under Deng Xiaoping in the late 1970s and early 1980s, while North Korea focused on perfecting its central planning mechanisms and eventually lost its growth momentum in the 1980s.

Throughout the Cold War, Kim Il Sung skillfully manipulated the Sino-Soviet split as a vehicle for enhancing his own tactical and strategic position, in the process maintaining a steady stream of aid alternately from China and the Soviet Union. Such maneuvering allowed Kim to play the great powers against each other in his efforts to gain security concessions, while simultaneously maneuvering to defend North Korea from "great power chauvinism."[8] In July 1961, Kim secured a treaty of friendship, cooperation, and mutual assistance from Moscow, and five days later secured a similar treaty from Beijing. These treaties formalized great power military commitments to North Korea in the context of US alliance commitments with Japan and South Korea.[9] However, even in the strategic context of the Cold War, and despite North Korea's efforts to preserve its independence through autarkic economic policies and avoid complete economic dependence on either the Soviet Union or China, a fundamental reality underlying Kim's management of his relations with Beijing and Moscow was North Korea's structural economic dependence on external assistance from both powers to ensure the survival and prosperity of its regime.

The opening of US-Chinese relations in the wake of visits by Henry Kissinger and Richard Nixon to Beijing in 1971 caught both Kim Il Sung and Park Chung Hee by surprise, leading to the first inter-Korean dialogue since the end of the Korean War.[10] Although Nixon's trip spawned a gradual opening in US-Chinese relations and eventual normalization in 1978, as well as the normalization of Sino-Japanese diplomatic relations beginning in the early 1970s, there was no similar move toward normalization of Sino–South Korean relations. In response to these developments, South Korea adjusted its policy to show greater "flexibility and sincerity" in relations toward China, showing a willingness to trade and offering to open negotiations on maritime boundaries in the Yellow Sea.[11] But China remained reluctant to open relations with South Korea out of consideration for North Korean sensitivities. In fact, the Nixon-Mao meetings were a sufficient shock to the leaders of both Koreas that the latter initiated secret contacts with each other, culminating on July 4, 1972, in a joint declaration that appeared to open the way for inter-Korean reconciliation and emphasized the need to pursue Korean reunification through their own autonomous efforts. A direct result of great power rapprochement was thus the recalibration on the part of both Koreas of the risks that accompanied their dependence on the great powers.[12] Another effect was to catalyze the pursuit of nuclear weapons in both South and North Korea as a way of augmenting security through their own autonomous efforts, in view of the perceived lack of reliability of great power sponsors.[13]

Beijing's Shift Toward Seoul

Despite the normalization of US and Japanese relations with China in the 1970s, the brief inter-Korean rapprochement surrounding the July 4, 1972, joint declaration did not last long enough to diminish inter-Korean competition on the international scene. Both Park Chung Hee and Kim Il Sung used the joint declaration for tactical purposes while international competition for legitimacy between the two Koreas intensified during the 1970s. A heated inter-Korean competition for international recognition extended as far away as Africa and Latin America. Reflecting the constraints Beijing felt given the intensity of the ongoing inter-Korean competition (and China's own pursuit of reunification with Taiwan), Deng Xiaoping explained to a visiting Japanese delegation from the *Yomiuri Shimbun* newspaper in March 1980 that it was not in the interest of China to develop a relationship with South Korea or for the United States to recognize North Korea. South Korean China specialist Chung Jae Ho believes that Deng's comment may have been designed to reassure Pyongyang as China began to open unofficial trade relations with South Korea.[14] Chinese and South Korean leaders sent periodic signals to each other throughout the 1980s that they were willing to improve economic ties even in the absence of an improvement in political relations.

During the 1980s, Chinese authorities limited South Korean travel to mainland China and economic interactions were closely monitored. Upon his first visit to Seoul to attend Asia Pacific Economic Cooperation (APEC) meetings in 1991, former Chinese foreign minister Qian Qichen described Seoul as a "forbidden zone."[15] Following complaints from North Korea about the rapid growth in Sino–South Korean trade and investment relations in 1980 (US$188 million) and 1981 (US$280 million), Chinese efforts to regulate trade with South Korea led to a significant decline in trade during 1982 (US$139 million) and

1983 (US$120 million), as well as to a one-year delay in the construction of the first Sino–South Korean joint venture, which began in 1986.[16] Since Sino–South Korean economic interactions were officially discouraged by Beijing, initial trade relationships were primarily indirect interactions via Hong Kong. Nonetheless, as South Korea's economic development progressed and South Korean companies began to venture abroad more actively to take advantage of newfound international economic opportunities, China itself became a natural object of interest within South Korea's private sector.[17]

Several crises during the 1980s led Chinese and South Korean diplomats to establish working relationships with each other that became the foundation for closer contacts between Seoul and Beijing. The shocking 1983 hijacking of a plane from Shenyang to Shanghai by Chinese civilians involved a forced landing at a US military base near Chunch'on in South Korea. This incident led China to send a team to Seoul to negotiate a memorandum that recognized the South Korean government's authority, but also required that China assure North Korea that these emergency negotiations did not signify a change in Chinese policy toward the Korean peninsula. In 1985, a Chinese navy torpedo boat set adrift in the Yellow Sea as a result of a mutiny found its way into South Korean territorial waters, where it was secured by South Korean naval forces. This incident required establishment of an emergency negotiating channel between Chinese and South Korean foreign ministry officials. In addition to "hijack diplomacy" and "torpedo diplomacy," "sports diplomacy" provided opportunities for official interaction as China decided to participate in the Seoul Asian Games and the Seoul Olympic Games in 1986 and 1988, respectively, to the disappointment of North Korea.[18] Another factor that cooled China's support for North Korea in the early 1980s was North Korean adventurism. North Korea's 1983 bombing attack on South Korean cabinet members in Rangoon, and the 1987 bombing of a South Korean airliner in advance of Seoul's hosting of the 1988 Olympics, dampened Chinese military cooperation with North Korea.[19]

The Tiananmen Square incident was another factor that may have initially contributed to a delay in China's normalization of relations with South Korea. Chinese leaders used Kim Il Sung's support for the Tiananmen crackdown to suggest that China was not completely isolated from the international community, highlighting Kim's support for China during his October 1991 visit to Beijing.[20] However, China's eagerness to strengthen relations with its neighbors following the Tiananmen incident probably served to facilitate its decision to normalize relations with Seoul.[21] In the aftermath of Tiananmen, China needed foreign policy victories to overcome its international isolation, and Seoul provided a confidence-builder as China launched a sustained effort to restore its international reputation and relationships.[22]

The Beijing Asian Games in 1990 provided further opportunities for "sports diplomacy." South Korean conglomerates were aggressive in supporting China as host of the games, donating US$5 million and over 400 passenger cars to support Beijing's sponsorship.[23] China also used its role as host of the games to set the stage for its decision to normalize relations with South Korea; it de-emphasized its relationship with North Korea and delinked the issues of Chinese and Korean reunification.[24] For the first time, China's Korea policy extended beyond its relations with North Korea to consider the entire peninsula.

Following the Beijing Asian Games of 1990, China and South Korea agreed to establish quasi-diplomatic trade offices in each other's capitals, and South Korea brokered the entry of China (along with Hong Kong and Taiwan) into APEC in 1991. During the same year, the China Council for the Promotion of International Trade and the Korea Trade Promotion Corporation signed bilateral trade and investment agreements that allowed mechanisms for protection and dispute arbitration. These developments stimulated further high-level exchanges among government officials and set the clock running toward official diplomatic recognition, which was finally achieved on August 24, 1992.

Factors That Drove Sino–South Korean Normalization

The end of the Cold War, South Korea's attempts to reach out diplomatically to socialist-bloc countries under Roh Tae Woo's Nordpolitik policy, South Korea's continued economic takeoff (combined with North Korea's stagnation), and China's economic opening all contributed to a positive environment for Sino–South Korean diplomatic normalization. The decision to pursue diplomatic normalization with South Korea involved political costs for China with North Korea, but also entailed clear economic and political gains with South Korea. Samuel Kim described China's post–Cold War diplomatic approach toward the Korean peninsula as "maxi-mini diplomacy," a "realist strategy of maximizing its interests while at the same time free riding on global arms control, human rights, and environmental issues" in which China maintained "geostrategic ties" with North Korea while simultaneously pursuing "geoeconomic ties" with the South.[25]

The end of the Cold War and the collapse of the Soviet Union partially changed the geopolitical context of the Korean peninsula, but these changes did not lead to the type of transformation in Asia that took place in Europe. Nonetheless, the absence of the Soviet Union as a strategic factor affecting the security order surrounding the Korean peninsula did have a number of critical effects on inter-Korean relations. As Sino-Soviet tensions subsided, the strategic value to Beijing of China's relationship with Pyongyang also declined, reducing the cost to China of political distancing from North Korea that might occur as a result of diplomatic normalization with South Korea.[26] Following Soviet normalization with South Korea and the collapse of the Soviet Union, China no longer found North Korea useful as a way of putting pressure on Moscow. For its part, North Korea faced a huge psychological and economic shock in the immediate aftermath of the Soviet collapse and lost maneuvering room to pursue its own interests by playing Moscow and Beijing against each other.

Partially in response to these developments, the two Koreas pursued eight rounds of inter-Korean high-level talks, led by their prime ministers, between 1990 and 1992. These talks culminated in the landmark Agreement on Reconciliation, Nonaggression, Exchanges, and Cooperation (widely known as the Basic Agreement), signed on December 13, 1991, and ratified in February 1992. The agreement contained provisions to promote exchanges and cooperation in a wide range of sectors and also endorsed concrete steps to promote confidence-building measures in the security sphere through measures designed to diminish perceived threats and enhance trust. Although the agreement was not implemented as envisioned, it contained the key provisions for inter-Korean reconciliation and signified a formal level of mutual recognition and coexistence between the two Korean states.

The ongoing inter-Korean high-level dialogue gave political cover for Japanese and US contacts with North Korea, which began to invite delegations of prominent Americans to Pyongyang for conversations with its foreign ministry–affiliated Institute of Disarmament and Peace as a way of bolstering its long-standing objective of normalizing relations with the United States. The United States also eased its policy of no contact with North Korean representatives through a periodic dialogue, undertaken in Beijing, that was approved near the end of the Ronald Reagan administration. These conversations took place against a different backdrop compared to previous North Korean proposals that had been overtly designed to create political dissension in the US–South Korean alliance; the North Korean leadership was clearly seeking to offset its loss of the Soviet Union as a major patron. North Korea also reached out to a high-level political delegation, led by Shin Kanemaru, in the fall of 1991, but in the end the emergence of the North Korean nuclear issue on the international stage destroyed the likelihood of Japanese and US normalization with Pyongyang, undermined implementation of the inter-Korean Basic Agreement, and froze the political evolution of Asian security relations with the Korean peninsula.

For South Korea, the end of the Cold War coincided with diplomatic opportunities made possible by the selection of Seoul as the host city for the 1988 Olympics, an event that provided a showcase to the world for South Korea's remarkable economic development. A further development that enhanced South Korea's international standing prior to the Olympics was the management of a peaceful transition from a military authoritarian government under President Chun Doo Hwan to a more open democratic system. Although many of the vestiges of political control remained in place as Chun's chosen successor, Roh Tae Woo, was elected as president, this transition further fueled liberalization of political expression in response to citizen demands for a more open society. All of these developments combined to support Roh's policy of Nordpolitik, launched in July of 1988 and inspired by West Germany's policy toward East Germany. The Nordpolitik policy was an expression of South Korea's political desire to establish new diplomatic relationships with Eastern Europe, the Soviet Union, China, and eventually North Korea. Through this policy, South Korea sought to attain an international environment favorable to unification, to take a prominent role in the region and in the world, and to promote national economic interests.[27]

The normalization of diplomatic relations between South Korea and the Soviet Union was consummated with a dramatic meeting between Presidents Roh Tae Woo and Mikhail Gorbachev in San Francisco in 1990. Following normalization with the Soviet Union (some would argue at an overly high financial cost)[28] and the negotiation of the Basic Agreement with North Korea, the last missing piece of the Nordpolitik policy for Roh Tae Woo was normalization of political relations with Beijing. Normalization with China was the objective that Roh prized most dearly. His desire to normalize relations with Beijing within his tenure may have come at the cost of overeagerness in managing diplomatic negotiations on normalization, even at the expense of frictions with Washington in the aftermath of the Tiananmen incident.[29] South Korea's normalization with the Soviet Union paved the way for China to consider normalizing with South Korea, but also provided an object lesson of the costs China would entail with North Korea if it handled the transition poorly. Soviet foreign minister Eduard Shevardnadze delivered the bad news during his September 1990 visit to Pyongyang, at which time North Korea warned that this development would "force Pyongyang to take certain actions to build certain types of weapons by our own means."[30]

Observing that the Soviets had squandered their influence with Pyongyang as a result of their sudden decision to normalize with Seoul, Beijing determined to make its own adjustment considerably more gradual, allowing itself to maintain a relationship with Pyongyang (albeit strained) despite eventually deciding to normalize with South Korea. At an early stage in this process, Deng Xiaoping had indicated that China should pursue enhanced economic relations with South Korea, but not at the expense of breaking relations with North Korea.[31] Pyongyang's strong reaction to the news of Soviet–South Korean normalization relieved the Soviet Union of its obligations to provide ongoing economic support for Pyongyang, but left unsettled a significant bilateral ruble debt accumulated during the Cold War that was virtually uncollectible at either friendship prices or cash valuations. The adjustment also made it possible for Moscow to insist on a market basis for economic transactions going forward, while heightening the severity of North Korea's economic need.

One effect of the collapse of the Soviet Union on Beijing was that North Korea's demands for additional economic assistance came right at the moment when Beijing sought to change the basis for the relationship from friendship prices to market value. Despite Beijing's best efforts to introduce market principles into the bilateral relationship, the collapse of support to North Korea from Moscow made such a transition impossible. Even today, North Korea receives its most significant foreign assistance from Beijing. The emergence of bilateral economic relations as an important factor in foreign policy was a significant new development for both China and North Korea.

As China embarked on the road of economic reform in the early 1980s, the success of other late industrializing nations such as Japan and the "four dragons" (Hong Kong, Singapore, Taiwan, and South Korea) provided guideposts for Chinese policymakers to consider in charting their own reform path. Among those newly industrializing economies, Hong Kong and Singapore were city-states, while newly industrializing Taiwan was a political competitor even while serving as an economic model. So South Korea's experience with economic opening, reform, and integration with the international economy may have served as an example for China's economic reformers.[32]

Under the guise of separation of economics and politics, China quietly allowed a growing trade relationship with South Korea during the mid-1980s, much of it conducted indirectly via Hong Kong, after having earlier opposed all economic interactions with South Korea on political grounds. South Korean goods were a better fit in terms of China's own needs in the early stages of its own reform and opening than higher-priced goods and technologies from more advanced countries. By the late 1980s, the pressure for political normalization, if only in support of greater efficiency in management of economic relations, clearly outweighed the political costs of damaged relations with an economically stagnant North Korea. Nonetheless, in view of long-standing fraternal ties with the leadership in Pyongyang forged during the Korean War, China sought to manage the development of its relationship with South Korea in such a way as to soften the blow on North Korea.[33]

This meant deferring the normalization of relations, downplaying or delaying the potential for strengthened political ties with South Korea, and, after normalization, emphasizing a formal policy of equidistance between North and South Korea. The opportunities associated with economic interdependence between China and South Korea far outweighed political costs, and in fact made possible the prospect of expanded political gains on both sides in the pursuit of their respective national and strategic interests on the Korean peninsula.

Key Issues in Chinese Policy

As China inched its way toward diplomatic normalization with South Korea on the basis of a gradual convergence of economic interests, three key political issues emerged in its management of policy toward the Korean peninsula: South Korea's decision in 1991 to pursue membership in the United Nations separate from North Korea; the question of "cross-recognition"—whether Japan and the United States might take steps to normalize relations with North Korea in rough parallel with Chinese and Soviet normalization with South Korea; and the emergence of international concern over North Korea's nuclear program, together with calls for China to play a role in managing this issue through its "special relationship" with North Korea.

China's decision in 1991 not to veto South Korea's bid to join the United Nations separate from North Korea was the clearest public signal of its impending shift to an equidistance policy and to dual recognition of the two Koreas. South Korea pushed the issue to the top of the policy agenda by abandoning its quest to gain international legitimacy through winning exclusive rights to a single Korean seat in the United Nations. But China's handling of the UN issue served as an early test case for how it might best manage the diplomatic task of normalizing relations with South Korea while minimizing political damage to its interests with North Korea. South Korea's UN bid on a nonexclusive basis presented China with a political choice at a critical juncture in the development of relations with South Korea. But the way the choice was framed did not require China to make a decision that would exclude North Korea from possible UN membership.

South Korea's UN bid also provided an opportunity to delink Korean reunification from questions related to Chinese reunification, since China had already won a UN seat, at the exclusion of Taiwan, in the early 1970s. From that time, China consistently used its position as a member of the UN to marginalize Taiwan from participation in UN-affiliated international organizations. By the early 1990s, South Korea was one of the most influential countries that still had formal diplomatic relations with Taiwan. Thus the simultaneous entry of the two Koreas into the UN facilitated China's normalization with South Korea, since Chinese normalization with South Korea could be used to marginalize Taiwan in the international community.

During a May 1991 visit to Pyongyang, Premier Li Peng conveyed to North Korea that China would not oppose South Korea's application for UN membership. North Korea surely did not appreciate China's decision not to block South Korea's bid. However, by handling the issue in this way, China successfully provided a symbolic exit for Pyongyang to save face by independently announcing its decision to pursue separate UN membership without being publicly humiliated by Beijing's abandonment of the North Korean position. As a result, North Korea was the first of the two Koreas to submit its formal application to join the UN. Chinese foreign minister Qian Qichen, during his June 1991 visit to Pyongyang, pledged to help ensure North Korea's simultaneous entry into the United Nations as part of the same "package."[34]

The second issue on which China's desires were ultimately not fulfilled was its interest in supporting North Korea's normalization with the United States and Japan in tandem with its own normalization with South Korea. Chinese leaders had long hoped that both Japan and the United States would improve their respective relationships with North Korea as a means of easing the pressure that North Korea would feel if China pursued diplomatic normalization with South Korea. It is even reported that Chinese leaders discussed this idea of cross-recognition with Kim Il Sung during his visit to Beijing, in May 1987.[35] In conversations with Roh Tae Woo during his first visit to Seoul for the October 1991 APEC meeting (only one month after North and South Korea simultaneously joined as members of the United Nations), Qian Qichen hinted at the desirability of cross-recognition of North Korea by the United States and Japan as part of the process of China's normalization with South Korea. The issue was discussed further between Kim Il Sung and Chinese president Yang Shangkun during his trip to Pyongyang in April 1992.

China's concern for cross-recognition apparently reflected North Korea's desires that Sino–South Korean normalization should occur in tandem with improvements in US–North Korean relations.[36] However, as North Korea's nuclear program became an international issue, the situation worked in precisely the opposite way. Not only did the nuclear program diminish prospects of North Korean diplomatic and political progress with Japan and the United States, but it also generated international pressure on China to communicate global concerns to North Korea at a time when the Sino–North Korean relationship was already under strain. Given its growing economic stakes in an improved relationship with South Korea, China decided to begin normalizing relations with South Korea while promising Kim Il Sung that it would continue to support North Korea's normalization with Japan and the United States. In light of China's failure to secure cross-recognition, and given North Korea's livid reaction when Soviet foreign minister Shevardnadze traveled to Pyongyang in September 1990 to deliver the bad news regarding Soviet normalization with South Korea, Qian Qichen was relieved at the relative civility of Kim Il Sung's response during Qian's one-day trip to North Korea in June 1992 to inform Kim of the imminent announcement of normalization of Sino–South Korean relations.[37]

The third political issue that arose during the process of China's decision to normalize its relations with South Korea was enhanced international scrutiny of North Korea's nuclear program. This issue was only beginning to emerge at the time of Sino–South Korean normalization, but became a significant challenge for China in the immediate aftermath of its decision to normalize, just at the moment when the Sino–North Korean relationship would have come under the greatest stress as a result of North Korean perceptions of betrayal by China.

As concern grew, expectations rose that China would restrain North Korea from persisting in its pursuit of nuclear weapons. But Chinese leaders must have been acutely aware of the limits of their influence in the aftermath of Sino–South Korean normalization, so they opted to play a passive role, by conveying messages to North Korea rather than joining any public efforts to press North Korea to respond to international concerns about its nuclear program. When the issue came before the UN Security Council following North Korea's threat to withdraw from the Nuclear Nonproliferation Treaty, China abstained from a presidential statement condemning North Korea's actions, making it possible to achieve unanimity within the Security Council. Even this approach was likely perceived among the North Korean leadership as a betrayal by China, given the close relations that the two countries had previously enjoyed.

China's Motives for Normalization

According to Qian Qichen's memoire, Deng Xiaoping had determined as early as 1985 that China should develop a healthy bilateral relationship with South Korea for two reasons: to benefit business and economic interests, and to help South Korea terminate its relations with Taiwan. But Deng also recognized that making this transition from a pro–North Korea policy to a two-Koreas policy would require delicacy and should be undertaken, if possible, with the understanding and support of North Korea. Given the economic complementarities between China and South Korea, it is remarkable that China was willing to wait over seven years to normalize relations with South Korea in deference to its ideological ties with North Korea.[38] When China finally did decide to move toward normalization with South Korea, Foreign Minister Qian justified the decision as one that would have the effect of "downing four birds with one stone." He argued that normalization with Seoul would (1) increase Taiwan's diplomatic isolation, (2) strengthen Beijing's growing economic cooperation with Seoul, (3) diminish Pyongyang's seemingly endless requests for more military and economic aid, and (4) enhance Beijing's bargaining power to defuse mounting US pressure from legislation known as "Super 301," which contained provisions requiring the US Trade Representative (USTR) to levy sanctions on offending countries if the USTR found that the offending country was engaged in unfair trade practices.[39]

Although the first and fourth justifications did not specifically address Chinese strategic objectives on the Korean peninsula, all four powerfully illustrated China's primary motivations and policy objectives in pursuing a two-Koreas policy. Two of the four objectives reinforced the idea that expanded expectations for the Sino–South Korean relationship—combined with diminished expectations for the Sino–North

Korean relationship—were key drivers behind China's decision to normalize relations with South Korea.

In a prescient analysis in *Asian Survey* on the eve of China's normalization with South Korea, Chinese analysts Jia Hao and Zhuang Qubing attributed the adjustment in China's policy toward the Korean peninsula to a revised Chinese calculation of the regional power equilibrium, adjustments in China's official ideology and domestic politics, and the growing importance of China's economic opening to the outside world. Among their recommendations were that (1) China should continue to seek bilateral and multilateral cooperation among the major powers, (2) China should seize the opportunity to play an active role in promoting regional economic cooperation, (3) China should recognize that it had become Pyongyang's single most important ally, a situation that gave China more leverage but also brought risks, (4) China should actively broaden comprehensive ties with Seoul to push for closer cooperation, and (5) China should work to guard against unilateral foreign interference in case of instability. Perhaps their most far-reaching observation illustrated the benefits to China of fashioning a policy that looked beyond North Korea and toward the peninsula as a whole: "While a unified Korea could be an important and energetic economic partner of China, a friendly relationship with [Korea] could also be conducive to safeguarding China's political and strategic position in the region."[40] All of these observations endure as key points that still inform of China's perspective and policy objectives toward the Korean peninsula since Sino–South Korean normalization.

South Korea's Motives for Normalization

For the administration of Roh Tae Woo, normalization of relations with China had become the holy grail of the Nordpolitik policy, one of the final tasks that remained incomplete in the waning days of his administration. Having normalized relations with the Soviet Union and having reached an agreement on reconciliation, nonaggression, exchange, and cooperation through high-level dialogue with North Korea, the last remaining piece of the puzzle (short of a summit meeting with Kim Il Sung) was the achievement of diplomatic normalization with Beijing.

South Korea's achievement of diplomatic relations with China would carry with it political and economic costs as a result of Seoul's willingness to dispense with its relations with Taiwan. Although it was clear that Roh Tae Woo had been actively pursuing relations with

Beijing as part of his Nordpolitik policy, South Korean failures to manage the repercussions of cutting off diplomatic relations with Taipei were in sharp contrast to the diplomatic efforts China invested in maintaining a relationship with Pyongyang. By the early 1990s, South Korea was one of the bigger countries that continued to have official representation in Taiwan, so the loss of relations with South Korea constituted a significant setback, especially given the political and economic similarities between the two as rapidly industrializing countries that had recently faced democratic transitions.

Not surprisingly, China maintained a hard stance—that South Korea should cut off not only formal diplomatic relations with Taiwan, but also all other forms of relations, including "unofficial" and "economic" exchange between representatives in Taipei and Seoul. In its eagerness to establish diplomatic relations with China before the end of Roh Tae Woo's term in office, South Korea gave up such ties and unceremoniously sent Taiwanese diplomats packing only days before announcing formal relations between Seoul and Beijing in 1992. This unceremonious end to formal relations between Taiwan and South Korea has had significant repercussions, and the political, diplomatic, and economic wounds have been slow to heal. It took over a decade just for national flag-carriers to resume operations between the two countries.

The actual negotiation of normalization was accomplished in only four months following Qian Qichen's proposal to his counterpart, Lee Sang Ock, during the latter's visit to Beijing to attend a meeting of the UN's Economic and Social Committee of the Asia Pacific in April 1992. From May to July, in an atmosphere of utmost secrecy, the negotiations were conducted in three preliminary rounds and one main round between the two foreign ministers. South Korea's code name for the negotiations was "Operation East Sea." In return for a summit meeting in China prior to the end of the Roh presidency, South Korea conceded on almost all points, including the handling of Taiwan-related issues. South Korea also failed to gain Chinese assurances of assistance in dealing with North Korea's nuclear program and in opening a South Korean consulate-general in Shenyang.[41]

President Roh Tae Woo's eagerness to achieve diplomatic normalization was made clear to Foreign Minister Qian Qichen through both formal and informal channels during the latter's first visit to Seoul for the October 1991 APEC meeting.[42] South Korean negotiators clearly understood the political imperative of achieving normalization with China before the end of Roh's term in February 1993. The August 24, 1992, announcement of normalization of relations was quickly followed by a South Korean presidential visit to Beijing the next month, during which Roh celebrated his long-sought achievement in triumphal language: "Following my inauguration as the president, I said that if I could not go directly to Pyongang, I would go there via Moscow and Beijing. This idea is at the heart of my northern policy. My visit to Beijing, following my visit to Moscow the year before last, signifies that the day of unification is drawing that much closer. . . . I hope to go down in history as the president who has built the foundations for democracy and laid the groundwork for unification."[43]

Though diplomatic normalization was achieved on the basis of enhanced prospects for economic growth, South Korea's expectations for the returns that a relationship with Beijing might yield toward achieving Korean reunification were inflated. South Koreans recognized that China was a close friend and backer of North Korea, and many may have hoped that China's betrayal of Pyongyang would be more complete. These individuals hoped that Beijing's choice to normalize relations with South Korea signaled the imminent delivery of North Korea into South Korean hands, along the model of German reunification fresh in everyone's minds. Clearly, if such expectations existed, they were not reflected in China's cautious approach, which for many years had in fact given up significant economic gains out of deference to longtime socialist allies. China had in mind a more complex game that did not involve complete betrayal of North Korea, but that did involve hedging its bets and minimizing its risks in light of the shifts in the relative economic strengths of South and North Korea.

Trade Expectations and Effects
of Sino–South Korean Normalization

Expectations for economic gains proved to be a more powerful rationale than ideological loyalty or "lips and teeth" fraternal ties between Beijing and Pyongyang. The story of China's calculations for economic gains, represented by its relationship with Seoul—as well as its effort to avoid being saddled with endless economic burdens, represented by its relationship with Pyongyang—provides ample evidence in support of Dale Copeland's "theory of trade expectations" as a decisive variable in determining the prospects for conflict between two countries that are economically interdependent. According to this view, whether two countries view the prospects for future trade as expanding or diminishing is a critical variable in understanding the impact of economic interdependence on the likelihood of political conflict or cooperation. High economic interdependence will promote peaceful cooperation as long as states maintain positive expectations for future trade, but if states have negative expectations for future trade, a highly dependent state may see conflict as a viable alternative to a peaceful situation if the benefits derived from trade continue to diminish.[44] The theory of trade expectations provides a useful framework for analyzing China's respective approaches to North and South Korea and its decision to pursue normal relations with South Korea despite the political cost to its relations with North Korea.

As Table 2.1 shows, the opportunities associated with normalization of economic relations were already very clear by the mid-1980s. Even in the absence of diplomatic relations, China and South Korea were

Table 2.1   China's Trade with North and South Korea, 1981–2005 (US$ millions)

	China's Imports from North Korea	China's Exports to North Korea	Total	Balance	China's Imports from South Korea	China's Exports to South Korea	Total	Balance
1981	231	300	531	69	205	75	280	−130
1982	304	281	585	−23	48	91	139	43
1983	254	273	527	19	51	69	120	18
1984	272	226	498	−46	229	205	434	−24
1985	257	231	488	−26	683	478	1,161	−205
1986	277	233	510	−44	699	621	1,289	−47
1987	236	277	513	41	813	866	1,679	53
1988	234	345	579	111	1,700	1,387	3,087	−313
1989	185	377	562	192	1,438	1,705	3,143	267
1990	125	358	483	233	1,553	2,268	3,821	715
1991	86	525	611	439	2,371	3,441	5,812	1,070
1992	155	541	696	386	4,493	3,725	8,218	−768
1993	297	602	899	305	5,151	3,927	9,078	−1,224
1994	199	424	623	225	6,200	5,460	11,660	−740
1995	64	486	550	422	10,293	6,689	16,982	−3,604
1996	68	497	565	429	12,481	7,511	19,992	−4,970
1997	121	531	652	410	14,929	9,116	24,045	−5,813
1998	57	355	412	298	14,995	6,268	21,264	−8,727
1999	42	329	371	287	17,226	7,807	25,033	−9,419
2000	37	451	488	414	23,207	11,292	34,499	−11,915
2001	167	571	738	404	23,376	12,528	35,905	−10,848
2002	271	467	738	196	28,568	15,534	44,102	−13,034
2003	396	628	1,024	232	43,128	20,094	63,222	−23,034
2004	585	799	1,384	214	62,234	27,811	90,045	−34,423
2005	499	1,081	1,580	582	76,820	35,107	111,928	−41,713

Source: China Statistical Yearbooks, various years.

already recording over US$1 billion per year in bilateral trade by 1985, not counting indirect trade via Hong Kong. South Korea's trade with China had already doubled the level of trade with North Korea, after having finally pulled even with North Korea in 1984. Although the trends were clear to Chinese leaders such as Deng Xiaoping, China waited seven more years before finally deciding to normalize relations with South Korea. This decision was driven by clear expectations of expanded trade that would accompany the Sino–South Korean economic relationship, but perhaps what is remarkable is the extent to which Chinese leaders exercised considerable patience in making their decision in light of special political considerations in the Sino–North Korean relationship, even utilizing political controls to tamp down economic gains in the early 1980s.

However, by the early 1990s, China's economic expectations for its new relationship with South Korea eventually overcame its concerns about political costs. Due to the economic opportunities created by the growth of China and South Korea, the question of normalization became a question of when and how China could minimize its political losses with Pyongyang while taking advantage of the clear potential that would accompany normalization of relations with South Korea. Or, as Samuel Kim has stated, "While the South Korean economy represents opportunities to be more fully exploited, the North Korean economy poses a continuing burden to be progressively lessened, although without causing any crash landing."[45]

A parallel assessment of the future of the Sino–North Korean economic relationship reveals a downward trend in China's expectations, given the floundering of North Korea's economy. While no one could have predicted the tremendous stresses that would befall the North Korean economy as a result of the collapse of the Soviet Union, China already understood that its relationship with Pyongyang was a net loser in economic terms. For this reason, in the early 1990s, China attempted to transition from "friendship prices" to a market basis for managing the relationship. However, this transition proved impossible to achieve in light of North Korea's extraordinary economic difficulties.

Pursuing Equidistance in China's Two-Koreas Policy

The prior discussion illustrates the role that expectations for expanded trade played in paving the way for Sino–South Korean diplomatic normalization, a set of developments that occurred at the expense of North

Korea. Perceived economic opportunity was the primary catalyst for and enabler of Sino–South Korean normalization. But despite the critical role of economic opportunity as a driver for closer diplomatic relations, political and strategic rather than economic calculations remained primary justifications in the thinking of both Chinese and South Korean leaders as they made the decision to normalize diplomatic relations. For South Korea's president, Roh Tae Woo, the end of the Cold War provided new opportunities to overcome long-standing enmities as part of his strategy of Nordpolitik, which ultimately was aimed at both gaining an advantage over and pursuing reconciliation with North Korea. Deng Xiaoping explicitly cited strategic gains vis-à-vis Taiwan as a reason for pursuing normalization with South Korea, despite the fact that such a course would involve betrayal of North Korea.

In neither case did the stated political rationales underlying the normalization decisions yield concrete returns. Instead, the tangible returns, benefits, and driving forces behind the further development of relations in the years following normalization occurred primarily in the economic sphere. Growth in the bilateral economic relationship served to dampen the possibility of protracted conflict on sensitive political issues, if for no other reason than that political conflict would serve as a potential obstacle to further economic gains. The economic effect of the political decision to normalize relations in turn expanded the breadth and depth of social and political interaction between the two countries in the early phases of the Sino–South Korean relationship, stimulating greater tourism and exchange and generating greater public consciousness.

Although China's relationship with the Korean peninsula was centuries old, its establishment of diplomatic relations with South Korea was in many ways new. South Korean experience with industrialization provided valuable opportunities to their Chinese counterparts, while South Korean attitudes and approaches toward North Korea, and by extension political expectations toward China's role as a third-party actor and intermediary in inter-Korean relations, were undergoing a profound evolution throughout the 1990s. The process of economic and political familiarization had a steep learning curve and yielded many unanticipated positive results, but also uncovered important political and security challenges for the future.

Meanwhile, North Korea's economic decline and its ongoing political and security confrontation with the United States (and South Korea) posed particular challenges for China and its ability to maintain formal equidistance. The possibility that China's strategic asset could be transformed into a strategic liability would raise acute dilemmas for Chinese policymakers as time went on. While China transformed itself economically and rose to prominence as a significant regional and global power, North Korea was stagnated, isolated, and unwilling to pursue Chinese-style reform of its feudalistic political system.

Notes

1. Zhang Xiaoming, "The Korean Peninsula and China's National Security: Past, Present, and Future," *Asian Perspective* 22, no. 3 (1998): 261.

2. Joanne Gowa, "Bipolarity, Multipolarity, and Free Trade," *American Political Science Review* 83, no. 4 (December 1989): 1245–1256.

3. Chen Jian, *China's Road to the Korean War: The Making of the Sino-American Confrontation* (New York: Columbia University Press, 1996). Interestingly, the only opportunity a Chinese representative had to address the United Nations prior to China's entry into the organization was during a November 1950 General Assembly discussion of the Korean War. Zhao Quansheng, "China, the United Nations, and the Korean Peninsula," in Kang Sung-hack, ed., *The United Nations and Keeping Peace in Northeast Asia* (Seoul: Institute for Peace Studies, Korea University, 1995), p. 163.

4. Suh Dae-sook, *Kim Il Sung: The North Korean Leader* (New York: Columbia University Press, 1988), pp. 107–157.

5. Jasper Becker, *Hungry Ghosts: Mao's Secret Famine* (New York: Henry Holt, 1998).

6. See Kongdan Oh and Ralph Hassig, *North Korea Through the Looking Glass* (Washington, DC: Brookings Institution, 2000), p. 178.

7. See Charles K. Armstrong, *The North Korean Revolution: 1945–1950* (Ithaca: Cornell University Press), 2003.

8. Suh, *Kim Il Sung*, pp. 176–210.

9. Lee Chae-jin, *China and Korea: Dynamic Relations* (Stanford: Hoover Institution, 1996), p. 59.

10. Don Oberdorfer, *The Two Koreas* (Reading, MA: Addison-Wesley, 1997), pp. 23–26.

11. Chung Jae Ho, *Between Ally and Partner: Korea-China Relations and the United States* (New York: Columbia University Press, 2006), pp. 29–31.

12. Oberdorfer, *The Two Koreas*, pp. 23–26.

13. Peter Hayes, *Pacific Powderkeg: American Nuclear Dilemmas in Korea* (Lexington, MA: Lexington Books, 1991); James Moltz, ed., *The North Korean Nuclear Program: Security, Strategy, and New Perspectives from Russia* (New York: Routledge, 1999).

14. Lee, *China and Korea*, p. 106. Lee's citation is from *Yomiuri Shimbun*, March 30, 1980. Chung, *Between Ally and Partner*, p. 57.

15. Qian Qichen, *Waijiao Shiji* [Ten Stories of China's Diplomacy] (Beijing: Shijie Zhishi Chubanshe, 2003), pp. 137–162.

16. Zhang, "The Korean Peninsula and China's National Security," pp.

259–272. See also Jia Hao and Zhuang Qubing, "China's Policy Toward the Korean Peninsula." *Asian Survey* 32, no. 12 (December 1992): 1144.

17. Chung, *Between Ally and Partner*, pp. 29–42.

18. Lee, *China and Korea*, pp. 106–112.

19. Jia and Zhuang, "China's Policy Toward the Korean Peninsula," p. 1142.

20. Zhao, "China, the United Nations, and the Korean Peninsula," p. 169.

21. Jia and Zhuang, "China's Policy Toward the Korean Peninsula," p. 1147.

22. Kim Hakjoon, "China's Policy Since the Tiananmen Square Incident," *Proceedings of the Academy of Political Science* 38, no. 2, *The China Challenge: American Policies in East Asia* (1991): 107–114.

23. See Chung, *Between Ally and Partner*, p. 45.

24. Kim, "China's Policy Since the Tiananmen Square Incident."

25. Samuel S. Kim, "The Dialectics of China's North Korea Policy," *Asian Perspective* 18, no. 2 (Fall–Winter 1994): 8.

26. Kim, "China's Policy Since the Tiananmen Square Incident."

27. Chung, *Between Ally and Partner*, pp. 67–74. Chung cites Park Chul-un, *Bareun Yoksa-Reul Wihan Jeungun* [Testimonies for Correct History], vol. 2 (Seoul: Random House Joong-Ang, 2005), pp. 24–25.

28. Gilbert Rozman, "Korea's Strategic Thought Toward Russia," in Gilbert Rozman, Hyun In-taek, and Lee Shinwha, *South Korean Strategic Thought Toward Asia* (New York: Palgrave Macmillan, 2008), pp. 203–224.

29. Chung Jae Ho, "South Korean Strategic Thought Toward China," in Rozman, Hyun, and Lee, *South Korean Strategic Thought Toward Asia*, pp. 159–161.

30. Valery I. Denisov, "Viewpoint: The U.S.-DPRK Deal—a Russian Perspective," *Nonproliferation Review* 3, no. 3 (Spring–Summer 1996): 75.

31. Qian, *Waijiao Shiji*.

32. Chung, *Between Ally and Partner*, pp. 26–28.

33. Qian, *Waijiao Shiji*.

34. Ibid.

35. Chung, *Between Ally and Partner*, p. 42.

36. Qian, *Waijiao Shiji*.

37. Ibid.

38. Ibid.

39. Kim, "The Dialectics of China's North Korea Policy," p. 15.

40. Jia and Zhuang, "China's Policy Toward the Korean Peninsula," p. 1156.

41. Chung, *Between Ally and Partner*, pp. 69–74.

42. Qian, *Waijiao Shiji*.

43. Bruce Cheeseman, "China Visit Helps Thaw Cold War, Says Roh," *South China Morning Post*, September 10, 1992, p. 10.

44. See Dale C. Copeland, "Economic Interdependence and War: A Theory of Trade Expectations," *International Security* 20, no. 4 (Spring 1996): 5–41.

45. Kim, "The Dialectics of China's North Korea Policy," p. 18.

3

The Transformation of Sino–South Korean Economic Relations

Economic opportunity has been the primary driver for expanded relations between China and South Korea since normalization in August 1992. On that occasion, no one could possibly have anticipated the rate at which economic ties would continue to grow. Trade grew at double-digit rates for over fifteen years, from US$2.56 billion in 1990 to over US$100 billion in 2005, and China surpassed the United States in 2004 as South Korea's largest trading partner. South Korea's investment in China as a share of its total foreign direct investment (FDI) rose from 4 percent in 1991 to a peak of 43 percent in 2006.[1] South Korean cumulative investment in China through September 2006 reached over US$16.3 billion, surpassing the cumulative level of South Korean investment in the United States.

Just as economic forces overcame political and strategic concerns to enable diplomatic normalization, rapidly rising economic interdependence created opportunities for expanded bilateral political cooperation. For the first time in the 1990s, a "China lobby" developed in Seoul composed of individuals and corporate interests who eagerly promoted expanded relations with China. In many sectors, the successful realization of business opportunities in China required government support in the form of official bilateral negotiations on specific issues between South Korea and China. The development of bilateral economic ties in turn strengthened domestic constituencies in support of the relationship, conforming to theories of international political economy that emphasize the power of globalization to create domestic constituencies in favor of international trade.[2]

For the most part, the rapid development of Sino–South Korean trade and investment ties has paved the way for development of closer bilateral political relations. But as the relationship has matured and especially as China has developed the capability to compete directly with South Korean firms on international markets in selected sectors, South Koreans have also expressed anxieties that economic dependency on China might leave them vulnerable if China were to attempt to utilize economic leverage to achieve its political goals through coercion. These concerns have not constrained continuing growth in trade or investment ties, but they have stimulated a strategic political response in the form of South Korean interest in negotiating a free trade agreement with the United States as a hedge against the centripetal pull of China-centered economic interdependence. South Korean fears of overdependence on China have played out primarily in the economic sphere, but the emergence of such anxieties imposes a potential limitation on prospects for expanded Sino–South Korean political cooperation as South Korea seeks instruments to hedge against perceived downside consequences of China's rise. The emergence of such fears also suggests that there is an inherent limit to China's ability to utilize South Korea's economic dependence on China as political leverage to demand specific quid pro quos as long as South Korea is able to identify alternative trade and investment partners in the international economy. South Korean anxieties themselves illustrate that South Korea desires to resist any possible attempt by China to condition further economic engagement on the achievement of its own political goals.

Overview of the Sino–South Korean Economic Relationship Since Normalization

The Sino–South Korean economic relationship developed in four distinct phases between 1992 and 2007. First was an initial phase of rapid growth, from 1992 through 1997, during which previously unavailable mutual economic opportunities were discovered and developed primarily through investments by small and medium-sized South Korean enterprises. Second was a period of readjustment following the South Korean financial crisis, which provided China with lessons for how to manage risks of financial liberalization and problems associated with nonperforming bank loans. Third was an expansion of trade and investment driven by China's entry into the World Trade Organization (WTO) and resulting large-scale expansion into the Chinese market by South Korean chaebols beginning in December 2001. And fourth was an adjustment phase, beginning in early 2006, during which issues of competitiveness, market access, and the political implications of South Korea's dependence on China and loss of competitive advantage in third-country markets began to make themselves felt as political issues in South Korea. For the most part, the economic relationship developed without regard to political considerations or easily overcame potential political obstacles through 2005. Around this time, South Korean concerns about the ramifications of their increasing dependence on Chinese economic growth, and concerns about maintaining their competitive edge vis-à-vis China, emerged as serious issues for consideration by policymakers in Seoul.

Sino–South Korean Economic Honeymoon, 1992–1997

The Sino-South Korean bilateral trade and investment relationship doubled twice in the six years following the formal establishment of diplomatic relations, totaling almost US$12 billion by 1994 and almost US$24 billion in 1997 (see Table 3.1). China's share of South Korea's

Table 3.1   Sino–South Korean Trade, 1991–2006 (US$ millions)

	China's Total Exports to South Korea	China's Total Imports from South Korea	Total Trade Between China and South Korea	South Korea's Total Exports	South Korea's Total Imports	South Korea's Total Trade	South Korea's Trade with China as Percentage of Its Total Trade
1991	1,003	3,441	4,444	71,870	81,525	153,395	3.0
1992	2,654	3,725	6,379	76,632	81,775	158,407	4.0
1993	5,151	3,929	9,080	82,236	83,800	166,036	5.5
1994	6,203	5,463	11,666	96,013	102,348	198,361	5.9
1995	9,161	7,424	16,585	125,058	135,119	260,177	6.4
1996	11,377	8,539	19,916	129,715	150,339	280,054	7.1
1997	13,572	10,117	23,689	136,164	144,616	280,780	8.4
1998	11,944	6,484	18,428	132,313	93,282	225,595	8.2
1999	13,685	8,867	22,552	143,685	119,752	263,437	8.6
2000	18,455	12,799	31,254	172,268	160,481	332,749	9.4
2001	18,190	13,303	31,493	150,439	141,098	291,537	10.7
2002	23,754	17,400	41,154	162,471	152,126	314,597	13.1
2003	35,110	21,909	57,019	193,817	178,827	372,644	15.3
2004	49,763	29,585	79,348	253,845	224,463	478,308	16.6
2005	61,915	38,648	100,563	284,419	261,238	545,657	18.4
2006	69,459	48,557	118,016	325,465	309,383	634,848	18.6

Source: Bank of Korea.

total trade doubled from 4.0 percent in 1992 to 8.4 percent in 1997 and reached over 16 percent of South Korea's overall trade in 2004, when China became South Korea's largest trading partner. South Korean investment in China as a proportion of its overall investment jumped from 3.8 percent (US$42 million) in 1991 to 26.8 percent in 1994 (see Table 3.2).[3] By 1997, China had already become South Korea's third largest trading partner, while South Korea was China's fourth largest trading partner and sixth largest foreign investor.[4]

This first phase in the development of Sino–South Korean economic relations was characterized by a growth in trade and investment ties largely focused on taking advantage of China's low land and labor costs to produce goods for export to third-country markets, especially the United States. The primary driver of this growth in its initial stages was Chinese demand for South Korean exports of industrial supplies and capital goods, while China initially exported mainly raw materials to South Korea. During the 1990s, South Korea's leading exports to China were industrial intermediate goods including electrical machinery, nuclear reactors and boilers, plastics, petrochemical products, and iron and steel. China's leading exports to South Korea during this period were primary products (products used as raw materials in the production of other goods), agricultural and fishery products, industrial raw materi-

Table 3.2 South Korea's Foreign Direct Investment in China, 1992–2006

	Number of Projects	Foreign Direct Investment in China (US$ millions)	South Korea's Total Foreign Investment (US$ millions)	South Korea's Investment in China/ Total Investment (%)
1992	170	141	1,216	12
1993	382	264	1,265	21
1994	840	635	2,304	28
1995	752	842	3,103	27
1996	740	929	4,462	21
1997	631	742	3,685	20
1998	264	696	4,798	15
1999	459	365	3,336	11
2000	775	712	5,075	14
2001	1,050	646	5,176	13
2002	1,383	1,042	3,758	28
2003	1,677	1,744	4,149	42
2004	2,144	2,381	6,083	39
2005	2,242	2,781	6,719	41
2006	1,762	3,201	7,455	43

Source: Export-Import Bank of Korea.

als, and some consumer goods, but the mix of exports from China to South Korea saw dramatic changes during this period. China began to export more intermediate industrial goods to South Korea, while the share of raw materials as a proportion of China's overall exports to South Korea decreased dramatically.[5]

South Korean investment in China grew rapidly in line with a global surge in foreign direct investment into China, since China's economic opening to FDI coincided with Sino–South Korean diplomatic normalization. In the early 1990s, China became the world's leading destination for foreign investment among developing countries, on the basis of efforts by foreign firms to take advantage of low Chinese labor costs and to establish bases for global exports in China's special economic zones. Given South Korea's geographic proximity with China, lagging competitiveness of South Korean labor costs, complementarities in Chinese and South Korean inputs, opportunities for China to move up the development ladder by gaining experience in South Korean–invested factories, and the right mix of quality and price for the US export market, the conditions were conducive for rapid expansion of South Korean trade and investment into China in order to take advantage of opportunities in the US market. As a result of these new conditions, South Korean manufacturing investment in China grew rapidly. The increase in Sino–South Korean investment and trade during this period reflected natural adjustments following the suppression of economic relations due to political factors during the Cold War.

Supporting the rapid expansion of trade relations, South Korean investment in China expanded dramatically in the mid-1990s until the advent of the South Korean financial crisis in 1998, and then expanded further following China's entry into the WTO in 2001 (see Table 3.2). By 1994, only a few years after diplomatic normalization, China became South Korea's primary destination for foreign investment, and this investment from South Korea remained at healthy levels until South Korea's financial crisis took its toll. A unique aspect of South Korea's foreign direct investment in China in the mid-1990s was that it was driven by small and medium-sized enterprises, especially in labor-intensive sectors such as electrical product manufacturing, machinery and equipment, petroleum and chemical products, and textiles. Although small and medium-sized firms routinely represent only about one-fifth of overall investment outflows from South Korea, in the mid-1990s these firms were responsible for about 40 percent of investment outflows to China.[6] By the end of 1997, South Korean investment in China had risen to about US$3.3 billion, consisting of over 3,500 projects. South Korean investments in China represented about 45 percent of the total number of projects and 20 percent of the total amount of South Korean overseas investments through 1997.[7]

The geographic proximity of China and South Korea enabled smaller South Korean firms, especially from labor-intensive industries that could no longer compete as a result of rising South Korean wages, such as textiles, shoes, transportation, mining, electronics, and chemicals, to survive by entering the Chinese market, where labor costs were approximately 7.5 times lower than in South Korea in 2002, a wage gap that had narrowed considerably compared to the mid-1990s.[8] The combination of South Korea's rising labor costs and resulting lack of competitiveness in labor-intensive manufacturing industries, and China's relative proximity and lower labor costs, stimulated extensive investment in China as an attractive manufacturing base for South Korean exports, especially in industrial sectors where wage levels for South Korean labor were no longer internationally competitive. Over 85 percent of South Korean investments throughout this period remained focused in the Chinese manufacturing sector. Since a variety of factors prevented South Korean production for the Chinese market, the dominant rationale for South Korea has been to use China as a production base for export to third countries.[9]

South Korean investment during this period was primarily centered in

Table 3.3 South Korea's Investment in China, 1992–2006 (US$ millions)

	South Korean Foreign Direct Investment	Global Foreign Investment in China	South Korea's Share of Total Investment in China (%)
1992	120	11,291	1
1993	381	27,770	1
1994	726	33,945	2
1995	1,047	48,132	2
1996	1,504	54,804	3
1997	2,227	64,408	4
1998	1,803	45,462	4
1999	1,274	40,318	3
2000	1,489	40,714	4
2001	2,151	46,877	5
2002	2,720	52,742	5
2003	4,488	53,504	8
2004	6,247	60,629	10
2005	5,168	72,405	7
2006	3,894	69,467	6

Sources: China Statistical Yearbook, various years; *China Commerce Yearbook,* various years.

the provinces closest to the Korean peninsula, including Shandong, Liaoning, Tianjian, and Jiangsu. South Korea's FDI in this region accounted for over three-quarters of its FDI in China, while most of the remainder focused on the southern economic zones at Guangdong, Fujian, Zhejiang, and Shanghai. Investments in those provinces accounted for about half of accumulated FDI entering China. South Korean investment in China was reinforced by government efforts beginning in the late 1980s to develop the west coast and Cholla provincial areas closest to Shandong and Liaoning provinces that had traditionally been neglected in the earlier phases of South Korea's industrial development. Through 1997, over three-quarters of South Korea's investment came from its less industrialized west coast, including Seoul, Incheon, and the Cholla provinces. Support from local political officials, economic liberalization policies, sociocultural factors, and enhanced transportation infrastructure investment interacted as mutually reinforcing factors in creating a cross-border economic zone across the Bohai Sea that dynamically linked the South Korean and Chinese economies in an unprecedented fashion.[10]

South Korea's investment in China's export processing zones had a direct impact on the trade deficits of both countries with the United States during this period (see Table 3.4). As South Korea scrupulously tried to avoid running up a large trade surplus with the United States so as to avoid further US pressure to open protected sectors of its market, its

Table 3.4   **United States–South Korea, United States–China, and South Korea–China Trade Balances, 1988–2000 (US$ millions)**

	United States–South Korea	United States–China	South Korea–China
1988	−8,899	−3,473	−1,014
1989	−6,277	−6,234	−1,267
1990	−4,081	−10,430	−1,683
1991	−1,513	−12,691	−2,438
1992	−2,043	−18,309	−1,071
1993	2,336	−22,777	1,222
1994	1,603	−29,504	740
1995	1,195	−33,789	1,742
1996	3,966	−39,520	2,838
1997	1,873	−49,695	3,455
1998	−7,456	−56,927	5,460
1999	−8,220	−68,677	4,817
2000	−12,477	−83,833	5,655

Sources: US Census Bureau (United States–South Korea and United States–China statistics), Korean International Trade Association (South Korea–China statistics).

investment in China became a useful safety valve for controlling its surplus with the United States, in effect transferring it to China. At the same time, South Korean investment in China generated higher trade flows as well as a structural surplus in South Korea's trade balance with China, especially since the resulting production was intended for export from China to the international market. A substantial part of South Korea's trade surplus with China is easily explained when one considers that South Korean investment in China played the role of a "pass through" for goods that were ultimately destined for sale in the United States.

The growing trade surplus between South Korea and China could also be explained by South Korea's relative position as a more industrialized country that provided capital and technology for joint projects, while China provided labor and land for production. This is the same role that Japan has long played in South Korea's development, which continues to be reflected in the latter's long-standing structural trade deficit with the former. The downside of this relationship lies in growing competitiveness of developing countries in sectors in which the more developed country has long sustained a significant market share.

Another critical factor that supported the development of Sino–South Korean economic relations was China's explicit identification of South Korea as a model for its own economic development. Among the newly industrializing economies of the 1980s, such as Singapore, Hong Kong, and Taiwan, South Korea was a more attractive model than Singapore or Hong Kong, which had built their economies on their unique roles as ports and as city-states. Political factors made countries like Hong Kong and Taiwan unattractive and politically incorrect as models for China's economic development. But the experience of South Korea's authoritarian political leaders with state-directed, export-led development appealed to China as a model for its economic reforms as early as the mid-1980s. South Korea's experience with economic development illustrated how China could productively utilize its central planning and state-owned enterprise structures as assets in the service of economic opening and reform.[11]

During the 1990s, South Korea began to supply China with long-term, low-interest development loans in support of the overall bilateral relationship. During Jiang Zemin's summit meeting with Kim Young Sam in Seoul in 1995, South Korea made a ten-year commitment to provide development loans to China, and by 2001 had disbursed almost US$100 million.[12] In addition, the Korean Overseas International Cooperation Agency reports sixty-three cooperation projects in China, valued at over US$36 million, through 2005.[13]

The first phase of development in the Sino–South Korean economic relationship exploited natural economic complementarities once the political obstacles that had previously blocked development of the relationship had finally been overcome. During the early and middle 1990s, no significant political issues arose, either as a result of the rapid growth in the economic relationship or as impediments to it. The natural development of bilateral trade and investment opportunities represented a "win-win" situation and fueled a "China fever" in South Korea on the basis of double-digit trade and investment growth and the complementarities between South Korea's capital and technology and China's low land and labor costs, especially in labor-intensive manufactures for export primarily to the US market. This first phase in the growth of Sino–South Korean trade and investment also laid the foundation for later opportunities, pending the further opening of the Chinese market with China's accession to the WTO in 2001.

South Korean Financial Crisis and Impact on Relations with China, 1997–2000

South Korea's financial crisis introduced a period of readjustment in the bilateral economic relationship, marking a pause in the growth of Sino–South Korean trade and investment relations as South Korea preoccupied itself with fixing its own financial problems and laying the basis for economic recovery. The South Korean financial crisis also had significant ramifications for a China that had taken South Korea and other newly industrializing economies as models in charting its own future development course. South Korea's experience gave China an opportunity to learn from the former's mistakes, while providing opportunities for South Korean specialists to gain practical knowledge in critical areas that might have direct applications to Chinese economic policy.

Analysis shows that the South Korean financial crisis started as a currency crisis in which the South Korean central bank was unable to sustain the value of the won due to the realization among international investors that South Korean companies were overexposed to short-term debt financed by international borrowing. The decline in the value of the South Korean won created a financial crisis for many South Korean firms—already operating under sizable debt-to-equity ratios—that could no longer generate the cash flows necessary to finance debt payments in dollars, which had effectively doubled due to the won's decline in value. The South Korean government's implementation of currency liberalization measures in the mid-1990s, including the lifting of restrictions on short-term capital inflows, posed an additional threat to South Korea's financial structure, which still relied inordinately on debt in light of the underdevelopment of equity and bond markets as sources of corporate financing.[14]

South Korea's financial vulnerability thus came about as a result of several structural factors. First, liberalization of an underdeveloped financial sector encouraged debt financing through international borrowing rather than through equity markets. Second, the nature of government-business relations provided reason for business owners to think that the government would bail them out in the event of failure. Third, chaebol strategies focused on growth and capture of market share at the expense of profitability. Fourth, lack of transparency in accounting (including complex cross–shareholding relationships among companies tied to the same primary shareholders) obscured the true state of debt loads. And fifth, the financial crisis drew the attention of international investors to the substantial debt burdens that South Korean companies carried. The financial crisis provided a shock to the real economy, since it influenced the availability of capital for firms to operate, resulted in layoffs that heightened unemployment, and made imported goods more expensive due to the dramatic weakening of the won in international currency markets.

In response to the crisis, a newly elected government under Kim Dae Jung signed on to an International Monetary Fund package, including loan pledges of up to US$57 billion. In return, South Korea committed to follow strict financial management guidelines that were intended to restore its credibility and to put in place reform measures that would reduce its financial vulnerabilities and put its companies onto a more stable financial footing. In addition to extensive efforts by the South Korean government to support financial workouts for heavily indebted South Korean companies, South Korea's reforms included renegotiation of international debt exposure of its companies and enhancement of transparency measures and accounting standards, regular publishing of corporate annual reports, and pressure to end cross-shareholdings among related companies through which debt risks could be obscured and malfeasance could be easily hidden.

The financial crisis distracted South Korean businesses from focusing on continued growth via offshore production using Chinese cheap labor, and made additional investment infrastructure in China extremely difficult due to the sudden shortage of capital that most firms faced. South Korean firms had to put investment plans on hold in order to focus on their own survival, so plans for expansion into China were postponed. Although China was praised for not devaluing its currency and not taking advantage of potential gains resulting from the distress of neighboring economies in Thailand, Indonesia, and South Korea, the crisis also provided an object lesson to Chinese economic planners regarding the importance of managing financial liberalization and the dangers inherent in the levels of nonperforming debt that were being accumulated in the Chinese banking sector as part of the process of financing China's economic takeoff.

Kim Jong Kil has analyzed lessons that China might learn from the Asian financial crisis. He observes that Chinese state enterprises suffer from mismanagement and declining profitability, contributing to unrecoverable debt and damaged balance sheets of major Chinese banks, and that the size of China's financial needs may compel liberalization measures that—if not properly handled—could require China to take risks similar to those taken by other Asian economies as they liberalized capital markets. China's state enterprises resemble South Korean chaebols, and government-, business-, and banking-sector relationships play a role in China's financial sector similar to that which existed in South Korea prior to the financial crisis. In other words, China's corporate-sector financing faces many of the same potential vulnerabilities that South Korea fell victim to during its financial crisis in 1997. Kim recommends South Korean reform measures to address poor corporate governance and financial-sector restructuring as lessons from the South Korean experience that might also apply to China.[15]

Based on South Korea's success in recovering from the 1997 financial crisis, officials from its quasi-governmental Korean Asset Management Corporation, created based on the model of the American Resolution Trust Corporation, the latter of which was established to manage the US savings and loan crisis of the 1980s, have worked actively with Chinese counterparts to share South Korean lessons from the financial crisis and to advise Chinese government and banking officials on methods for managing their considerable financial exposure to nonperforming loans, estimated to constitute up to 50 percent of China's loans overall. Although the nonconvertibility of China's currency was a factor that helped to insulate it from the Asian financial crisis in 1997–1998, its exposure to the international financial community continues to grow as Chinese firms increasingly seek financing through both international equity and bond offerings.

China also faces increasing pressure to liberalize its currency given a ballooning trade surplus with the United States. As China manages its own integration with the international financial community, South

Korea's experiences with financial liberalization, including hard lessons learned through financial crisis, will provide relevant expertise.

China's WTO Entry and Revitalized
Economic Relations with South Korea, 2001–2004

China's entry into the World Trade Organization triggered a lowering of tariffs that had previously inhibited entry of foreign firms into many sectors of the Chinese market. In combination with changes in Chinese laws that eased conditions for foreign investment and removed some restrictions on sale of foreign goods in the Chinese domestic market, this sparked another round of global investment flows into China, this time in major manufacturing sectors such as steel, automobile manufacturing, electronics, and computers, in which China became the processing and production base for the global market. Global companies poured investment into large-scale plants in these significant manufacturing sectors. South Korean firms joined the race among multinational firms to use China as a foothold for pursuing a global production strategy in which China was at the start of a production chain to meet global consumer demand. In the case of South Korean firms, companies would supply inputs for assembly and export to South Korean and third-country markets. In addition, China's market liberalization created new opportunities to meet rising domestic demand in the Chinese market for South Korean–made mobile phones and automobiles.

China's liberalization stimulated a second "China fever" in South Korea, driving growth in trade at an annualized rate of over 30 percent from 2001 through 2005 and stimulating unprecedented levels of South Korean investment in China. According to the Export-Import Bank of Korea, South Korean investment in China dramatically increased from 1,383 contracted projects worth US$1.0 billion in 2002, representing 5.2 percent of all foreign investment in China during that year, to 2,144 projects worth over US$2.4 billion in 2004, representing over 10 percent of all foreign investment in China. South Korea has consistently been one of the top five sources of foreign direct investment in China in recent years and was the third largest source of foreign investment in China (and the largest source of nonethnic Chinese investment) during 2004, behind only Hong Kong and the Virgin Islands. One curious twist in South Korea's investment patterns during this period that distinguishes it from the overall trend is that while the total amount of foreign investment in China continued to increase by double-digit rates, from US$53.5 billion in 2003 to US$60.6 billion in 2004, total levels of investment in China from Taiwan, Singapore, and the United States dropped in 2004.[16] During the first quarter of 2004, South Korea accounted for 16 percent of FDI in China, while Japan represented 13 percent; the United States, 11 percent; and Taiwan, 9 percent.[17]

The focus of investment flows since 2001 has shifted from the pattern in the 1990s of localized labor-intensive, export-oriented processing operations, toward larger-scale and technology-intensive sectors such as electronics, communications, automobiles, and intermediate goods from which products are being made for sale in the local consumer market. Since China's opening of its domestic market in accordance with WTO obligations in 2001, a surge in investment has been led by large South Korean firms such as Samsung, SK Telecom, LG, Hyundai, and Posco, and such large-scale investment projects have tended to be located in Shanghai, Jiangsu, and Zhejiang provinces in coastal China, in and around Beijing and Tianjian, and in Shenzhen province. Although labor and land costs are highest in these areas, many larger South Korean firms have decided to focus their investments in these areas in order to partner with local companies that have the capacity to sell to the local market. This means that size, financial capacity, technology, and relationships with government are more important as criteria for choosing a joint venture partner and therefore as factors in determining the location of investments in China.[18] This investment also affected smaller South Korean suppliers, especially in the auto parts manufacturing sector, which sought to relocate its production bases near South Korean–invested factories in pursuit of labor-cost advantages. The proportion of small to medium-sized firms investing in China jumped from 83.7 percent in 1999 to 93.6 percent in 2004, based primarily on efforts by small and medium-sized suppliers to follow larger investments by their major customers in China.[19]

The rapid increase in South Korean foreign direct investment in China that derived from China's market opening drove a surprisingly strong growth in Sino–South Korean bilateral trade, from US$24 billion in 1999 to over US$100 billion in 2005. (In 2002, the two governments had projected that the US$100 billion mark in trade would be reached by 2008, but the mark was achieved three years early.) On the basis of the growth that had occurred during the 1990s, South Korea had already become China's fourth largest trading partner, representing 7 percent of China's overall trade by 2001 (compared to only a 3 percent share of China's overall trade in 1992). China had become South Korea's third largest trading partner by 2001, with an 11 percent share of China's overall trade. The second takeoff in bilateral trade relations would consolidate China as South Korea's leading trade partner (representing 18 percent of South Korea's overall trade) by 2004.

An examination of the core drivers of growth in Sino–South Korean trade relations reveals the importance of the information technology, automobile, steel, and chemical-processing sectors as catalysts for the expansion of the relationship since 2001. Compared to the 1990s, information technology, large-scale manufacturing, and heavy industry have become major growth sectors for South Korean exports. South Korean exports to China are primarily composed of intermediate goods (80 percent in 2004). With China's entry into the WTO, larger South Korean firms could make large-scale investments in sectors such as computers, telecommunications, and automobiles that would ultimately target and depend on the local Chinese market rather than manufacturing for export to third-country markets.

A new development in the bilateral economic relationship beginning in 2000 was the emergence of Chinese overseas investment, including in South Korea. Chinese investments in South Korea were initially small-scale and experimental, focused primarily on enhancing branding opportunities for Chinese-made products, securing means for entry into foreign markets, and acquiring new technology that would support China's effort to climb the development ladder. Chinese investment in South Korea has primarily been focused on automobiles, information technology, iron and steel, and research and development. South Korea's Ministry of Commerce, Industry, and Energy recorded almost 600 investment projects from China with a value of $1.165 billion in 2004 (see Table 3.5).[20]

The most significant Chinese investment in South Korea has been the takeover of financially distressed Ssangyong Motors by the Shanghai Automotive Investment Corporation (SAIC) in October 2004.

Table 3.5 China's Foreign Direct Investment in South Korea, 1988–2007

	Number of Projects	Value (US$ millions)
1988–1999	658	80
2000	1,165	77
2001	812	70
2002	442	249
2003	522	50
2004	596	1,165
2005	672	68
2006	334	39
2007	365	385

Source: Republic of Korea, Ministry of Commerce, Industry, and Energy.

This investment provided an opportunity for Chinese management to gain access to new technology and provided Chinese owners with an important avenue for distribution to the South Korean market. Despite automobiles as a strategically significant sector in which South Korea enjoyed an international competitive advantage, the South Korean government did not employ economic protectionism and allowed the investment to go forward (unlike the attempt by China National Overseas Oil Corporation to invest in the US-owned Unocal Corporation). However, efforts by Ssangyong laborers to protect their own positions and privileges, demand additional Chinese investment in South Korean plants, and thwart possible Chinese attempts to apply South Korean–based technology to investment in new Chinese factories have led to incessant labor-management conflict between Ssangyong's labor union and Chinese management, culminating in a prolonged walkout in the fall of 2006.

Another trend in the Sino–South Korean economic relationship that underscored China's interest in South Korea as a model for its own economic development was the emergence of overseas training contracts for Chinese laborers to spend time in South Korea. These short-term training contracts offered South Korea the opportunity to utilize China's low-cost labor while also providing Chinese participants with new skills and experience in South Korean business and manufacturing processes. South Korean overseas training contracts with China peaked in 2001, when 555 labor contracts, worth US$230 million and involving approximately 43,500 Chinese workers, were executed.[21]

The period following China's 2001 entry into the WTO was characterized by remarkable growth in Sino–South Korean economic relations, which for the most part paralleled China's rapid rise to prominence as the world's manufacturing hub. However, South Korea's proximity to China and the complementarity of its level of development with that of China offered unique opportunities for rapid growth as China continued its integration with the global economy. China needed many of the intermediate or end products that had propelled South Korea's industrialization, but was only beginning to develop the critical industrial infrastructure that would eventually allow its products to compete directly with South Korean products in third-country markets. South Korean manufacturers of mobile phones, automobiles, and information and communication technology struck gold during this period as they rushed to meet the opportunities posed by the opening of China's domestic market in critical sectors. In 2003–2004, as South Korea's domestic economic growth slowed, its exports to China boomed, mitigating the effects of its domestic economic stagnation.

However, as Chinese domestic capital investments began to provide Chinese firms with indigenous production capacity in key sectors such as automobiles, steel, port infrastructure, and information and communication technology, South Korean firms began to feel the impact of Chinese competition in international markets. The emergence of this competition spawned an increase in both South Korean and Chinese charges of dumping and unfair practices, leading to charges of antidumping in the WTO. For both sides, the lure of unparalleled opportunity, undergirded by double-digit rates of growth in trade and investment, far outweighed the longer-term risks of economic or political conflict, and during this period the possible costs that might accrue from enhanced economic interdependence remained, for the most part, unexamined.

The "China Threat" in the Economic Sphere: South Korean Dependency

Beginning in 2005, a steady stream of economic studies began to emerge from South Korean research institutions showing that South Korean economic competitiveness vis-à-vis China was declining as Chinese firms closed the technological lead that had been enjoyed by South Korean firms in many critical sectors. Economic statistics showed that the market share of exports from China was growing rapidly in third-country markets, while the South Korean market share began to decline. South Korea's anemic growth rates and the apparent stagnation of its domestic economy further added to anxieties about its future competitiveness in the context of China's economic rise.

In March 2006, South Korean finance and economy minister Han Duck Soo publicly raised the alarm about competitiveness in third-country markets, warning that "it is of the utmost importance to appropriately understand the changes coming from China's rapid rise and how to come up with ways to best cope with the challenge."[22] Han's comments arguably mark the start of a fourth phase in Sino–South Korean economic relations, during which the increased price competitiveness of Chinese products began to challenge South Korean products in areas where South Korea had traditionally enjoyed a strategic advantage, leading to structural changes in economic relations and enhancing the likelihood that economic tensions could become a political issue between the two countries.

As new Chinese production came online, South Korea's international competitiveness faltered. South Korea's Ministry of Commerce,

Industry, and Energy reported that a January 2006 survey of 300 South Korean companies had revealed a belief by over 86 percent of respondents that technology was developing faster in China than in South Korea. The ministry assessed that South Korea was less than three years ahead of China in developing appliances containing liquid crystal displays, and had only a two-year lead in the development of rechargeable batteries. The gap was even narrower in the manufacture of mobile phone and communication equipment, for some aspects of which South Korea had only a one-year lead over China. Faring better, the South Korean automobile sector had a three- to eight-year lead in the production of many key parts and systems, and the South Korean shipbuilding sector had a decade lead.[23]

The impact of increasing competitiveness of Chinese products, which were even making inroads in sales to South Korean customers, marked a structural shift in Sino–South Korean trade relations that has led to gradual reductions in South Korea's long-standing trade surplus with China, but has also called into question South Korea's long-term competitiveness and stimulated strategic thinking among South Korean government and business leaders regarding how to respond. Just as South Korean steel-makers and shipbuilders gradually took a greater share of the global market in these sectors from Japanese companies, Chinese companies (many of which have enhanced their production capacity and moved up the technological ladder thanks to investment from South Korean partners) are poised to undercut South Korean manufacturers in the steel, automobile, and shipbuilding sectors in both domestic and international markets. A major challenge for South Korea is how to maintain a technology and innovation edge over China in product exports while finding ways to maintain price and design competitiveness against sophisticated high-tech products from Japan and other industrialized-country competitors.

By November 2006, Korea International Trade Association chairman Lee Hee Beom expressed concerns that the decline in growth of South Korean exports to China from a 30 percent rate of growth during 2003–2005 to a 12 percent increase through the first ten months of 2006 may have resulted from China's increased production capability and competitiveness. Lee cited semiconductors, computers, liquid crystal displays, mobile phones, steel, and synthetic fiber as sectors in which enhanced Chinese production challenged South Korea's competitive advantage.[24]

Another example of the shift in the structure of trade relations was felt in the steel sector, where South Korean companies experienced the direct effects from enhanced Chinese competition in 2006 as Chinese steel companies began to compete for supply contracts to South Korean buyers on the basis of both improved quality and lower cost. The previous bilateral trend in which South Korea mainly exported steel to China was replaced by a new trend in which Chinese exports to major South Korean consumers were priced 15 to 20 percent cheaper than South Korean steel products. In the first ten months of 2006, South Korean exports of steel products to China dropped by 14 percent to 3.4 million tons of steel, while Chinese imports to the South Korean market increased by 46 percent to 8.4 million tons.[25] The same trends have also occurred in other sectors as Chinese manufacturing production levels have become competitive with those for South Korean products.

While South Koreans were becoming anxious that economic interdependence with China was transforming itself into economic dependency as China continued to develop and grow as a global economic player, Chinese leaders began to focus on achieving a "harmonious society" due to internal social divisions resulting from uneven economic development. As Chinese leaders searched for ways to mitigate the growing economic gap between rural and urban areas, they borrowed once again from South Korea's development experience under Park Chung Hee by studying the *saemaul* movement, which was designed to promote equitable development in South Korea's agricultural regions as well as in urban areas that were rapidly industrializing during the 1970s. China's model involved unprecedented government investments in rural infrastructure and social welfare projects as part of its eleventh five-year program. The Chinese government sought to counter growing social protests driven by perceptions of inequitable development and collusion with local government officials to use agricultural land for development purposes.[26]

Political Challenges of Burgeoning
Sino–South Korean Economic Relations

The expanded intensity of Sino–South Korean economic relations resulting from growth in trade and investment ties carried with it the likelihood that conflicts would arise. If such conflicts became serious enough, they would require management by political leaders on each side. Some of the problems that arose were associated simply with success, such as natural frictions resulting from increased competition despite the overall mutual benefits derived from expanded trade volumes. For example, during the "garlic wars" of 2000, an escalating trade dispute became a bilateral political issue. In other cases, new problems arose because the respective governments needed to protect their societies from the negative impact of increased international competition—for instance, through the relatively frequent use by both China and South Korea of WTO antidumping provisions, to restrain each other in key industrial sectors.

In the investment sphere, South Korea faced domestic political challenges posed by the "hollowing out" of South Korean industry. In addition, South Korean officials considered the risks and long-term implications of Chinese investment in strategic sectors such as the South Korean automobile industry. Technology transfer provided an incentive for China to open its domestic market to foreign investment in order to learn new skills while benefiting from local production of state-of-the-art consumer products such as telephones and automobiles. But the desire to gain technology also fed illicit attempts to steal or copy intellectual property from South Korean–invested plants in China, and to seek partners inside South Korean companies who were willing to risk illegally selling proprietary technology to Chinese firms. Finally, the long-term strategic implications of growing economic interdependence—or the strategic risks that might accompany excessive economic dependency—remained relatively unexplored, but were critical factors likely to influence the nature and structure of the political relationship. All of these areas must be considered as potential political and strategic implications of growing Sino–South Korean economic interdependence.

Lessons from the "Garlic Wars"

The most politically serious Sino–South Korean trade dispute to date occurred in 2000, one year prior to China's entry into the WTO. At that time, there was a rapid influx of low-cost Chinese garlic into the South Korean market at prices that threatened the livelihood of South Korean garlic farmers. Controversy first arose in South Korea as the result of a complaint from South Korea's National Agricultural Cooperative Federation to its Ministry of Finance and Economy regarding alleged dumping of Chinese garlic in South Korea. The resulting investigation revealed that Chinese exports to South Korea had risen from less than 10,000 tons in 1996 to over 36,000 tons in 1999 at a market price one-third to one-fourth that of South Korean garlic. Based on this finding, South Korea slapped punitive tariffs of up to 315 percent on imports of Chinese garlic in June 2000. China responded one week later by banning imports of cell phones and polyethylene from South Korea, sectors that represented a significantly larger portion of South Korea's exports to China worth hundreds of millions of dollars per year compared to the garlic trade, which was valued in the millions annually.[27] Under considerable pressure from China's sledgehammer-like reaction, the South Korean government pledged to purchase 32,000 tons of Chinese garlic in 2000, followed by increasing amounts through 2002, totaling slightly less than the equivalent level of Chinese garlic exports to South Korea in 1999.[28]

As a result of China's threat of trade retaliation against South Korean polyethylene and mobile phone exports, the trade dispute spilled over into the political sphere. South Korean garlic growers decried their government's failure to protect domestic producers, but the deal served to keep the lucrative Chinese market open to South Korean polyethylene and mobile phone exports. However, South Korea's managed-trade efforts with China continued to be a source of political friction between the two countries for at least two more years. In the spring of 2001, as the South Korean government prepared to honor its garlic import pledge, the price of garlic declined in the South Korean domestic market but Chinese garlic prices rose. Now lacking sufficient funds to meet its commitment, the South Korean government asked telecommunications and polyethylene exporters to help shoulder the financial burden of the garlic agreement. The dispute engendered public resentment in South Korea against China's perceived bullying approach in managing its trade relations. In order to calm protests from South Korean garlic producers, several South Korean ministries split the bill for the imports and reexported the garlic on the international market, after having offered it to North Korea (which promptly rejected the offer) under the guise of humanitarian aid.[29]

South Koreans learned in 2002 about their government's secret pledge to completely open the South Korean garlic market to Chinese imports beginning in 2003. South Korean farmers were again enraged, but by then there was little that could be done. In a ruling that ultimately led to the resignation of its chairman, the Korean Trade Commission decided that the commitment would stand, and South Korea reopened its market to Chinese garlic imports in 2003.[30]

The "garlic wars" between South Korea and China illustrated the pressure on South Korean officials to take defensive actions against the flood of cheap Chinese agricultural goods, which began to undercut South Korean producers. South Korean interlocutors also came to realize that, on trade matters, China was willing to play hardball and would use its market size and growth potential, as well as harsh retaliatory measures, as political weapons to achieve its own market-opening objectives. But China's entry into the WTO in 2001 provided some relief for South Korea, since the WTO provided guidelines for applying retaliatory measures and for managing trade disputes among member countries. WTO regulations have muted prospects for retaliatory actions in unrelated sectors and have provided internationally recognized mechanisms for leveling the playing field between China and South Korea.

As South Korea pursued higher levels of trade liberalization, South Korean agriculture became increasingly threatened by the prospect of a market opening that would expose the sector to greater competition from Chinese producers. But South Korea consistently adopted a pragmatic stance—that it had far more to gain from opportunities in higher-tech sectors provided by China's liberalization than it had to lose from the liberalization of agricultural markets in which the cost of China's exports to South Korea were relatively insignificant compared to the benefits of market access. Nonetheless, the trade-offs imposed by these economic choices did not come without the domestic costs of a political backlash against the government by South Korean farmers. The psychological scars from this experience may be the single greatest reason for South Korea's relative reluctance to enter into bilateral free trade negotiations with China.[31]

Antidumping and Other Bilateral Trade Disputes

Following China's entry into the World Trade Organization, Sino–South Korean trade disputes did not disappear, although the WTO provided new tools by which both sides could seek relief from a rapid rise in imports that threatened their domestic interests. Reflecting their rapid economic growth and trade, China and South Korea became the first and second leading exporters, respectively, to face antidumping measures under the WTO in the initial years following China's membership in the organization.[32]

The Korean Trade Commission reported in 2003 that South Korea was the most common target of Chinese antidumping lawsuits (eighteen out of twenty-three), in sectors such as optical fiber, stainless steel, cold-rolled steel plates, newsprint, and polyester.[33] The Korea International Trade Association reported in 2005 that South Korea was the primary target for Chinese antidumping actions; between 1997 and 2005, China imposed restrictions on twenty-six South Korean export items, primarily in the petrochemical and steel sectors.[34] Likewise, the flood of Chinese steel exports into South Korea during 2006 led to calls that South Korea initiate antidumping actions against China under the

WTO. As China's production capacity in key industrial sectors expands, it is likely that South Korea will take more actions against Chinese goods under the WTO's antidumping provisions. Thus far, however, the WTO has served as an effective mechanism for keeping Sino–South Korean economic disputes depoliticized.

Another area in which chronic problems have negatively affected the image of Chinese products in South Korea is consumer safety, specifically related to inferior and tainted Chinese food imports and other substandard materials that have found their way into the South Korean market. Consumer safety has a broad impact on South Korean public perceptions of China, but has rarely risen to the level of serious political dispute. Nonetheless, reports of defective, spoiled, fake, tainted, unhygienic, and otherwise unsafe Chinese exports to South Korea have been steadily reported in the South Korean media since 2000, when an uproar arose over Chinese exports of blue crabs and swellfish contaminated by lead weights that had been inserted in order to increase package weight and therefore cost.[35] These problems damaged perceptions of the quality of Chinese exports long prior to the emergence of similar issues in the United States regarding Chinese exports of components for pet food and other consumer goods to the North American market in the summer of 2007.

In 2005, a dispute arose over safety concerns connected with South Korea's rapidly growing reliance on Chinese imports of kimchi, South Korea's national dish, when the Korean Food and Drug Administration revealed that these imports contained ringworm eggs at higher than expected levels. The national outcry among South Korean consumers temporarily halted kimchi imports from China, but follow-up investigations revealed two facts that undercut South Korean consumer reaction and damaged the position of the Korean Food and Drug Administration. First, it was revealed that South Korean–made kimchi also contained ringworm eggs, albeit at lower quantities than in the Chinese imports. Second, most of the increase in kimchi imports from China was led by South Korean companies that had relocated their production operations to China to take advantage of lower labor costs.

China announced its own concerns about contamination of South Korean–made chili paste, imposed sanctions on a number of South Korean producers, and also expressed concerns about the safety of some materials used in South Korean–made cosmetics that were enjoying a rising popularity in the Chinese market. However, it turned out that none of the South Korean companies cited by China were exporting to the Chinese market. China received the psychological satisfaction of imposing retaliatory sanctions on South Korean companies, but at no tangible cost to either side. This time the dispute was quickly settled; both sides sought mechanisms for improving safety inspections at Chinese factories and for improving oversight by the Korean Food and Drug Administration.

As trade disputes in various sectors have grown, so has the sophistication of bilateral mechanisms for managing them while avoiding escalation of retaliatory measures. Thus far, it has been possible for China and South Korea to contain the political fallout from bilateral trade disputes, especially through appeals to international dispute resolution mechanisms under the WTO. However, on both sides, public perceptions that the benefits of the trade relationship are flowing only in one direction rather than being mutually advantageous could possibly force economic disputes back onto the political agenda.[36]

The "Hollowing Out" of South Korea's Domestic Economy

A negative impact of the rush by South Korean small and medium-sized firms to invest in China since the mid-1990s has been the "hollowing out" of manufacturing jobs in many low-end sectors in which South Korean wage structures are no longer competitive. The temptation to move increasingly high-end production processes from South Korea to China to take advantage of low labor costs has hurt South Korean employment and made South Korea's own economic growth dependent primarily on companies involved with production of exports to China. The boom in South Korean exports to China, fed in large part by South Korean investment in China, has created tremendous opportunity for South Korean companies, but also carries with it costs to the vibrancy of South Korea's own industrial manufacturing base.

The hollowing out of South Korea's economy has been a serious domestic political issue, but South Korea's economic slowdown in 2002–2004 was blamed primarily on poor economic management policies by the South Korean government rather than on competitiveness of Chinese labor costs.[37] Another factor that has mitigated politicization of the transfer of South Korean manufacturing plants to China through foreign direct investment is that those jobs have for the most part been replaced by higher-end manufacturing and services jobs as South Korea's economy continues to move up the economic value chain, both as a result of its own development and in response to China's growth.[38] South Korean labor has focused more on protecting privileges of its own members by taking actions against South Korean management than on mobilizing campaigns to vilify Chinese labor for unfair competition or attacking South Korean firms for moving to China. The ability of South Korea to manage the political ramifications of its rising investment in China stands in dramatic contrast to the US political debate over multinational "off-shoring" in China, in which China's low-cost labor and the decisions of US companies to move production bases to China have become political obstacles to investment by Chinese companies in the United States.

A negative aspect of South Korean investment in China has come in the form of higher risks to South Korean businesses that seek to take advantage of lower labor and land costs in order to enhance their competitiveness in international markets. Risks accompanying South Korean investment in China come in several different forms. For instance, South Korean multinationals seeking to invest in China must negotiate arrangements with authorities at the local and central government levels, often in competition with other companies that are also seeking preferential access to the Chinese market. As China's economy has grown, it has benefited from higher levels of technology transfer and other investment gains to the local economy, while discouraging investments in labor-intensive sectors. When Hyundai Motors negotiated the opening and expansion of a new plant in 2004 in Beijing, Chinese officials sought significant technology transfer pledges as a quid pro quo for approving Hyundai's request.[39] This shift in Chinese investment policies has posed new obstacles for some South Korean investors that had intended to take advantage of low Chinese labor costs for production and export to the United States and other global markets.

Under China's new policies for foreign direct investment, it has become necessary for South Korean products to compete for domestic market share on the basis of a combination of quality and affordability, usually through a reputation for greater dependability compared to Chinese-made products, and for greater affordability compared to Japanese-made products. Production for China's domestic consumer market requires significant cultivation of marketing, sales, and distribution networks inside China in order to compete for local market share. The transition from investments designed to take advantage of low labor costs in producing goods for export, to investments that must take into account strategies for competing locally, has proved to be a frustrating new challenge for South Korean invested firms in China. For South Korean firms, enhanced competition, for instance in the home appliances sector, comes from three directions: South Korean companies that assemble products in China, local Chinese competitors that export to South Korea, and Japanese companies that are also relying on Chinese factories for assembly and reexport.[40]

A 2006 survey by South Korea's Export-Import Bank showed that only about 20 percent of South Korean exports to China were being sold in the domestic market. Cheong Young-rok has analyzed Chinese trade statistics to determine that over half of South Korea's US$20 billion surplus with China is generated by intrafirm transactions between South Korean companies and their plants in China. Since South Korean intrafirm transactions are usually involved in the manufacture of products for export from China to third-country markets, Cheong concludes that South Korea's trade surplus with China is almost equivalent to the contribution of South Korean companies to China's trade surplus with the rest of the world.[41]

Chinese Investment in South Korea: SAIC and Ssangyong Motors

The emergence of Chinese overseas direct investment is a relatively new phenomenon; the fact that many Chinese investments have been targeted at sensitive sectors involving technology-rich firms has already become a political issue in both the United States and South Korea. However, unlike the United States, which forced the China National Overseas Oil Corporation to withdraw a bid for the US company Unocal under political pressure, the South Korean government has approved Chinese investment in some sectors that are central to South Korea's international manufacturing competitiveness, including semiconductors and automobiles. The most significant Chinese investment to date has been the takeover of financially troubled Ssangyong Motors by the Shanghai Automotive International Corporation in October 2004, which involved a heated competition against another Chinese firm, Blue Star, that had no automotive experience. SAIC's purchase of Ssangyong has stimulated skepticism and opposition within Ssangyong's labor union but has not spread to stimulate serious political opposition more broadly within South Korea. Building on joint ventures with General Motors and Volkswagon, the purchase of Ssangyong represented SAIC's first venture into a foreign market and the first step in a goal by SAIC's leadership to become a manufacturer for the global market.[42]

Since SAIC's purchase of Ssangyong for US$552 million, SAIC management has faced a number of difficult challenges in the South Korean market, including the contentious labor-management relationship in South Korea. Relations between leaders of Ssangyong's labor union and SAIC's Chinese management were contentious from the moment SAIC took over management responsibilities at Ssangyong.

Ssangyong's labor union went on strike, protesting the new management as well as its decision to replace the South Korean chief executive officer in late 2005. Ssangyong's labor union accused the new management of planning to transfer Ssangyong's core technologies to China and of failing to fulfill the promised investment plans that had been submitted as part of SAIC's original bid to take over the firm. Union leaders even traveled to Shanghai in an attempt to meet with SAIC's chairman to voice their grievances, leading to a commitment by SAIC to invest US$1 billion in Ssangyong over five years.[43]

However, tensions boiled over again during the summer of 2006 as workers protested the appointment of former General Motors executive Philip Murtaugh to a senior position in SAIC. One of Murtaugh's responsibilities within SAIC has been to manage the Ssangyong acquisition. The hiring of Murtaugh provided Shanghai Automotive with the international standing to more effectively pursue its goal of becoming an international player in the automotive sector, given Murtaugh's long experience in the industry. The appointment of a non-Chinese as a senior manager responsible for Ssangyong has diminished fears that SAIC is working primarily to advance Chinese interests (at the expense of the interests of Ssangyong in South Korea).[44]

The labor union also challenged alleged management decisions to move production of Ssangyong's sport utility vehicles to China under a licensing agreement worth US$25 million (10 percent of the true commercial value of the technology, according to critics of the agreement) and attempted to hold SAIC's management to commitments made upon purchase of Ssangyong to invest in a South Korean plant. During the course of the strike, the labor union and a South Korean civic group named Spec Watch Korea, dedicated to monitoring activities of foreign investors, jointly filed a lawsuit against SAIC's board of directors. The strike ended following an agreement by SAIC management to drop planned job cuts and a pledge to invest US$1.25 billion over four years to develop new models and engines.[45] Publicity surrounding Ssangyong's labor-management difficulties has raised fears in South Korea that Chinese shareholders could use acquisitions to transfer core technologies to Chinese competitors.

Shanghai Automotive has its own ambitions to become an automobile manufacturer for the global market, feeding Ssangyong's fears that the priorities of its Chinese owners lie elsewhere. But it may turn out that SAIC is not so much interested in Ssangyong's production or technology but rather in its international distribution channels to Europe and other markets. Shanghai Automotive has announced plans distribute its first brand, the Roewe, based on the British MG Rover. But the Roewe will be selling years in advance of what many had expected, due to Shanghai Automotive's decision to sell the cars in Europe under the Ssangyong name.[46] Thus far, other Chinese attempts to acquire South Korean firms have included a bid by Lenovo to acquire South Korea's third largest computer manufacturer, Trigem, from court receivership, and the 2003 purchase of Hydis, which manufactures liquid crystal displays, by Beijing Orient Electronics, but neither case by itself has stimulated a political response in South Korea.[47]

"Technology Leakage" and the Costs of Industrial Espionage

Another type of threat to South Korea's technology advantage vis-à-vis China comes from within, either by intent or by stealth. The fundamental incentive for any developing country to open itself to foreign investment from abroad is to access capital and technology that presumably can be used to help that country move up the development ladder. In turn, the investor gains access to an otherwise closed market or enhances its global competitiveness through reduced land and labor costs. But the costs of such an arrangement include the possibility that the developing country might gain new technologies that enable it to become a direct competitor. Or, local competitors might hire outside talent to facilitate technology transfer, as has been the case for certain Chinese firms that have hired South Korean engineers in the semiconductor sector.[48] This hope lies behind China's strategic approach to sectors such as automobiles, semiconductors, steel-making, and shipbuilding, in which South Koreans have been major investors.

It is possible to climb the development ladder faster through industrial espionage or if subcontractors gain access to confidential company data. In some cases, South Korean and Chinese company employees have attempted to steal company secrets and set up their own plants, in order to eventually compete directly with South Korean rivals. Hyundai has faced both of these problems: a Chinese subcontractor involved with information systems at Hyundai's Beijing plant may have stolen sensitive data, and it is also suspected that Chinese employees at Hyundai may have shared secrets with potential challengers in the Chinese market. The problem of Chinese knockoffs is especially severe as a challenge to South Korean profitability, particularly in China's local market. Stolen technology enables Chinese companies to open new factories that could then directly compete with the original manufacturers, cutting into profit margins and diminishing business.

One factor that has unfairly aided China has been industrial espionage involving the sale of proprietary technology developed by South Korean firms to Chinese competitors. Other efforts to promote technology transfer have involved negotiations in which Chinese local authorities demand technology concessions as a condition for opening new plants in China, and Chinese subcontractors' providing services to South Korean automotive firms and then stealing proprietary information. At the November 2006 Beijing Motor Show, Hyundai executives suspected that Chinese companies such as Liaoning SG Automotive and Tianma Auto may have acquired proprietary technology and design information for some of its popular automobile models, such as the Santa Fe. Those suspicions appear to have been justified. In May 2007, nine current and former employees of Kia were charged with industrial espionage for sharing proprietary information with a Chinese company. According to the prosecution, a former employee set up a consulting company and acquired proprietary data from current employees; these data were then sold to the Chinese firm. The Korean National Intelligence Service reported over a hundred known cases of industrial espionage against South Korea between 2003 and 2006, at a cost to South Korea of at least US$100 billion. The estimated damages from undetected industrial espionage could amount to an additional US$100 billion.[49]

Another trend is that leading South Korean shipbuilders are starting to invest overseas, including in China. For instance, Samsung Heavy Industries and Daewoo Shipbuilding have recently invested in China. Some shipbuilders have expressed concern about South Korean shipbuilders such as STX, which has aggressively expanded its market presence and has also invested in the construction of complete production facilities at a shipyard near Dalian.[50] Other South Korean shipbuilders are concerned that such investments might increase the possibility of technology leakage to Chinese competitors; there have already been indictments of employees of South Korean shipbuilding firms for trying to leak proprietary technologies to China.[51] China's emergence as a potential competitor in shipbuilding, as well as South Korea's exploitation of cheap North Korean labor in order to maintain its comparative advantages in the sector, have made shipbuilding a priority for potential inter-Korean economic cooperation since the 2007 inter-Korean summit.[52]

Strategic Implications of Economic Dependency vs. Economic Interdependence

Initially, as South Korea's trade and investment with China increased, the lure of economic opportunity overwhelmed any consideration that economic interdependence might carry with it long-term costs in the form of excessive economic dependency. Instead, South Korea's primary concerns were traditionally focused more on international competitiveness vis-à-vis China in international markets. But by early 2006, these factors converged, leaving South Korea wary of its growing economic dependency on China and its international competitiveness in critical sectors. Rising recognition of South Korea's economic dependence on China has been evidenced by the sensitivity of the South Korean stock market to measures by the Chinese government to rein in economic growth, as well as by the fact that in 2004, South Korea's growth in gross domestic product was dependent primarily on China-related exports.

South Korea's economic dependency on China has stimulated a variety of reactions among South Korean policymakers and business leaders. One reaction had been to utilize China's growing competitiveness to spur more effective South Korean–led growth and innovation. In January 2007, Samsung chairman Lee Kun Hee publicly raised the question of whether South Korea's economic growth will be "sandwiched" by its geographic position between high-tech Japan and low-cost manufacturing powerhouse China.[53] But others maintain that such a possibility is exaggerated, emphasizing that China's continued growth will bring greater opportunities.

A second, more practical effect of the emergence of South Korea's economic dependency on China as a political concern has been South Korea's sudden interest in negotiating a free trade agreement (FTA) with the United States before proceeding with stalled FTA negotiations with Japan or initiating FTA negotiations with China. That a free trade agreement with the United States could serve as a hedge against China's growing economic dominance was one motivation to move forward in 2006. Roh Tae Woo commented in an interview about the advisability of going forward with a China–South Korea FTA in mid-May, but in so doing revealed the core of South Korea's worries concerning the impact of such an FTA on its agricultural sector: "An FTA with China is inevitable. Some have asked why China was not first, but frankly, our agricultural situation would have needed major restructuring for such a deal. We need to strengthen the agricultural sector first with an FTA with the United States before heading for China."[54] Negotiation of a US–South Korean FTA might also be seen as a means to strengthen South Korea's competition with China and Japan in the US market and as a way of promoting diversification of South Korea's trade to forestall South Korea's growing dependence on the Chinese market.

China has been pushing for a free trade agreement with South Korea for several years, since the launch of a quasi-official binational study of a potential FTA in 2004. During a press conference prior to his visit to Seoul and at a meeting of the Korea-China Friendship Association also in Seoul, Chinese premier Wen Jiabao called for FTA negotiations to begin based on the results of the joint study. The study apparently projects that South Korea's agriculture, fisheries, clothing, and leather sectors would be badly hit by a Sino–South Korean FTA, but it might provide significant benefits to the automobile, steel, and petrochemical sectors. The Korean Institute for International Economic Policy estimates that a Sino–South Korean FTA would add 2.3 percent per year to South Korea's economic growth. A Korea Trade-Investment Promotion Agency (KOTRA) survey of Chinese business leaders revealed enthusiasm for a Sino–South Korean FTA, with over three-fifths of those surveyed indicating that they might benefit directly from the conclusion of such an agreement. Chinese business leaders saw such an FTA as likely to promote a more positive environment for Chinese exports to South Korea.[55]

Political and Security Implications of Sino–South Korean Economic Integration

This chapter has surveyed the nature and manifestations of the rapidly growing economic interdependence between China and South Korea. For the most part, the economic relationship has developed unfettered by political concerns. But the intensity of economic interdependence and structural changes in the nature of the relationship from one in which the geographically larger party sought to emulate the economic successes of the smaller party, to one in which the geographically larger party threatens to overtake the smaller party in key sectors, has raised new questions, at least in Seoul, about the strategic implications of South Korean economic dependency. This set of concerns about economic dependency derives at least in part from the fact that China has become South Korea's largest trading partner, largest destination for foreign direct investment, largest recipient of exports, and even its most important source of economic growth. China, on the other hand, does not appear concerned about increasing economic interdependence with South Korea or about economic dependency on South Korea, in part because China's own growth remains diversified and South Korea is not China's largest trading partner or largest source of foreign investment. However, the emergence of these concerns in South Korea as an issue of political debate diminishes the likelihood that China would be able to utilize South Korean economic dependency as political leverage, given that the natural South Korean response to concerns about overdependence would be to promote diversification in international markets so as to deny China the desired political benefits or any potential leverage that might derive from such dependency.

A second set of concerns in Seoul has derived from China's increasing competitiveness and the possibility that China could overtake South Korea as a key competitor and supplier in international markets. This structural change in the nature of the relationship may well affect its future. In the words of one South Korean observer, "We have the perception that China is still lagging behind still so that's the reason we have confidence on China and actually look down on China still, but it is a matter of time until China is equal and then rising above us. Koreans have overconfidence about China, but it will be transformed into a kind of competition and then a China problem and then a China threat as time goes by."[56]

An additional issue highlighted in this chapter is whether South Korea may have prematurely compromised its competitiveness with China through loss of proprietary technologies in key sectors. Though there is evidence that "China fever" has in fact resulted in significant losses, it is hard to conclude that South Korea has done a poor job of managing its economic relations with China, given the relative success to date of South Korean companies in providing China with intermediate and capital goods. However, there are risks associated with South Korean investment in China as the latter increasingly looks for higher-value-added technology and restricts continued overseas investment—including from South Korea—in labor-intensive and low-end manufacturing projects for export to the United States. One result is that some South Korean investments in labor-intensive sectors have been pushed out—for instance, China's adjustment of its labor law in 2008 spiked "fly by night" departures of South Korean investors who were no longer financially viable.

But most of the problems related to rapid expansion of trade and investment between China and South Korea are those that derive from success. Addressing these problems requires the creation of new mechanisms for effectively managing disputes and regulating the negative consequences for particular social sectors that accompany broader economic gains. Effectively regulating unfair trade practices such as dumping, and punishing illicit activities such as technology theft and industrial espionage, also require the establishment of strengthened regulatory and enforcement capacities and bilateral mechanisms for effectively managing disputes as they arise.

The potential long-term consequences to competitiveness that might result from investment and technology sharing are harder to gauge. Likewise, fears of economic dependency are most acute when there are no alternative partners available, but this is not the case for South Korea. The most worrisome question for South Korean business should be the challenge of maintaining competitiveness internationally. The outcome will depend in part on the ability of South Korean companies to meet the challenge by innovating and finding new product areas in which to compete that rely less on labor-cost advantages and more on knowledge and design inputs, so as to preserve competitiveness in the global market.

The psychological impact of perceived South Korean economic reliance on China has had a direct influence on South Korean markets. Witness the response of the South Korean stock market to China's efforts to bring its domestic growth under control, which suggests that South Korea's prospects for economic growth are now just as psychologically influenced by China's economic situation as they are by what happens in the United States or Japan. The South Korean stock market's response underscores the extent of South Korea's stakes in China's success, while also suggesting that South Korea is already so interdependent with China that it would face serious consequences if China's economy were to stagnate or become unstable.

Broadly speaking, these concerns have grown with China's rapidly rising importance in regional economic and political affairs, but there is little evidence thus far that economic interdependence has decisively influenced South Korean political choices or that South Korea's level of trade or investment dependency on China has risen to the extent that an industrialized South Korea operates as China's economic satellite. In fact, South Korea's trade with other countries remains well-diversified. Though China represents about 20 percent of South Korea's trade, the United States, Japan, and the European Union remain strong trade partners. Likewise, though South Korean investment in China reached over 40 percent of all South Korean investment during 2004, it has since declined, and the investments that took place through 2004 were driven by South Korean firms that engaged China as an opportunity, not a threat. Moreover, South Korea's dependency on China is far less than its past economic and political dependency on the United States during the Cold War.

Does South Korea's reliance on China as an economic growth opportunity provide China with leverage that could be used to influence South Korean foreign policy or strategic choices in ways that inhibit cooperation with the United States? To the extent that closer economic ties have enabled the development of a "strategic partnership," one might argue that such ties have enhanced Beijing's voice and influence in Seoul. In fact, there are now analysts who advocate that not only South Korea's economic but also its political future lies with China rather than with the United States, but such voices remain relatively rare.

Although it is unprecedented that an alliance partner would depend to a greater extent for its economic growth on a third party and former combatant than on the United States, South Korea's economic dependency on China does not yet appear to have limited its political and military cooperation with the United States. However, given the vibrancy of the Sino–South Korean economic relationship, its potential to constrain South Korea's security alliance with the United States remains an important concern.

Notes

1. Figures on Korean investment in China are available from the website of the Korea Export-Import Bank, http://www.koreaexim.go.kr.

2. See Etel Solingen, *Regional Orders at Century's Dawn: Global and Domestic Influences on Grand Strategy* (Princeton: Princeton University Press, 1998).

3. See Lee Jung-yoon and Jean-Paul Rodrigue, "Trade Reorientation and Its Effects on Regional Port Systems: The Korea-China Link Along the Yellow Sea Rim," *Growth and Change* 37, no. 4 (December 2006): 602.

4. See Kim Jong Kil, "Economic Relation Between Korea and China: Implications of Korean Economic Crisis for China," *Southeast Asia Studies* 8 (1999): 249–285. For 1997, see *China Statistical Yearbook 1998* (Beijing: China Statistical Publishing House).

5. See Ahn Joong-young, "Economic Relations Between Korea and China," *Korean Journal of International Studies* 29, no. 1 (Spring–Summer 2002): 61–81.

6. Ibid., p. 78.

7. Kim, "Economic Relation Between Korea and China," pp. 255–256.

8. Japan External Trade Organization (JETRO), as cited in Lee and Rodrigue, "Trade Reorientation and Its Effects on Regional Port Systems," p. 600.

9. Lee and Rodrigue, "Trade Reorientation and Its Effects on Regional Port Systems," p. 603; Kim Byungsoo, "The Effect of Social Structural Factors on Foreign Market Entry," unpublished diss., Stanford University, 2005, pp. 8–25.

10. Chen Xiangming, "The Bottom-Up Remaking of Asian Regionalism: Views from the Geoeconomic Core and Periphery," paper prepared for the con-

ference "From Commerce to Community: Korea's Role in East Asia," Georgetown University, December 13–15, 2006, pp. 12–26.

11. Chung Jae Ho, *Between Ally and Partner: Korea-China Relations and the United States* (New York: Columbia University Press, 2006), pp. 26–28.

12. *Yearbook of China's Foreign Economic Relations and Trade, 2001* (Beijing: China's Foreign Economic Relations and Trade Publishing House), p. 391.

13. See the Korean Overseas International Cooperation Agency website, http://www.koica.go.kr.

14. South Korean failure to develop equity and bond markets is attributable to Park Chung Hee's desire to retain the ability to direct Korean corporate strategies.

15. Kim, "Economic Relation Between Korea and China," pp. 249–285.

16. Kim, "The Effect of Social Structural Factors on Foreign Market Entry," p. 13.

17. Andrew Ward, "S. Korea Moves Ahead of Japan: A Strengthening Economic Relationship Is Leading to Closer Political and Cultural Ties Between South Korea and China," *Financial Times,* June 23, 2004.

18. See Lee Sung-cheol and Jung Sung-hoon, "Impact of Market, Institution, and Technology on the Location of FDI: The Case Study of Korean Samsung CDMA FDI in China," *Journal of the Korean Geographical Society* 39, no. 2 (2004): 241–255.

19. Kim, "The Effect of Social Structural Factors on Foreign Market Entry," p. 19.

20. *China Statistical Yearbook 2004,* compiled by the National Bureau of Statistics of China (Beijing: China Statistics Press, 2004), p. 257.

21. *China Statistical Yearbook 2002,* compiled by the National Bureau of Statistics of China (Beijing: China Statistics Press, 2002), p. 391; *China Statistical Yearbook 2003,* compiled by the National Bureau of Statistics of China (Beijing: China Statistics Press, 2003), p. 256.

22. Kim Sung-jin, "Finance Minister Warns Against China Threat," *Korea Times,* March 22, 2006.

23. Cho Jin-seo, "China Closes Tech Gap with Korea," *Korea Times,* March 6, 2006.

24. Lee Hee-beom, "Raising the Bar for Korean Exporters," *Korea Herald,* December 22, 2006.

25. Scott Snyder, "Political Fallout from North Korea's Nuclear Test," in Brad Glosserman and Sun Namkung, eds., *Comparative Connections* 8, no. 4 (2006): 115–124.

26. Josephine Ma, "Balm for China Rural Areas Unlikely to Bring Calm," *South China Morning Post,* January 3, 2006, accessed at http://www. opensource.gov, doc. no. CPP20060103517007. See also Kim Tong-hyung, "Korea to Share Rural Development Experience with Asian Neighbors," *Korea Times,* March 9, 2006.

27. See Scott Snyder, "Beijing at Center Stage or Upstaged by the Two Kims?" in Ralph A. Cossa and Eun Jung Cahill Che, eds., *Comparative Connections* 2, no. 2 (April–June 2000): 82–88; Scott Snyder, "The Insatiable

Sino-Korean Economic Relationship: Too Much for Seoul to Swallow?" in Ralph A. Cossa and Eun Jung Cahill Che, eds., *Comparative Connections* 2, no. 3 (July–September 2000): 84–91.

28. "ROK-PRC Trade Resolution on Garlic Sparks Debate," *Korea Herald,* April 24, 2001.

29. "Are Cell Phone Exporters Garlic Sellers?" *Donga Ilbo,* April 13, 2001, accessed at http://www.opensource.gov, doc. no. KPP20010413000100.

30. Kim Mi-hui, "Trade Commission Chairman Quits over Garlic Issue," *Korea Herald,* July 31, 2002.

31. Jung Sung-ki, "President Wants Free Trade Pact with China," *Korea Times,* May 21, 2007.

32. See the World Trade Organization website, http://www.wto.org. On antidumping measures by exporting country, see http://www.wto.org/english/tratop_e/adp_e/adp_stattab6_e.pdf, accessed on January 19, 2007.

33. See Kim Mi-hui, "China: Friend or Foe to Korea's Trade?" *Korea Herald,* July 7, 2003.

34. "Korea Becomes China's Chief Import Restriction Target," *Korea Times,* May 17, 2005.

35. "Lead-Tainted Chinese Crabs," *Korea Herald,* August 29, 2000.

36. Scott Snyder, "Hu Visits the Two Koreas," in Brad Glosserman and Sun Namkung, eds., *Comparative Connections* 7, no. 4 (October–December 2006): 99–108.

37. See Ha Byung-ki, "De-Industrialization or Hollowing Out?" *Korea Herald,* August 19, 2004.

38. See Andrew Ward, "South Korea Feels the Chill in China's Growing Shadow: As Manufacturing Jobs Decamp Across the Yellow Sea, Seoul Is Facing Up to Change," *Financial Times,* September 25, 2003, p. 24.

39. Yang Sung-jin, "Hyundai Motor Faces Tough Competition in China," *Korea Herald,* August 18, 2006.

40. Cheong Young-rok, "Impact of China on South Korea's Economy," in *Dynamic Forces on the Korean Peninsula: Strategic and Economic Implications,* Joint U.S.-Korea Economic Studies no. 17 (Washington, DC: Korea Economic Institute of America, 2007), p. 76.

41. Ibid., pp. 61–82.

42. Alex Taylor III and Zhang Dahong, "Shanghai Auto Wants to Be the World's Next Great Car Company," *Fortune,* October 4, 2004, p. 102.

43. "Ssangyong Union Accuses Shanghai of Siphoning Off Core Technologies," *Korea Times,* November 10, 2005; "Ssangyong CEO Fired," *Korea Times,* November 7, 2005; Kim So-hyun, "Ssangyong to Focus on Chinese Joint Production," *Korea Herald,* November 8, 2005; "Ssangyong Dispute Boils Over," *Korea Times,* December 8, 2005; Kim Yon-se, "Shanghai Commits $1 Billion to Ssangyong," *Korea Times,* December 23, 2005.

44. Alysha Webb, "Murtaugh's Charge: Make Ssangyong Strong for SAIC," *Automotive News,* August 7, 2006.

45. Park Hyong-ki, "Can Ssangyong's New CEO Wield Hatchet?" *Korea Times,* August 17, 2006; Kim Yon-se, "Ssangyong Motor Union Starts Strike," *Korea Times,* August 12, 2006.

46. Alysha Webb, "Shanghai Automotive Industry Corp.," in "2007 Guide to China's Auto Market," *Automotive News,* May 14, 2007, p. C27.

47. Kim Tae-gyu, "Chinese Takeovers Raise Concerns," *Korea Times,* August 31, 2006.

48. Cheong, "Impact of China on South Korea's Economy," p. 73.

49. Song Jung-a, "Seoul Raises Defences Against Industrial Spies," *Financial Times,* June 28, 2007, p. 10; "Nine Charged for Leaking Auto Tech to China," *Korea Herald,* May 11, 2007.

50. Park Hyong-ki, "STX to Build Plant in China," *Korea Times,* April 1, 2007.

51. Shim Sun-ah, "Four S. Koreans Indicted over Shipbuilding Technology Leakage," *Yonhap News Agency,* July 31, 2007.

52. See text of the October 4, 2007, Inter-Korean summit declaration at http://english.hani.co.kr/arti/english_edition/e_national/240541.html, accessed on December 7, 2007.

53. Yoon-mi Kim, "Samsung Chief Renews Warning on Economy," *Korea Herald*, June 2, 2007, accessed via Nexis News Service, www.nexis.com.

54. Jung Sung-ki, "President Wants Free Trade Pact with China," *Korea Times,* May 21, 2007.

55. Scott Snyder, "Strategic Maneuvers for the 'Sandwich Economy,'" in Brad Glosserman and Sun Namkung, eds., *Comparative Connections* 9, no. 2 (April–June 2007): 121–129.

56. Author interview in Seoul, October 2007.

4

Emerging Political Challenges in the Sino–South Korean Relationship

I n parallel to rapid growth in Sino–South Korean economic relations, the bilateral political relationship has expanded considerably
since diplomatic normalization in 1992. The development of the political relationship corresponds to the stages in the expansion of economic
ties described in the previous chapter. The respective political and
strategic objectives of the two leaderships have also evolved considerably since 1992, yielding new points of convergence and exposing fundamental contradictions in the respective strategic interests of the two
countries.

Growth in Sino–South Korean economic relations has promoted the
convergence of mutually held priorities in support of maintaining
regional stability, but this convergence has not eliminated some basic
contradictions in the respective Chinese and South Korean foreign policies that have become more visible since 2004, for instance over the relative influence of China and South Korea in North Korea and over historical and territorial issues. It remains to be seen whether these disputes
may come to reflect deeper strategic conflicts. The rapid growth of the
economic relationship has provided an incentive to manage political
conflicts efficiently so that they do not become obstacles to the further
development of the economic relationship.

Political tensions have thus far not limited the growth of the bilateral economic relationship, but they do represent a source of potential
conflict that may eventually put the brakes on the development of
Sino–South Korean relations, especially if the rate of growth in economic relations begins to stagnate. For instance, specific political issues
such as the Koguryo history dispute or China's management of North

Korean refugees might be more politically sensitive in South Korea if the Sino–South Korean economic relationship were not so vibrant.

Development of Sino–South Korean
Political Relations Since Normalization

Chinese policy toward South Korea in the period since normalization has undergone three distinct phases of development. These phases roughly correspond to three periods in South Korea's management of policy toward China, defined by the differing policies and styles of three South Korean administrations through 2007. During the initial phase in Sino–South Korean relations following normalization, China attempted to maintain a relatively passive policy toward the Korean peninsula that emphasized formal political equidistance between North and South Korea despite rapidly growing Sino–South Korean trade ties. South Korea's hopes for the political relationship with China during the Kim Young Sam administration were closely linked to expectations that good relations with Beijing (and strict adherence to Beijing's conception of "one China") would yield understanding, if not appropriate quid pro quos, in support of South Korean interests related to North Korea, including the achievement of an early Korean unification. The rapid growth of the Sino–South Korean economic relationship during this period was perceived in Seoul as a tool by which to gain leverage and expand influence with Beijing at the expense of North Korea. The erosion of China's equidistance policy was one fruit of South Korean policy, but it is unlikely that this erosion came as a result of enhanced South Korean economic influence in China. Instead, China's own economic liberalization led to a greater interest in regional stability in the context of its sizable humanitarian and strategic response to North Korea's famine in the 1990s. Ironically, it was Beijing's prioritization of regional stability that forestalled hopes of early Korean reunification under Kim Young Sam.

By 1997, China's policy of maintaining equidistance between the two Koreas was no longer feasible. North Korea's political weakness led the Chinese leadership to focus on preservation of regional stability as a priority over the need to maintain the perception of political equidistance in managing political relations with the two Koreas. China's change in policy led to greater political cooperation between China and South Korea and a trend in which Chinese policies toward North and South Korea were no longer directly linked with each other, especially on issues that might heighten political tensions or lead to a change in the status quo on the Korean peninsula. With the inauguration of Kim Dae

Jung, South Korean policy toward North Korea dramatically shifted toward prioritizing inter-Korean reconciliation and embracing North Korea, which also implicitly prioritized regional stability. This approach coincided with the Chinese objective of promoting stability in areas along its periphery, including the Korean peninsula, in ways that brought South Korean and Chinese interests in regional stability into line with each other and enhanced prospects for political cooperation.

The third phase of China's policy toward the Korean peninsula coincided with a political transition between Jiang Zemin and Hu Jintao and the simultaneous emergence of the second North Korean nuclear crisis, in early 2003. In this phase, China has undertaken a more active role as host and mediator in the context of the six-party talks, while the administration of Roh Moo Hyun has continued a "peace and prosperity" policy that continues to promote engagement and economic integration with North Korea. China's mediating role has provided it with opportunities to enhance its influence on the Korean peninsula by strengthening high-level political relations with both North and South Korea, but at risk of coming into direct conflict with South Korea's interest in enhancing its political influence with North Korea as a precursor to the eventual realization of Korean reunification. While the emergence of the second North Korean nuclear crisis further reinforced South Korean and Chinese priorities on the maintenance of regional stability under Roh Moo Hyun's "peace and prosperity" policy, fundamental strategic differences between China and South Korea emerged over conceptions of regional cooperation, the future of North Korea, and conflicting interpretations of the historical significance and "ownership" of the Koguryo kingdom. Throughout this period, China has succeeded in influencing South Korea to adhere to a "one China" policy that is more strictly in line with its own conception compared to the policies of either the United States or Japan.

The December 2007 election of Lee Myung Bak has introduced some uncertainty into the future direction of Sino–South Korean political relations, despite the declaration of a "strategic partnership" during Lee's first visit to Beijing, in May 2008. The transition to a fourth phase appears to be under way, but the characteristics and direction of the relationship remain to be defined.

China's Transition from Formal Equidistance to Regional Stability, 1993–1998

The emergence of the first North Korean nuclear crisis, early in Kim Young Sam's administration, set the tone for inter-Korean relations during his term and shaped the context for the administration's early political interactions with China. Throughout the crisis, South Korean foreign minister Han Sung Joo actively pursued consultations with his counterpart, Chinese foreign minister Qian Qichen, in an attempt to enhance South Korea's cooperation with China in order to pressure North Korea to give up its nuclear program. Han met with Qian no fewer than six times during 1993 as part of efforts to manage the first North Korean nuclear crisis (see Appendix B), but it is not clear that South Korea's new relationship with China delivered the anticipated strategic benefits vis-à-vis North Korea.

China received public acknowledgment from South Korea and the United States for behind-the-scenes interventions with Pyongyang in support of US negotiations with North Korea, but it is not clear what precise actions China took to restrain North Korea or convince it to reach an agreement with the United States. China distanced itself from the implementation of the Geneva agreed framework by choosing not to become involved with the Korean Peninsula Energy Development Organization (a technical body created to implement the agreed framework by constructing two 1,000-megawatt light-water reactors in North Korea), preferring to maintain its own bilateral channels for relations with North Korea.

Although the rapid growth in Sino–South Korean trade and investment relations during the Kim Young Sam period provided a basis for enhancing South Korea's influence in Beijing while North Korea's economic and political influence with Beijing waned, South Korea was unable to convert its economic advantage vis-à-vis North Korea during this period into leverage sufficient to decisively influence Chinese policies toward the Korean peninsula, as China strictly adhered to a policy of formal equidistance in relations with the two Koreas through the mid-1990s.

For the Chinese government, the task of maintaining an equidistance policy was complicated following the death of Kim Il Sung on July 8, 1994. As a result of North Korea's extended leadership transition, its top leaders became even more internally focused than usual, especially since Kim Il Sung's son and designated successor, Kim Jong Il, observed a three-year period of reclusion and mourning following his father's death, a Korean tradition inherited from Confucian practice. As a result, high-level exchanges in the Sino–North Korean relationship experienced an extended hiatus (see Appendix A, which shows that there were virtually no Sino–North Korean high-level contacts throughout this period). Figure 4.1 illustrates the lack of high-level leadership

Figure 4.1   North and South Korean High-Level Interactions with China, 1992–2005

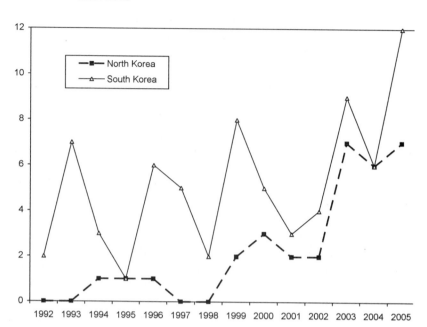

visits between North Korea and China during this time, while Sino–South Korean high-level ties grew and were even given a boost by the successive North Korean nuclear crises.

China's objective of maintaining formal equidistance between Seoul and Pyongyang was also complicated by increased levels of hostility in inter-Korean relations in the aftermath of Kim Il Sung's death. Although Kim Young Sam had agreed to hold a summit with Kim Il Sung only weeks prior to the latter's sudden death, Kim Young Sam publicly criticized Kim Il Sung following his death, stimulating a strongly vituperative reaction from North Korea and destroying near-term opportunities for inter-Korean reconciliation during the Kim Young Sam presidency. In turn, Kim Young Sam characterized North Korea as a "broken airplane," and many in South Korea anticipated North Korea's collapse and a German-style Korean reunification process.[1] However, a sudden influx of North Korean refugees into Chinese territory following North Korean floods in the summer of 1996 stimulated China to provide extensive food assistance to North Korea in 1997 and 1998 in an effort to forestall political instability there, effectively dashing hopes within the

Kim Young Sam administration for a political collapse that might lead to Korean reunification.

China's intervention came into direct conflict with the Kim Young Sam administration's policy toward North Korea during this period, although there was little that South Korean authorities could do but grouse that China had denied an opportunity for Korean unification on South Korean terms.[2] North Korea's own political weakness and the negative impact on China's national interests of instability on the Korean peninsula led to an adjustment in China's policy. It opted to abandon an emphasis on equidistance in favor of supporting regional stability, even at the expense of exposing political gaps with Pyongyang. Although China's priority on regional stability exposed political differences with North Korea to an unprecedented degree, these differences did not necessarily mean that China supported South Korean policies, especially if they were perceived as likely to result in greater instability on the Korean peninsula.

Jiang Zemin's visit to Seoul in 1996 marked the first visit for a Chinese president to South Korea. Despite China's efforts to portray a veneer of equidistance, the visit itself was evidence that China could no longer afford to observe equidistance between North and South Korea. China still handled political and strategic issues vis-à-vis the strategic balance on the Korean peninsula with care, but had too much at stake in its developing economic relationship with South Korea to limit political relations with Seoul in deference to Pyongyang.

During Jiang's visit to Seoul, he and Kim Young Sam found common cause in criticizing Japan for failing to address its historical legacy of imperialism in Northeast Asia. This issue was significant in bringing South Korea and China together and served as an indirect challenge to relations between Washington and Tokyo that resulted in reaffirmation of the US-Japanese alliance. This development was almost as unwelcome in Seoul as it was in Beijing. China attempted to exploit South Korean frustrations with the US–South Korean alliance, although there was no serious prospect at that time that such frustrations might yield strategic gains for China.[3] However, South Korean frustrations provided a potential strategic opportunity for China to improve its relations with South Korea, thereby strengthening its strategic position on the Korean peninsula. In this way, Beijing attempted to lay the groundwork for an enhanced relationship with Seoul in the event of Korean reunification.

China's shift in policy coincided with its participation in the four-party talks, initially proposed by Presidents Kim Young Sam and Bill Clinton in April 1996 (North Korea finally agreed to participate in

December 1997).[4] Although those talks made little progress in reducing tensions on the Korean peninsula, they did bring China's foreign ministry into consultations with its South Korean and US counterparts, providing new opportunities for the Chinese government to understand the views of South Korea and the United States and enhancing multilateral consensus on steps needed to enhance prospects for regional stability.[5]

Another major event that exposed the limits of China's transition from a policy of equidistance toward Pyongyang and Seoul to a policy that emphasized stability on the Korean peninsula was the March 1997 defection of Hwang Jang Yop and his colleague Kim Dok Hong at the South Korean consulate in Beijing. This incident required China to make hard choices about the relative importance of its long-standing fraternal ties with North Korea versus international diplomatic practice and the ramifications of closer relations with South Korea. Following weeks of complex negotiations, North Korean accusations that Hwang had been kidnapped by South Korea, and a thwarted North Korean attempt to enter the South Korean consulate and take Hwang back by force, China agreed to allow Hwang and his colleague to depart Beijing for the Philippines en route to their defection in South Korea.[6] China's handling of this incident further illustrated the erosion of its equidistance policy and served as the first practical precedent in handling North Korean refugees as an ongoing challenge that would beset China's relations with both Koreas.

Inter-Korean Reconciliation, Regional Stability, and Multilateral Cooperation, 1998–2003

Kim Dae Jung's inauguration as president and adoption of his Sunshine policy in February 1998 marked a sea change in South Korea's policy toward North Korea. This policy, together with rapidly growing Sino–South Korean economic ties during the 1990s, provided the foundation for a convergence in Chinese and South Korean priorities on maintaining regional stability, the use of Asian regional institutions as vehicles for promoting inter-Korean reconciliation, and North Korea's integration into the region. In the early stages of his administration, Kim Dae Jung simultaneously laid the framework for inter-Korean reconciliation, promoted consolidation of Sino–South Korean political relations, and improved South Korea's relations with the United States and Japan.

Kim Dae Jung understood that international support from all of the major powers, including China, would be necessary if his efforts to promote inter-Korean reconciliation through the Sunshine policy were to succeed. Following visits to Washington and Seoul, Kim visited Beijing in November 1998 as the next step in consolidating an expanded "cooperative partnership for the twenty-first century" with Beijing. Building on the trend of improving Sino–South Korean economic relations, Kim Dae Jung's main emphasis during this visit was to reassure Pyongyang that Sino–South Korean cooperation would not be detrimental to North Korea, while Jiang Zemin underscored Beijing's willingness to take an active and constructive role in supporting inter-Korean relations.[7] China indicated its support for the Sunshine policy and reaffirmed its core commitment to maintaining peace and stability on the Korean peninsula. China also welcomed efforts to enhance mutual trust through inter-Korean dialogue, and pledged to play a constructive role in promoting reconciliation. Two years later, in October 2000, the "cooperative partnership" was elevated to an "all-around" cooperative partnership during Premier Zhu Rongji's state visit to South Korea in conjunction with the Asia-Europe Meeting.[8] In light of inter-Korean summit developments, China signaled its willingness to further expand its cooperation with South Korea into the political sphere. During this period, South Korea and China initiated regular senior-level military exchanges.

South Korea's Sunshine policy, which focused on engagement and dialogue with North Korea and eschewed strategies of containment, converged with China's efforts to ensure stability in its simultaneous relations with the two Koreas. A fundamental premise underlying inter-Korean reconciliation was that it removed the basis for a competitive relationship between Pyongyang and Seoul. This change in South Korean policy relieved psychological pressure on China to choose between the two Koreas. A second prerequisite of the Sunshine policy was the need for a benign international security environment. Therefore, the policy prioritized regional stability as an important objective and condition for promoting inter-Korean reconciliation. The pursuit of regional stability as a necessary precondition for other objectives (in China's case, its continued economic development, and in South Korea's case, implementation of inter-Korean exchanges and cooperation that would lead to reconciliation) brought Chinese and South Korean foreign policies into alignment and created a space for political cooperation and multilateral consultation on security issues involving North Korea.

In addition to promoting regional stability by reducing tensions, an indirect benefit for China of the Sunshine policy and the inter-Korean summit was the possibility that "independent" efforts of the two Koreas in pursuit of reunification might diminish the strength of the US–South Korean military alliance and eventually push US forces off the peninsula. In the immediate aftermath of the inter-Korean summit, several Chinese analysts put forward the view that inter-Korean reconciliation would pose significant political challenges for the alliance.[9]

South Korean policies toward regional cooperation under Kim Dae Jung also coincided with a transformed Chinese attitude toward Asian regional institution building in the late 1990s. China determined that globalization and regional integration, rather than resulting in isolation, would facilitate its economic development; based on this assessment, the Chinese leadership began to more constructively participate in Asian regional bodies. South Korean policies toward regional cooperation were based on the idea that inter-Korean reconciliation and regional integration and development would go hand-in-hand, and many of Kim Dae Jung's policy initiatives designed to build a regional community were seen as the natural endpoint and precondition for achieving inter-Korean reconciliation. Establishment of an East Asian "vision group" and promotion of Asian dialogues, including dialogue among China, South Korea, and Japan, were ideas that Kim Dae Jung initiated or strongly supported, and coincided with the development of Chinese policy toward regional cooperation.

Consolidation of Relations, Emergence of New Challenges, 2003–2008

On the basis of a rapidly expanding economic relationship following China's entry into the World Trade Organization, the scope of cooperation between South Korea and China continued to expand. China's political transition from Jiang Zemin to the fourth-generation leadership under Hu Jintao coincided with the start of Roh Moo Hyun's presidential term. The second North Korean nuclear crisis has taken prominent space on the political agenda since Roh and Hu took power in early 2003. In addition, new challenges have emerged in the Sino–South Korean political relationship requiring greater effort by both sides to manage effectively.

At their first summit meeting in Beijing in August 2003, Presidents Roh and Hu met and reviewed political and economic objectives in the region with the objective of affirming the Sino–South Korean "comprehensive, cooperative partnership." During this meeting, both leaders agreed on the desirability of handling the North Korean nuclear issue through diplomatic means. Seoul and Beijing independently pressed the

United States and North Korea to show greater flexibility in their respective approaches to the nuclear standoff.

Both leaders agreed to enhance bilateral cooperation in energy and high-technology sectors, such as information technology and biotechnology, through the establishment of a Korea-China "industrial cooperation committee." At the time, it was predicted that the bilateral trade volume between China and South Korea would more than double by 2008, to US$100 billion, a mark that was reached in 2005, three years earlier than projected. At a luncheon with South Korean executives in Beijing, Roh encouraged South Korean businesses to participate in building China's infrastructure, including projects related to the "Great West Development," the 2008 Beijing Olympics, and the 2010 Shanghai exposition. There was also discussion about the need to apply environmental technologies to reduce the negative impact of "yellow dust," which affects the Korean peninsula each spring. But China also made clear its lack of enthusiasm for Roh Moo Hyun's vision of South Korea as a regional hub, given Shanghai's future aspirations and potential capacity to play such a role.[10]

During 2004, a number of structural challenges to improved Sino–South Korean political relations became evident. The most significant challenge was a dispute over whether the ancient Koguryo kingdom (37 B.C.E.–C.E. 667) and the Manchuria-centered Parhae (Bo-hai) kingdom (698–926) should be referenced in historical narratives as precursors to the Korean and Chinese states. In February 2002, the Chinese Academy of Social Sciences had launched a project on "Northeast Asian history," a research effort to document the historical antecedents to modern China. The initial controversy arose beginning in 2001 over whether China or North Korea had the right to petition the UN Educational, Scientific, and Cultural Organization (UNESCO) to add Koguryo mural paintings to the World Heritage list (UNESCO dodged the issue by granting both petitions on July 1, 2004). A major political backlash to this project developed in South Korean media and political circles during the summer of 2004, when the Chinese foreign ministry removed information about pre-1948 Republic of Korea from the Korea section of its website. The revision galvanized South Korean public and elite sentiment, requiring the foreign ministries to negotiate a five-point verbal agreement to resolve the issue.[11]

Chronic problems involving South Korean consular protection for North Korean refugees continued to surface during this period. In 2005, South Korean media reports about China's growing economic influence in North Korea received a great deal of public attention in South Korea. South Koreans were worried about new Chinese investment in North

Korea in sectors that remained closed to the South, despite the Roh government's efforts to advance inter-Korean relations through the Kaesong industrial complex. Other nagging issues included China's annual emissions of "yellow dust," which contained hazardous particles, from its factories; consumer health problems connected with Chinese food imports; and an increasingly heavy-handed approach by China toward South Korea on cross-strait issues. But none of these mounting political challenges were allowed to sour the official diplomatic relationship.

Prior to the November 2005 Asia Pacific Economic Cooperation meetings in Busan, Presidents Roh and Hu held their second summit in Seoul. The Sino–South Korean joint communiqué that was released following this summit emphasized that the "comprehensive, cooperative partnership" that had been affirmed during President Roh's July 2003 visit to Beijing had developed beyond expectations and that exchanges and cooperation should be further deepened and expanded. Hu and Roh welcomed the joint statement that had been negotiated by the six-party talks less than two months prior to their meeting, and encouraged the concerned parties "to demonstrate sincerity and flexibility, implement the statement in earnest, and continue to make progress in advancing the process of talks." Both leaders affirmed the desirability of deepening political contacts at the highest levels among executive, legislative, and party representatives of the two countries, pledged to strengthen foreign affairs coordination, and pledged "to continue strengthening dialogue and contact between the two nations in the realms of national defense and security and to expand exchanges between the two militaries."[12]

The day after the Roh-Hu summit, Hu Jintao addressed the South Korean National Assembly, laying out his vision for the relationship and for China's rise and regional role. Hu asserted that "Sino–South Korean relations have entered the best stage in history," and suggested that the relationship between China and South Korea was a model of peaceful coexistence between countries with different social systems, that the two countries should be "friends" and could "learn from and complement each other," and that "Sino–South Korean ties have gone beyond the scope of bilateral relations against the backdrop of a multi-polar world and economic globalization."[13]

Emerging Challenges in Sino–South Korean Political Relations

Despite a convergence between China and South Korea in their respective priorities toward the North Korean nuclear issue, focused on regional stability and cooperation, many bilateral political issues that have emerged since 2004 have deep roots and cannot be easily resolved. Although the Roh Moo Hyun administration has been tempted to work more closely with China (at the expense of the alliance relationship with the United States, some have alleged), the costs of such a move—despite opportunities for tactical coordination in dealing with North Korea—are apparent, especially in the context of possible renewed regional rivalry between China and Japan (to be dealt with in greater detail in Chapter 8). Despite common interests and visions of enhanced regional cooperation, South Korea and China have differing motivations and visions even in areas where political cooperation is feasible, including Korea's initiative to establish a hub for regional cooperation in Northeast Asia.

During the first decade following diplomatic normalization, the Sino–South Korean relationship faced few difficulties. But by 2004, challenges that had been effectively swept under the rug for the sake of economic opportunity were no longer easily dismissed. Political problems have required more active management since 2004, including the dispute over the Koguryo kingdom (an expression of rising nationalism in China and South Korea and a South Korean litmus test for the political intentions behind China's rise), an incipient competition for influence over North Korea (revealing a direct conflict over whether China or South Korea would exert greater political influence in North Korea), the handling of North Korean refugees (highlighting value and differences between the Chinese and South Korean political systems), and even the broader question of the role of the United States and the structure of the regional order in East Asia. Tensions over these issues have also produced secondary dilemmas for South Korean foreign policy concerning the extent to which South Korea and China should undertake a coordinated response to Japan's handling of historical issues as well as China's expectations for South Korea in managing relations with Taiwan.

The Koguryo Kingdom Dispute and Unresolved Sino-Korean Border Claims

The public tempest in South Korea over China's "Northeast Asian history" project became a full-scale confrontation in the summer of 2004, deeply influencing South Korean public and elite opinions toward China. An April 2004 poll by *Donga Ilbo* showed that the majority of Uri Party members of the National Assembly believed that South Korea "should focus more on China than the US in our foreign policy of the future," and that 84 percent of the public agreed that it was important to give "serious consideration of China."[14] However, a January 2005 *Chosun Ilbo* survey showed that only 40 percent of the South Korean public held favorable attitudes toward China, revealing the extent of political damage to China's image that occurred as a result of the Koguryo issue.[15] Chinese "claims" on the ancient Koguryo kingdom had hit a nerve with South Koreans, whose reaction seemed well out of proportion to the immediate cause of the furor; on the other hand, the issue received little mention in China and hardly registered a reaction among the Chinese public.

Some analysts attribute the motivations behind China's "Northeast Asian history" project, a government-funded effort to reexamine historical and archaeological issues in Manchuria, to concerns that Korean ethnically based claims of historical control over the Manchurian region might stoke ethnic nationalism in the Yanbian Korean ethnic autonomous region of Jilin province, located just across the Tumen river from North Korea. Chinese diplomats and scholars have expressed irritation with occasional nationalist claims by some South Koreans to large portions of Manchuria on the basis that Koguryo was originally Korean territory. In turn, the history of the Koguryo kingdom has served as an example of Korean national pride in standing against Chinese aggressors, and every Korean schoolchild is taught that Koguryo is one of the three kingdoms out of which a unified Korean nation eventually emerged.[16]

At first glance, the dispute seems nonsensical, since the modern concept of nation-state did not come to Asia until the nineteenth century and the Koguryo kingdom certainly would not have defined itself as either Chinese or Korean. But as a historical reference point designed to bolster respective forms of Chinese and Korean national pride, the Koguryo dispute takes on greater significance and drastically limits options for compromise on either side. An early-twentieth-century Korean nationalist, Sin Ch'ae Ho, attempted to define "nation" in the context of ethnicity rather than geographical territory while Korea was under Japanese rule. Park Chung Hee made references to Koguryo as a historical inspiration for nation building, and Koguryo artifacts were used in modern Korean historical exhibitions to "symbolize Korea's national historic past." These claims have persisted throughout the twentieth century as an alternative Korean narrative of national survival and endurance in the context of the loss of the Korean nation and its rebuilding.[17]

As the Koguryo dispute became politicized into an emotional grievance that South Koreans held against China's handling of the issue,

Chinese diplomats were quick to negotiate a secret, verbal understanding of a modus operandi for managing the problem. But given the informal nature of the agreement and the inability of either side to ensure that the terms of the agreement would be implemented among its populace, it seems inevitable that the Koguryo dispute will continue to resurface, as was the case in 2006 when South Koreans reacted negatively to the release of Chinese research papers that perpetuated the idea that the Parhae and Koryo kingdoms were founded by ethnic Chinese rather than ethnic Koreans.[18] Concerns remain on both sides that the dispute will continue to be used as a tactical tool for extracting political gains. South Koreans remain suspicious that a Chinese policy of "internalization of border areas" *(bianjiang neidihua)* would impinge on Korean autonomy, while Chinese fear a unified Korean territorial claim to large swaths of Manchuria.[19]

By evoking historical precedents in which China played a central role in a hierarchical relationship with its Korean tributary, the Koguryo issue has captured substantial media attention in South Korea and instigated fears that China desires to replicate a China-centered East Asian order rather than an order in which South Korea can fully exercise its sovereignty or autonomy. Yonsei University professor Kim Woo Jun told the *New York Times* in August 2004 that "the anti-U.S., pro-China atmosphere has changed recently as we saw the hegemonic side of China."[20]

For Koreans, how China handles the issue of the Koguryo kingdom has become a litmus test for its intentions in Northeast Asia, whether hegemony on the Korean peninsula, or truly peaceful development based on notions of equality and mutual benefit. For instance, in response to perceived Chinese arrogance in handling the Koguryo issue in the summer of 2004, South Korean National Assembly members demanded that China turn over territory ceded to it by Japan under the Gando Treaty in 1909. Since South Korea was under the protection of Japan at that time and could not exercise its sovereignty in protesting the treaty, South Koreans view the treaty as invalid, even though the basis for a prior Korean claim to land on the other side of the Tumen river may also be regarded as weak. Even during the Cold War, disputes over Sino–North Korean border claims were never completely resolved; such territorial issues are bound to resurface in the event that China someday shares a border with a unified Korea.[21]

Chinese concerns with separatism by minority ethnic groups have extended to the Yanbian Korean autonomous region, despite the fact that Chinese Koreans have generally been a model minority ethnic group.

The Korean autonomous region of Yanbian has been a showcase for Chinese ethnic tolerance and official bilingualism, but Chinese concerns about separatism rose in the 1990s with a growing influx of South Korean tourists into Yanbian. During this period, Seoul became an alternative center for ideas, cultural influence, and financial success for ethnic Koreans in China, despite Chinese policies that initially discouraged South Korean businesses from trade and investment opportunities in Yanbian. By the mid-1990s, opportunities for ethnic Koreans to work and study in South Korea, where income potential and career opportunities were considerably broader than in Yanbian, were widening. Since then, more and more ethnic Koreans, especially women, have been drawn to South Korea for "short-term" work opportunities as migrant workers in sectors that pay as much as twenty times the wages for similar work at home. As South Korean investment centered in Shandong and around Shanghai has developed in recent years, these work opportunities have also driven demand for bilingual employees who can bridge Korean and Chinese culture, stimulating additional employment opportunities for Korean Chinese workers in other parts of China. One result is that Yanbian is in danger of losing its status as a Korean ethnic autonomous region due to Korean outmigration combined with a steady influx of Han Chinese into the region. Contradictory cultural and economic influences are thus serving to weaken Yanbian as a base for ethnic Koreans in China, even as South Korean cultural influences spread rapidly due to the "Korean wave" of pop music, television dramas, and films, even within Han Chinese society.[22]

Competition for Strategic Influence over North Korea

A second area of competition between China and South Korea derives from China's expanded economic influence over North Korea, which many South Koreans regard as their own natural sphere of influence. A long-standing assumption behind South Korea's unification policy under every modern administration has been that, eventually, South Korea will restore its proper influence over North Korea and that the inter-Korean process will be pursued according to the independent efforts of the two Koreas. An unstated corollary to this assumption in South Korea is that major powers such as the United States, Japan, and China have the capacity to thwart South Korean aims, especially by developing economic ties with North Korea and possibly using economic leverage to thwart prospects for Korean reunification.

China's expanded trade and investment ties with North Korea since

2004 have drawn considerable public attention and anxiety in South Korea, especially since China has gained concessions in critical sectors such as mining and natural resource development, to which South Korea has long sought access through the gradual process of improving inter-Korean relations. Instead, North Korea has confined South Korean influence to Mount Kumgang and the Kaesong industrial zone while allowing Chinese entrepreneurs and investors much wider-ranging access to many sectors of the North Korean economy. Most notably, the rapid growth of Sino–North Korean trade and investment since 2005 has stimulated anxieties in South Korea over the level of China's economic influence in North Korea and the possibility that such influence could be used to thwart South Korean dreams of eventual Korean reunification. These anxieties appear to have also served as a catalyst for South Korean interest in negotiating expanded inter-Korean economic cooper-ation agreements, as illustrated during the 2007 inter-Korean summit. This summit resulted in an agreement to expand joint economic cooper-ation to a wide range of new sectors, most notably including pledges to expand inter-Korean natural resource development and to establish new shipyards in Anbyon, North Korea.[23] An antecedent to such anxieties, in a dramatically different policy context, was the disappointment shown by South Korean officials during the Kim Young Sam era when China's large-scale provision of economic assistance in 1996 and 1997 may have forestalled North Korea's economic collapse.[24]

The significance of South Korean anxieties over China's influence in North Korea is directly related to the question of whether China, as a great power, might ultimately dash South Korea's long-standing hopes that good diplomatic relations could lead to Chinese support for its own strategic objectives on the peninsula (including a South Korea–led Korean unification process), should China act to preserve North Korea as a strategic buffer and sphere of Chinese influence. As China's diplomatic role and influence in Korea-related diplomacy expands, it will increas-ingly have the ability both to veto developments on the Korean peninsula contrary to Chinese interests, and to ensure that any possible outcome on the peninsula will be neutral if not beneficial to its security needs.

North Korean Refugee Issues

Since the defection of Hwang Jang Yop to the South Korean consulate in Beijing in February 1997, the management of North Korean refugees has been a constant source of low-level friction between the Chinese and South Korean governments. Although the two governments have managed the issue strictly through negotiating secret verbal protocols (often while intentionally looking the other way when these protocols are broken, to avoid escalation), the North Korean refugee issue involves direct conflicts between South Korean and Chinese conceptions of human rights and the scope of allowable actions by foreign citizens under democratic versus authoritarian systems of government.

No other issue in the Sino–South Korean political relationship has greater power or longer-lasting grassroots impact in shaping public perceptions than the management of North Korean refugees. The issue has persisted for over a decade on virtually a daily basis, leading to permanent double-duty for South Korean consular officials in China, who serve as de facto managers of temporary way stations that process hundreds of North Korean refugees each year, handle periodic breaches of protocol, and provide consular services for South Korean media representatives, activists, religious figures, and other nongovernmental actors who face difficulty on Chinese soil.[25] But the real impact of the issue lies in the potential for individual cases to poison broader public support for the Sino–South Korean relationship. Both South Korean policies toward the handling of North Korean defectors, and Chinese policies of unscreened repatriation of North Korean refugees in violation of international humanitarian conventions, have come under criticism by a growing network of South Korean and international activists who target both North Korea and China as human rights violators.[26]

A growing number of South Korean humanitarian networks have developed in an attempt to assist North Korean refugees, who face constant personal risk of repatriation or exploitation on Chinese soil. Some South Koreans have been detained by authorities for protesting Chinese policies or defying Chinese laws while assisting North Korean refugees. Technology and loosened political controls within North Korean society have facilitated movement and communication between North and South Korea via China, through letters, brokers, and temporary meetings and reunions of divided families, further challenging the diplomatic and political relations between South Korea and China and clearly illustrating wide gaps in social and humanitarian priorities.

In the first few years following the North Korean famine of the late 1990s, China's primary policy approach to South Korean humanitarian efforts on behalf of North Korean refugees was to look the other way. Even when South Korean media and nongovernmental representatives took direct action to respond to the needs of North Korean refugees, punishments were relatively light. Chinese policy did not allow for active assistance of North Korean refugees, nor did it allow the UN High

Commissioner for Refugees (UNHCR) to become involved. But Chinese policy also clearly did not allow for prevention of refugee flows, nor for targeting refugees from North Korea. Following the famine and the refugee flows of 1996–2000, North Korean refugees were a common sight on the streets of Yanbian, as were North Korean refugee children outside the terminal at Yanji airport, begging for handouts.[27]

An early incident that drew public attention in South Korea was the repatriation of an entire family of seven North Korean refugees who had sought to contact the UNHCR in 1999. This family had initially crossed from North Korea into Russia and then entered China, where they were caught. The Chinese authorities repatriated the North Koreans to Russia, but in 2001 the family again escaped to Beijing, where they were finally granted refugee status by the UNHCR.

China's initial crackdown on North Korean refugees in Yanbian occurred in the context of a nationwide anticorruption campaign in which each province chose to address a specific problem. In Jilin province, the 2001 "Strike Hard" campaign focused on rounding up North Korean refugees through door-to-door searches and active detaining and repatriation of North Koreans who had illegally entered China. Networks involved with trafficking of North Korean female refugees also became more established during this period. But the focus on rounding up North Korean refugees in provincial regions intensified as a result of the organized efforts of North Korean refugees to seek asylum in diplomatic compounds in Beijing and Shenyang in March 2002, often with the active support of South Korean nongovernmental and human rights groups. These asylum cases were designed to publicly humiliate China for its handling of North Korean refugees and to attract international attention to their plight.[28]

In response to these developments, China developed a two-pronged policy toward the North Korean refugee issue. On the one hand, Chinese authorities intensified monitoring and repatriation of North Korean refugees in areas near the border with North Korea. On the other hand, if refugees had come under international protection at foreign embassies or consulates, the Chinese government allowed those refugees to leave China, usually after requiring them to submit to a background check to confirm that they were North Korean citizens and not ethnic Korean citizens of China.

During this period, Chinese and South Korean authorities negotiated a verbal protocol by which the South Korean government pledged to minimize media reporting on North Korean refugee issues and by which South Korean authorities would care for North Korean refugees who came under their protection but would not undertake active efforts to invite North Korean refugees to defect to South Korea. In return, Chinese authorities allowed North Korean refugees to be transported to South Korea, but only following a background investigation; Chinese processing requirements sometimes took up to a year. Since so many North Korean refugees in China sought asylum in South Korean diplomatic facilities, one way that Chinese authorities could limit their numbers was through delaying departure approvals, since such approvals would create physical space for new refugees to take their place. These de facto limits that China imposed on South Korean diplomatic compounds coincided with a South Korean policy to discourage refugee flows within China, in deference to the wishes of the Chinese government. As a result, many North Korean refugees sought passage through China to countries as far afield as Mongolia, Thailand, and Vietnam prior to seeking asylum in South Korea.

Even with a verbal protocol in place for managing North Korean refugees, a number of ongoing issues have required periodic attention. In early 2005, South Korea's Ministry of Unification announced that it would try to more effectively screen North Korean refugees to avoid admitting criminals, spies, and Chinese ethnic Koreans. The policy spawned an opposition National Assembly fact-finding investigation to Yanji and a dispute with Chinese authorities over the disruption of a planned press conference in Beijing, which itself became a minor diplomatic incident. When South Korean National Assembly members tried to call a press conference in a Beijing hotel to release their findings, Chinese plainclothes security agents cut the power to the conference room; in protest over the incident, the opposition urged that the South Korean ambassador to China be recalled.[29]

With South Korean nongovernmental organizations so actively involved in assisting refugees in China, complete control over South Korean media reporting of these cases has proved impossible. Likewise, China has imposed increasingly strict jail sentences on South Korean citizens caught aiding North Korean refugees, creating yet another issue of contention between China and South Korea. In addition, unscrupulous and shadowy brokers have been involved in bringing North Koreans out of China to meet with South Korean family members, raising the possibility of financial fraud or other exploitation of South Korean citizens in China.[30] An even stickier issue for the two countries involves protecting the rights of South Korean prisoners of war, abductees, and refugees from North Korea who have become citizens of South Korea. In some cases, former North Korean refugees who have obtained South Korean citizenship have undertaken the dangerous return to China to help their refugee relatives. The handling of abducted South Korean citizens who had been detained against their will in North Korea or who had managed to escape to China create further coordination challenges for both South Korean and Chinese authorities, since many of these individuals have rights to consular protection as South Korean citizens, but do not have the documentation necessary to prove those rights, given that they had been held for long periods of time in North Korea. Mishandling of these and similar cases could easily stimulate public outrage among South Koreans, directed at both the South Korean foreign ministry and the Chinese government for failure to preserve the rights of South Korean citizens.

The Role of the United States

Some Chinese scholars cite the US–South Korean alliance as the biggest obstacle that restrains the Sino–South Korean relationship from reaching its full potential.[31] However, it is not clear that Chinese and South Korean visions of a future relationship would converge even if the US–South Korean alliance were to unravel. Chinese scholars have characterized the US-led bilateral alliance structure as "Cold War thinking" that should be abandoned in favor of regional cooperative security arrangements. During Lee Myung Bak's first visit to China, the spokesman for the Chinese foreign ministry rehearsed Chinese objections to the alliance as an indirect way of criticizing Lee's prioritization of a US–South Korean "strategic alliance," saying that "the Korean-U.S. alliance is a historical relic. The times have changed and Northeast Asian countries are going through many changes and transformations. We should not approach current security issues with military alliances left over from the past Cold War era."[32] The Chinese view coincides with the thinking of some South Korean observers who define the "dismantling of the Cold War structure on the Korean peninsula" as the elimination of confrontation on the Korean peninsula and who see the US–South Korean security alliance as blocking conditions for peace.

The role and future of the security alliance with the United States remains a matter of political debate within South Korean society, although a majority of the public appear to support the maintenance of US security ties. Some South Korean progressives appear eager to rush into the arms of China simply in order to escape the clasp of the US security alliance, but what the Sino–South Korean political and security relationship would look like if it were to become the main pillar for a new South Korean security strategy has not yet been envisioned.

South Korea's diplomatic orientation vis-à-vis China and the United States became a challenge under Roh Moo Hyun in the context of managing the North Korean nuclear issue as part of six-party talks. Despite South Korea's security alliance with the United States, its priorities for maintaining regional stability have converged with those of China, sometimes contradicting the imperatives for institutional and political coordination required by its alliance with the United States. South Korea's maneuvering in the context of six-party talks represents an initial glimpse at the future political challenges that South Korea might face, especially in the context of Korean reunification. If Korean unification were to occur, the de facto balance of influence on the Korean peninsula, which is physically represented by a division into spheres that favor China and the United States, would be erased, and could result in a heightened strategic competition for influence on the peninsula (to be dealt with in more detail in Chapter 7, which examines the triangular interaction among China, South Korea, and the United States).

Management of Cross-Strait Relations and Tibet

South Korea has persistently sought Chinese understanding of and cooperation with its efforts to enhance influence on the Korean peninsula in ways that might create a favorable environment for Korean reunification. In return, South Korea has attempted to meet Chinese expectations that it strictly support Chinese policies in managing cross-strait relations. Just as South Korea has been disappointed with China's use of economic instruments to strengthen political influence in North Korea, China has sometimes expressed disappointment with South Korea's positions vis-à-vis Taiwan.

For the most part, however, the South Korean government has exercised strict discipline in support of China's policies, to the point of public criticism and even absurdity. The ability of the South Korean government to walk the line between public expectations of sovereignty on cross-strait matters, and expectations strictly in line with Chinese policy, is increasingly eroding.

South Korea has been so judicious in avoiding any offense to Beijing that it refused the application for political asylum of Xu Bo, an alleged Tiananmen dissident, in 2001. Xu subsequently won a contest, conducted by the Seoul metropolitan government in the fall of 2002, that encouraged foreigners to give suggestions on how to improve life in Seoul. When the city government discovered that a Chinese dissident had won the prize, it canceled the award ceremony and gave Xu a cash prize instead, presumably to ensure that there would be no record of the transaction. Meanwhile, deportation proceedings against him continued; he was forced to depart Seoul in early 2003.[33]

Another example of South Korean efforts to avoid diplomatic conflict with Chinese authorities has been South Korea's handling of issues related to the Dalai Lama and Tibet. Despite a large population of Korean Buddhists who have sought to invite the Dalai Lama to visit Seoul on several occasions, the South Korean government has consistently refused permission for the visit, at the behest of Beijing. In 2001, South Korean authorities even prevented the Dalai Lama from taking a transit flight to Mongolia on South Korea's Asiana airlines.[34]

Given South Korea's great desire to avoid political offense to Beijing on cross-strait matters, in addition to the lingering bitterness of Taiwanese authorities regarding the unceremonious manner in which they were forced to depart, despite having received assurances from senior South Korean government officials only months prior to the August 1992 normalization of relations between Seoul and Beijing, it is perhaps unsurprising that over a decade passed before flag-carriers resumed service between Seoul and Taipei.

In 2004, despite efforts by the South Korean government to avoid offending Beijing on cross-strait issues, the South Korean public reacted negatively to the warnings and threats that Beijing transmitted to South Korean National Assembly members, and even to former South Korean president Kim Young Sam, not to attend the presidential inauguration ceremony of Chen Shui Bian. The heavy-handed manner by which Beijing threatened to "remember" lawmakers who attended the ceremony was perceived by the South Korean public as an insulting and arrogant intrusion. Violence by Chinese students against pro-Tibetan and North Korean refugee protesters during the Olympic torch rally in April 2008 incited a firestorm of public opinion in South Korea, to the extent that the South Korean government weighed the possibility of repatriating any Chinese students whose involvement in the violence could be proved.[35] South Korean scholars have suggested that Seoul might consider improvement in unofficial relations with Taipei as a tactical response if Beijing becomes too overbearing on strategic issues of central importance to South Korea.[36]

Prospects for Sino–South Korean Economic Relations

Serious political disputes between China and South Korea have thus far been contained from directly impacting the bilateral economic relationship. This seeming isolation of political challenges from the economic relationship is similar to the "economics hot, politics cold" mantra that has characterized Sino-Japanese relations. But it is still possible that a political dispute might have a spillover effect on the economic relationship, or that perceptions of South Korea's economic dependency might lead China to believe that economic opportunities could be held hostage in the pursuit of political interests.

Most of the political issues that have emerged thus far in the Sino–South Korean relationship are unlikely to threaten its economic aspects. Only if core national security interests were at stake would it be possible to imagine either South Korea or China utilizing economic instruments for retaliation in a political dispute—for instance, if South Korea were to openly challenge China's policies in managing cross-strait relations, or if China were to pursue policies hostile to South Korea's vital security interests and objectives vis-à-vis North Korea. Even if South Korea or China were to use economic measures to achieve political objectives, however, the likelihood that such tools could be used successfully appears low. Most of the political issues that have emerged thus far, such as management of refugees, the Koguryo kingdom dispute, and even the emergence of Sino–South Korean economic competition for influence inside North Korea, have had a negligible effect on the bilateral economic relationship.

It is far more difficult to assess the extent to which increased mutual economic interdependence might inhibit forms of political cooperation with third parties, for instance in the context of political tension between the United States and China. If South Korea eventually were to find itself in China's "economic orbit" as a result of increasing economic dependency, in what ways might South Korea hesitate to cooperate politically with third parties such as the United States on political issues? In a situation in which US-Chinese relations are characterized by a mixture of cooperation and competition, it is hard to imagine cases where either side would be able to utilize economic measures alone to effectively compel a third party to provide political support for a specific initiative.

Conversely, it has been argued that South Korea effectively utilized economic engagement with China during the 1990s in order to promote China's integration into the international community.[37] South Korea's pursuit of economic opportunities in China in the early stages following diplomatic normalization might have indirectly encouraged China to follow the South Korean economic model, but such effects were probably incidental to core economic and business motives for engagement by South Korean businesspeople. Once the political barriers that had inhibited economic cooperation had been removed, politics became incidental to the maturation of the economic relationship. Only a significant change in the strategic orientation of either party would be likely to change the trajectory of the bilateral economic relationship—for instance, in the unlikely event that the United States and China were to engage in a major conflict.

Although there is little evidence of a direct linkage between the bilateral economic relationship and specific political issues, there is no question that Sino–South Korean economic ties have brought the two countries closer together, enhancing the likelihood that some political conflicts might be magnified as issues of disparity as well as increasing the possibility that some political conflicts might be overlooked for the sake of economic growth that leads to mutual prosperity. It also remains to be seen whether the remarkable change in economic ties between the two countries will resonate in setting the context for strategic choices, including the question of how to value regional relations vis-à-vis third parties, including the United States and Japan.

Notes

1. "Kim Likens North Korea to Broken Airplane, Warns of Security Threat," *Agence France Press,* February 29, 1996.
2. See Scott Snyder, *North Korea's Decline and China's Strategic Dilemmas: Report on a June 1997 Research Trip to Beijing, Shenyang, Yanji, and Changchun* (Washington, DC: US Institute of Peace, October 1997), p. 12.
3. Cameron Barr, "A 'Whale' and a 'Shrimp' Gang Up on Japanese," *Christian Science Monitor,* November 15, 1995, p. 6.
4. "2nd Round of Korea Peace Talks Slated for March 16," *Japan Economic Newswire,* December 10, 1997.
5. Scott Snyder, "Six Party Talks: 'Action for Action' and the Formalization of Regional Security Cooperation in Northeast Asia," *International Journal of Korean Unification Studies* 16, no. 1 (2007): 1–24.
6. Andrew Pollack, "Defector Says North Korea Seems Intent on War," *New York Times,* April 21, 1997, p. 8; "Chronology of Events As North Korean Defector Arrives in Seoul," *Agence France Presse,* April 20, 1997.
7. "ROK-China Partnership Not Intended to Isolate NK," *Korea Times,* November 12, 1998.
8. Piao Jianyi, "China's Policy Toward the ROK: An All-Around Cooperative Partnership," unpublished paper sent via communication with author, January 2006.
9. Wang Xiaohui, "Summit Meeting Opens a New Era in North-South Korea Cooperation," *Zhungguo Xinwen She* (Beijing), in Chinese, June 15,

2000, accessed at http://www.opensource.gov, doc. no. CPP20000615000116; Yu Meihua, "Ice-Breaking Trip Takes Place After Being Expected for Half Century: On Successful DPRK-ROK Summit," *Shijie Zhishi* (Beijing), July 1, 2000, pp. 8–9, accessed at http://www.opensource.gov, doc. no. CPP20000712000051.

10. Hwang Jang-jin, "Korean Leader Has Limited Success in Beijing," *Korea Herald,* July 11, 2003.

11. For more detail on the initial phases of the controversy, see Peter Hayes Gries, "The Koguryo Controversy, National Identity, and Sino-Korean Relations Today," *East Asia* 22, no. 4 (Winter 2005), pp. 3–17; Scott Snyder, "Can China Unstick the Korean Nuclear Standoff?" in Brad Glosserman and Vivian Bailey Fritschi, eds., *Comparative Connections* 6, no. 1 (January–March 2004): 97–102; Scott Snyder, "A Turning Point for China-Korea Relations?" in Brad Glosserman and Vivian Bailey Fritschi, eds., *Comparative Connections* 6, no. 3 (July–September 2004): 109–116.

12. "'Full Text' of Joint Communiqué Issued by China and the Republic of Korea in Seoul on 17 November," *Xinhua Domestic Service,* in Chinese, November 17, 2005, accessed at http://www.opensource.gov, doc. no. CPP20051117078040.

13. "Chinese President Calls for Further Cooperation Between China, South Korea," *Xinhua General News Service,* November 17, 2005.

14. "Public Polls About China," *Donga Ilbo,* May 4, 2004, accessed at http://www.opensource.gov, doc. no. KPP20040503000103.

15. Chung Jae Ho, "Dragon in the Eyes of South Korea: Analyzing Korean Perceptions of China," in Jonathan D. Pollack, ed., *Korea: The East Asian Pivot* (Newport, RI: Naval War College Press, 2004), pp. 253–267.

16. See Gries, "The Koguryo Controversy," p. 5.

17. See ibid., pp. 9–10.

18. "S. Korea-China History Dispute over Ancient Kingdoms Resurfaces," *Yonhap News Agency,* September 7, 2006.

19. Chung, "Dragon in the Eyes of South Korea," p. 262.

20. James Brooke, "Seeking Peace in a Once and Future Kingdom," *New York Times,* August 25, 2004, p. 3.

21. Daniel Goma, "The Chinese-Korean Border Issue: An Analysis of a Contested Frontier," *Asian Survey* 46, no. 6 (2006): 867–880.

22. Kim Jung Min, "Dissolution of Korean Minority Families in China: Socio-Demographic Changes in the Yanbian Korean Autonomous Prefecture," in *Study on Women and Family Life* vol. 9 (Seoul: Myongji University Institute of Women and Family Life), pp. 67–87.

23. "Full Text of Inter-Korean Agreement," *Korea Times,* October 4, 2007, accessed at http://www.koreatimes.co.kr/www/news/nation/2007/10/120_11295.html on June 11, 2008.

24. Atsushi Ijuin, "Playing It Cool with N. Korea," *Nikkei Weekly,* October 17, 2005.

25. Author interviews with South Korean diplomats in Beijing and Washington, DC, November 2005 and March 2007.

26. The North Korea Freedom Coalition, an international network focused on North Korean human rights issues, has held annual conferences since 1999. The coalition has held annual events in Washington, DC, to call attention to North Korean human rights issues, since 2004. See Carl Gershman, "Promoting Democracy in the Post-9/11 World: The Case of North Korea," October 11, 2002, accessed at the National Endowment for Democracy website, http://www.ned.org/about/carl/oct1102.html, on August 4, 2007.

27. Author's personal observations from periodic visits to Yanji in 1998–2001.

28. Jasper Becker, "Refugees Strike Blow for Truth," *South China Morning Post,* March 17, 2002, p. 11.

29. Philip P. Pan, "Chinese Agents Storm Briefing by South Korean Lawmakers," *Washington Post,* January 13, 2005, p. A16.

30. Bill Powell, Matthew Cooper, and Donald MacIntyre, "Running Out of the Darkness; With the Aid of American Christians, North Koreans Are Risking Their Lives to Reach Freedom—The Inside Tale of One Escape," *Time,* May 1, 2006, p. 32.

31. Author interviews with Chinese scholars in Shanghai, October 2006.

32. Michael Ha, "Chinese Official Calls Korea-U.S. Alliance 'Historical Relic,'" *Korea Times,* May 28, 2008.

33. Kwak Young-sup, "Chinese Man Allegedly Faces Deportation Threats," *Korea Herald,* September 26, 2002; "Dastardly City Officials," *Korea Herald,* September 16, 2002; "No Excuse for Shameful Delay," *Taipei Times,* February 24, 2003.

34. Angus McDonald, "Dalai Lama Cancels Trip to Mongolia Due to Travel Restrictions," *Associated Press,* August 30, 2002.

35. "Chinese Student Faces Arrest for Seoul Torch Relay Violence," *Korea Herald,* May 2, 2008; Cho Ji-yun, "Seoul Slams Chinese Torch Relay Violence: Deputy Foreign Minister Delivers Message of Regret After Chinese Scuffled with Police," *Korea Herald,* April 29, 2008.

36. Author interview with South Korean scholar in Seoul, September 2005.

37. Victor D. Cha, "Engaging China: Seoul-Beijing Détente and Korean Security," *Survival* 41, no. 1 (Spring 1999): 73–98.

5
China's Evolving Economic and Political Relations with North Korea

Following the collapse of the Soviet Union, China carried the burden of being North Korea's only remaining economic patron. North Korea's loss of face and gradual distancing from Beijing following China's decision to establish diplomatic relations with South Korea made the management of relations with Pyongyang even pricklier. China's normalization of diplomatic ties with South Korea—and the consummation of its betrayal of North Korea, from the perspective of the leadership in Pyongyang—marked the beginning of a unique challenge in China's formulation of policies toward the Korean peninsula: that of maintaining good relations with both Koreas simultaneously.

Ironically, North Korea's dependence on China had never been higher than it was following the fall of the Soviet Union, a period that coincided with China's diplomatic normalization with South Korea. This period marked the peak of China's economic leverage over an economically dependent North Korea. Despite its apparent economic leverage over North Korea, China appeared to be a hostage to the specter that North Korea's economic collapse would engender political instability, which in turn might spill over and affect China's northeastern provinces. North Korea's leadership owes its survival to its ability to turn its own economic dependency into an obligation and a liability for the donor rather than allowing the subsidies on which Pyongyang depended to become a source of leverage for its erstwhile patrons.

To the extent that China maintained the distinction of being the only major power to have cordial relations with both Koreas, the situation was also a subtle reminder of an unfulfilled promise that Chinese leaders had made to Kim Il Sung to promote the normalization of North Korea's relations with Japan and the United States. The existence of relations with both Koreas created an opportunity for Beijing to enhance its influence on the Korean peninsula and to play a diplomatic brokering role between Pyongyang and Seoul, Washington, and Tokyo. This was a role to which Beijing begrudgingly acquiesced in the 1990s, given China's keen awareness of the deterioration in Sino–North Korean relations caused by the decision to normalize diplomatic relations with South Korea. But China took on a much more active mediating role through the six-party talks during the second North Korean nuclear crisis, beginning in early 2003. China's special role and relationship with North Korea placed extra responsibilities and expectations on Beijing in the eyes of the international community, resulting from the fact that China was North Korea's only regular channel of communication with the outside world.

China's management of its own economic policies toward the Korean peninsula became a critical component of that challenge, especially given that South Korea and the United States had their own strong views on how China might utilize its economic leverage with North Korea to achieve desired political goals of denuclearization and regime transformation. But China had its own interests in promotion of regional stability, which cast the economic instruments at China's disposal—and the economic policy instruments China would be willing to consider in achieving those objectives—in a very different light. Given these circumstances, economic instruments were always very closely linked to the politics of managing the Sino–North Korean relationship, and North Korea's own approach reinforced that linkage by subordinating economics to politics and intensely politicizing any decision that China might make regarding management of economic policy toward North Korea.

Overview of Sino–North Korean Economic Relations, 1992–2005

The immediate challenge for China in managing economic relations with North Korea in the early 1990s was its desire to lessen the aid burden from North Korea by promoting greater market-based trade, especially in the areas of oil and grain provision. Following the collapse of the Soviet Union, North Korea had lost a key patron and a source for considerable economic assistance, creating an immediate and severe economic crisis for Pyongyang. Beginning in 1990, North Korea's gross national product dropped precipitously due to the loss of assistance from

Moscow (see Table 5.1). At the same time, Beijing desired to adjust the economic relationship from one based on assistance to North Korea to a more market-oriented basis, but Pyongyang was clearly unprepared to respond to such requests. The impact of Beijing's efforts reinforced the political estrangement in Sino–North Korean relations resulting from China's normalization of relations with South Korea. Sino-North Korean bilateral trade dropped from almost US$900 million in 1993 to US$550 million in 1995 and US$565 million in 1996 (see Table 5.2).[1] The dramatic drop in trade mirrored an overall decline in North Korea's external trade.

China's share in North Korea's overall trade dipped from about 32 percent in 1993 to under 20 percent in 2000 (with an exception to the trend in 1997, due to China's bump in grain exports to North Korea at the height of the latter's famine), reflecting political difficulties in the relationship, but China's share of North Korea's overall foreign trade jumped from 20 percent in 2000 to 28 percent in 2001. As China sought to enhance its political influence on North Korea beginning in 2003, its share of North Korea's overall trade reached 33 percent that year, and has continued to rise since, to over 43 percent in 2005. China has become North Korea's external lifeline and major source of economic exchange.

Chinese analysts speak about the goal of making the Sino–North Korean economic relationship more "normal" (one conducted on a market basis, without subsidies), but there is little indication that Chinese

Table 5.1   North Korea's Gross National Product, 1995–2006

	Gross National Product (US$ millions)	Gross National Product per Capita (US$)	Gross Domestic Product Growth Rate (%)
1995	22,300	1,034	–4.1
1996	21,400	989	–3.6
1997	17,700	811	–6.3
1998	12,600	573	–1.1
1999	15,800	714	6.2
2000	16,800	757	1.3
2001	15,700	706	3.7
2002	17,000	762	1.2
2003	18,400	818	1.8
2004	20,800	914	2.2
2005	24,200	1,056	3.8
2006	25,600	1,108	–1.1

Source: The Bank of Korea.

Table 5.2   China's Trade with North Korea vs. Inter-Korean Trade, 1993–2006 (US$ millions)

	China's Imports from North Korea	China's Exports to North Korea	China's Total Trade with North Korea	North Korea's Total Trade	China's Share of Total Trade (%)	Total Inter-Korean Trade	South Korea's Share of Total Trade (%)
1993	297	602	899	2,833	32	187	6
1994	199	424	623	2,295	27	195	8
1995	64	486	550	2,339	24	287	12
1996	68	497	565	2,228	25	252	11
1997	121	531	652	2,485	26	308	12
1998	57	355	412	1,664	25	222	13
1999	42	329	371	1,813	20	333	18
2000	37	451	488	2,395	20	425	17
2001	167	571	738	2,673	28	403	15
2002	271	467	738	2,902	25	642	25
2003	396	628	1,024	3,115	33	724	22
2004	585	799	1,384	3,557	42	697	20
2005	497	1,085	1,582	4,057	43	1,056	26
2006	468	1,232	1,700	4,346	39	1,350	31

Sources: Ministry of Unification, South Korea; KOTRA; KEIA.

leaders would be willing to pursue such a goal, given the potential negative impact on China's economically lagging northeastern provinces and concerns that withdrawal of Chinese assistance from North Korea might induce political instability or an economic collapse. Chinese analysts justify assistance to North Korea, estimated at approximately 40 percent of China's overall development assistance in 2006 (up from an estimated 33 percent in 2002), as "strategic" in nature, handled through high-level leadership channels rather than through the channels in China's Ministry of Commerce that are responsible for overseas development assistance. China's General Administration of Customs reports that China's oil exports to North Korea in 2007 amounted to 523,160 tons.[2] The International Crisis Group reports that China supplies North Korea with 500,000 tons of food and 300,000 to 1 million tons of heavy oil annually.[3] Chinese analysts affirm continuing supplies of oil to North Korea on a concessional basis ("the DPRK is very unsatisfied with our oil supply"), as well as glass (from a Chinese-built factory near Pyongyang), the latter classified as development assistance, but beyond this, relatively little is known about the amounts and types of assistance that China is currently providing to North Korea.[4]

There are no official figures available that capture the level of direct bilateral assistance that Pyongyang receives from Beijing. These statistics remain classified by the Chinese government.[5] Moreover, there are multiple channels, including military-to-military ties, local cross-border relationships, and provincial-level relationships with North Korea, through which such assistance might be made available, either at the direction of or outside the direct approval of Beijing's central leadership.[6] In addition, it is hard to judge what portion of bilateral economic interactions are captured in official Chinese trade data, given the possibility of unrecorded official or quasi-official transfers among fraternal institutions, military-to-military transfers handled through special ties, illegal or unrecorded cross-border or barter transfers (for instance, "after hours" activity that might take place after customs officials have left work), and other such bilateral economic activity. Some Chinese analysts report that unrecorded border trade through various unofficial means could equal the level of official trade.[7] Thus, no comprehensive evaluation of the extent of China's economic assistance to North Korea is available. However, "mirror statistics" reflecting China's official trade with North Korea have been reported to the United Nations and are available for scrutiny, even if they are only partially representative of the overall trade relationship.

As one examines North Korean "mirror statistics," several trends become apparent. First, China has consistently run a structural trade deficit with North Korea of about US$400 million annually since the late 1980s.[8] This structural deficit itself provides partial evidence of ongoing Chinese subsidies to North Korea, but does not fully capture the entire scope of China's assistance. Many Chinese firms that have conducted trade with North Korea have suffered from the unwillingness or inability of North Korean counterparts to pay for their goods. In addition, smuggling may prove to be the easiest and most profitable way for small-scale Chinese traders to work with North Korean counterparts. For Chinese state-owned enterprises that have lost money through trade deals with North Korean counterparts, North Korean failure to pay for goods ultimately constitutes an additional subsidy to the North Korean economy.[9]

The Chinese and North Korean central governments have traditionally and regularly negotiated assistance packages, and have incorporated these packages into their respective central budgets. For instance, up to 1993, Beijing was reported to have supplied 1.2 million tons of crude oil to North Korea, of which 650,000 tons were provided through barter trade and 550,000 tons were provided on credit. But Chinese media reports indicate that Beijing served notice that it would demand cash payments for such trade beginning in 1993.[10] However, Chinese premier Li Peng and North Korean vice premier Hong Song Nam are reported to have agreed in May 1996 that over the course of the successive five years, China would provide 500,000 tons of grain (half for free and half at a "friendship price"), 1.3 million tons of petroleum, and 2.5 million tons of coal annually.[11] Despite Beijing's long-standing desires to move to market-based bilateral trade with Pyongyang, the negotiation of successive government-to-government aid agreements illustrates the difficulty of breaking away from the old model of central government planning. Based on this precedent, it is likely that North Korea and China negotiated similar agreements in 2001. Likewise, the two leaders are reported to have negotiated a five-year economic aid and development plan in 2006 worth approximately US$2 billion that incorporates a more market-oriented approach than previous agreements, but that may simply reflect China's desire to continue to honor its long-standing energy and food commitments to North Korea.[12]

The overall trend of Sino–North Korean trade appears to serve as a barometer for the relative health of political relations between the two countries. The economic relationship declined steadily from 1993 to 1996 following China's decision to normalize with South Korea, possibly reflecting strained relations with North Korea. In his analysis of North Korean food trade, Nicholas Eberstadt went so far as to suggest that China's grain shipments to North Korea, which averaged 800,000 tons per year in 1992 and 1993, dropped to under 280,000 tons in 1994 as China began to require that trade with North Korea be conducted on market-based terms rather than on the basis of "friendship" prices.[13] Thus the decline in bilateral trade could have reflected Chinese efforts to establish a more market-oriented relationship with North Korea following diplomatic normalization with South Korea.

Despite the overall downward trend in the Sino–North Korean bilateral trade relationship, one notable exception can be observed. During the height of the North Korean famine, Chinese exports of grain to North Korea increased from US$29 million in 1995 to US$129 million in 1996 and US$195 million in 1997 (see Table 5.3). As humanitarian support from UN agencies and South Korea came online, China's export of grain declined gradually, to US$54 million in 1999 and US$41 million in 2000.

Another interesting feature of China's recorded exports to North Korea is the level of petroleum as a component of the overall trade relationship. Petroleum, representing the largest single component of the Sino–North Korean bilateral trade relationship, grew to over a quarter of

Table 5.3   China's Petroleum and Grain Exports to North Korea, 1990–2005 (US$)

	Petroleum	Grain	Total Exports
1990	66,969		358,143,602
1991	145,683		524,771,479
1992	152,382	81,708	541,065,162
1993	158,962	103,633	602,297,933
1994	106,459	31,294	424,459,357
1995	154,837	28,595	485,997,873
1996	135,413	129,399	496,980,844
1997	92,045	194,753	534,646,444
1998	74,610	76,894	355,676,480
1999	56,757	53,843	328,668,694
2000	108,659	41,427	450,774,930
2001	138,530	73,882	573,064,114
2002	98,649	40,208	467,506,921
2003	158,780	58,808	627,699,154
2004	190,334	32,693	799,450,316
2005	273,157	78,768	1,081,103,675

Source: United Nations ComTrade Database, DESA/UNSD.

all Chinese exports to North Korea by 1995 (see Table 5.3). With the start of heavy oil shipments from the Korean Peninsula Energy Development Organization as part of the agreed framework, North Korea's dependence on China for petroleum supplies declined steadily thereafter until 1999, but increased dramatically beginning in 2003, following the end of the heavy oil shipments.

Despite China's desire to put the relationship onto a more market-oriented basis, it continued to aid and trade with North Korea in an effort to forestall the latter's collapse and to keep refugees from flowing into China at the height of the famine. China's trade with North Korea increased in 1996 and 1997 given North Korea's overwhelming need to sell anything it could in order to purchase food from China. Both exports and imports to North Korea rose due to North Korea's continuing need for food, after having dropped steadily during the four years prior to 1996.

A second change occurred beginning in 2000, when Chinese exports to North Korea increased by approximately 30 percent. In 2001, North Korea's exports to China increased by 400 percent, to US$166 million, while Chinese exports continued to expand at double-digit rates, to US$573 million. This increase corresponded with the initial stage of China's efforts to repair its relationship with North Korea, including

Kim Jong Il's visits to Beijing in June 2000 and January 2001, and Jiang Zemin's visit to Pyongyang in September 2001. A further dramatic increase in the Sino–North Korean trade relationship occurred in 2003, coinciding with the start of recorded Chinese investment in North Korea and Chinese diplomatic efforts to support the six-party process during the second North Korean nuclear crisis. Sino–North Korean trade jumped by almost 40 percent during 2003 compared to 2002, and continued to grow at double-digit rates through 2005, coinciding with China's increased diplomatic mediation efforts. Based on the available data, there seems to be a close correlation between the size and growth of the bilateral trade relationship and the health of the political relationship between China and North Korea.

In addition, China's rapid economic development, its central role as a destination for global investment (to finance its expansion), and its search for energy and natural resources (to fuel its expansion) have provided it with previously nonexistent economic tools that might become a factor in Sino–North Korean relations. China is rapidly increasing its share of global trade, and is also becoming an important overseas investor in states deemed critical to its energy security interests. These factors have contributed to China's steadily expanding foreign exchange surplus and reserve holdings of US dollars. Chinese overseas investment had been discouraged until the Chinese Communist Party's sixteenth congress, in 2002, when the leadership began to encourage enterprises to "step out." However, the Chinese government carefully regulates such investments, increasing the likelihood that they can be used to support China's overall policy interests. Thus far, state owned enterprises have been the dominant actors in overseas direct investment, further underscoring that China's overseas investments, while primarily designed to support its economic objectives, may also be used in support of its political objectives.[14]

China's investment in neighboring states that lag in development may also be regarded as a new tool for maintaining regional stability along its periphery, as relatively low levels of trade and investment in comparison with China's overall economy may be sufficient to stabilize failed economies such as North Korea. China's foreign investment in developing countries along its periphery jumped dramatically between 2003 and 2004. Chinese investment in Myanmar, Cambodia, and Bangladesh nearly doubled during that time, and Chinese investment in Nepal started in 2004.[15] Chinese investment in North Korea was reported to be relatively constant during that time, at US$2.4 million and US$2.7 million in 2003 and 2004, respectively, but increased dramatically to US$15.0 million in 2005. The Chinese embassy in Pyongyang reported that approved Chinese investment in North Korea doubled from US$67 million for nineteen projects during the first ten months of 2005, to US$135 million for forty-nine projects through October 2006. Over thirty-eight companies were reported to have invested in mining, vehicle manufacturing, and food processing, representing approximately 70 percent of all investments in North Korea.[16]

Strained Sino–North Korean Relations and the First North Korean Nuclear Crisis, 1993–1996

Although China's diplomatic normalization with South Korea marked a major turning point in its economic (and by extension, political) interests on the Korean peninsula, the Chinese government took great pains in the years following Sino–South Korean normalization to present a picture of formal equidistance between the two Koreas, characterized by Chinese scholars as pursuit of "special relations" with North Korea and pursuit of "normal state relations" with South Korea.[17] Reporting of diplomatic developments between China and the two Koreas in the Chinese media was scrupulously even-handed during this period: if there was a high-level visit between Beijing and Seoul, great efforts were expended to portray an equivalent exchange or development in relations with Pyongyang. These gestures masked an increasingly strained Sino–North Korean relationship, even as China was being asked to play an active role as diplomatic liaison for messages from Seoul and Washington related to North Korea's nuclear program.

Nonetheless, Beijing still derived benefit from being a diplomatic conduit to North Korea, even if Beijing couldn't deliver North Korea's cooperation in managing the nuclear issue. During the first North Korean nuclear crisis, US diplomats requested Chinese counterparts to use their influence with North Korea, despite their passive role in managing the crisis.[18] Analysts argued at the time that China's own proliferation record and denial of responsibility for North Korea's actions contributed to this passivity, but the main reason for China's inaction appears to have been an acute awareness of the limits of Beijing's influence with Pyongyang.[19] Nonetheless, such an approach paid off for Beijing: China was lauded for its influence and cooperation behind the scenes as the United States and North Korea negotiated the agreed framework. In the words of an anonymous US government official, "The consensus [within the Bill Clinton administration] is that China is the key to solving the North Korea crisis."[20]

During US–North Korean negotiations over the nuclear issue, North

Korea actively sought to expand bilateral dialogue to include direct negotiations on a peace regime with the United States. North Korea sought to use crisis escalation tactics to draw the United States into a further dialogue on military issues as a means to marginalize both South Korea and also China. In particular, North Korea sought to dismantle infrastructure associated with the Military Armistice Commission, first by announcing its own withdrawal, then by pressing China to withdraw. A September 2, 1994, communiqué negotiated between Vice Foreign Minister Tang Jiaxuan and his counterpart Song Ho Gyong during a period of ongoing US–North Korean negotiations in Geneva announced that China would withdraw, "taking into consideration the request by the DPRK."[21] Subsequent North Korean actions included eviction of the Polish delegation from the Neutral Nations Supervisory Commission and a proposal that the US military establish a bilateral "military liaison office" in Panmunjom to replace the armistice commission, the latter in response to North Korea's detainment of airman Bobby Hall, who had accidentally crossed by helicopter over the demilitarized zone, for several weeks in December 1994.

Although China went along with withdrawal from the armistice commission as a symbolic measure, given that the commission had already been rendered ineffective, it was alarmed by such maneuvers on the part of North Korea. But the Geneva Agreed Framework, in which the United States pledged to support the provision of light-water reactors to North Korea in return for the latter's dismantlement of graphite nuclear reactors, appeared to offer a solution to the nuclear crisis. Still, Chinese policymakers insisted on staying outside multilateral interactions with North Korea undertaken through the Korean Peninsula Energy Development Organization, which had been established to provide North Korea with light-water reactors under the agreed framework.

The death of Kim Il Sung, North Korea's founder and chairman, who had first-generation ties to China's political leadership, further strained Sino–North Korean ties during the lengthy period of Kim Jong Il's accession. Chinese scholar You Ji suggested, based on interviews with Chinese diplomats, that because of Mao Zedong's and later Deng Xiaoping's reluctance to accept Kim Il Sung's plan to name Kim Jong Il as his successor, Kim Jong Il's attitudes toward the Chinese have been described as unfriendly at best.[22]

China's Policy Shift from Formal
Equidistance to Stability, 1996–1998

Throughout the first nuclear crisis, North Korea had consistently rejected South Korea's efforts to involve itself in the official dialogue. When

South Korean president Kim Yong Sam proposed a "two plus two" forum in August 1995 that would include both Koreas in the dialogue, together with the United States and China, North Korea rejected the offer. A revamped April 1996 joint proposal for four-party talks, put forth by Presidents Bill Clinton and Kim Young Sam, was more difficult for North Korea to turn down, especially in light of its desperate need for international assistance at the height of its emerging famine.

In the summer of 1996, at an initial "briefing" in Beijing to explain the revamped proposal, North Korea seemed particularly uncomfortable with the idea of China's inclusion in the four-party process, a rare public revelation of the high levels of strain in Sino–North Korean relations. But North Korea finally accepted the proposal and the first round of four-party talks was held in December 1996 in Beijing. China's inclusion in the four-party talks provided it an opportunity to participate, but it became clear during the talks that China neither unconditionally supported the North Korean position nor fully supported the South Korean position. Chinese diplomats were clearly focused on stability, as defined by Chinese interests on the peninsula, rather than equidistance or South Korea's growing economic influence.

Following torrential flooding in the summer of 1996, North Korea made an unprecedented decision to allow international workers to respond to its growing famine. The food shortages had actually begun in the early 1990s with the end of Soviet assistance, which resulted in a curtailing of rations through North Korea's public distribution system. According to refugee reports, this system came to a virtual standstill in the northeastern provinces in the early 1990s. Other evidence included an official "two meals a day" campaign by the government to cover up the severe food shortage. At the same time that North Korea had begun to negotiate rice assistance from Japan and South Korea to meet the structural shortfall, large parts of North Korea were hit by massive flooding from a typhoon in July 1996, providing pretext for a broader appeal for assistance from the international community. The resulting shortfalls precipitated hoarding and a more intensive state effort to extract grain from North Korean farmers, adding to the severity of the food crisis and precipitating flows of North Korean refugees, who were desperate for food, into China.

The refugee flows constituted a serious burden for the local population in northeastern China and fixed the attention of Chinese policymakers on the political risks associated with a possible decline in economic and political stability in North Korea. The local ethnic Korean population on the Chinese side of the border had sought refuge in North Korea when China faced famine at the time of the Great Leap Forward in the late 1950s, and were willing to help their North Korean relatives during this time of need. But the severity of conditions inside North Korea—at a time when the North Korean leadership situation had not yet been fully normalized following the death of Kim Il Sung—fixed the attention of Chinese analysts on prospects for stability in North Korea.

The Chinese government officially forbade scholars to comment on the North Korean issue, underscoring the sensitivity of the situation. However, there was an active internal debate over prospects for North Korea's survival among Chinese scholars and policymakers, with some specialists arguing that North Korea's collapse was not a matter of if, but when.[23] At the same time, the Chinese government at the local and national levels provided as much food as possible to North Korea in order to stabilize the situation. This effort is clearly reflected in UN trade statistics, and China may have provided as much as 1 million tons of food assistance in 1997. Chinese assistance was unmonitored and probably was used to feed the North Korean military. This Chinese assistance constituted the earliest international response to the North Korean food crisis and went a long way toward stabilizing the immediate situation during 1996–1997. During this period, international humanitarian assistance operations were responding to a humanitarian crisis while simultaneously contending with political controls imposed by North Korean authorities.[24] The food crisis further underscored for China the dangers of instability that might derive from North Korea's collapse, and raised concerns in Chinese circles about early reunification. At the same time, officials at South Korea's Ministry of Unification who were closely following the North Korean famine under the Kim Young Sam administration privately despaired that Chinese food assistance in large amounts most probably served to defer an early opportunity to achieve Korean unification through South Korea's absorption of North Korea.

The dilemma of managing a potential failed state in North Korea while recognizing that the future of the Korean peninsula would likely depend more on Seoul than Pyongyang were most dramatically illustrated by China's response to the defection of high-ranking North Korean official Hwang Jang Yop and his colleague Kim Dok Hong at the South Korean embassy in Beijing on February 12, 1997.[25] The incredibly contentious and politically charged incident required delicate negotiations involving China and both South and North Korea. The crisis also coincided with the death of Deng Xiaoping and the eighth National People's Congress, further extending the negotiations. During the five-week standoff, North Korean embassy officials stood guard outside a security cordon surrounding the South Korean embassy to ensure that South Koreans did not try to take Hwang out of the country, and even attempted to break through the cordon and take Hwang back into North Korean custody.[26] If Hwang were allowed to defect, North Korea would publicly lose face and the rift with China would be further exposed and widened. But South Korea had the backing of international law and international opinion, despite China's assertion that it did not recognize the right of diplomatic asylum.[27] Eventually, North Korea was forced to give up its efforts to secure the return of Hwang and his aide; Hwang was released via the Philippines, where he stayed for a few days at an undisclosed location before traveling to Seoul.

The Hwang Jang Yop incident underscored Beijing's focus on stability over equidistance, and set a precedent in its handling of refugee cases: in high-profile refugee appeals—those that came to the attention of the international community or involved contact with foreign officials— China would accommodate South Korea's requests, despite its long-standing relationship with North Korea. This precedent became the basic guideline for China's handling of other asylum cases involving North Korean defectors who were able to enter diplomatic compounds, despite the fact that China and North Korea had a bilateral repatriation agreement as part of their friendship treaty. Although this arrangement came into direct contradiction with China's international obligations under covenants regarding the handling of refugees, China continuously honored its bilateral commitment in North Korean refugee cases that involved no public contact with foreigners or South Koreans.

Recovery of Sino–North Korean Relations, 1999–2002

In April 1999, following an extended suspension of high-level interaction between Pyongyang and Beijing, Chinese foreign minister Tang Jiaxuan visited North Korea. In March 2000, North Korea reciprocated, sending Kim Yong Nam, president of the Supreme People's Assembly, together with a fifty-person delegation, to China. During the April 1999 exchange, Tang Jiaxuan and Zhu Rongji reached "common ground" and acknowledged that "friendly relations between China and the DPRK have experienced new growth in recent years." They also acknowledged that senior-level exchanges between the two countries were being discussed.[28] During that visit, Tang promised that China would provide North Korea with 150,000 tons of grain and 400,000 tons of coal.[29] Tang made a second visit to Pyongyang the following October to mark the fiftieth anniversary of the establishment of Sino–North Korean relations.

These high-level visits played a critical role in overcoming tensions that had beset the relationship, and set the stage for reopening more active leadership exchange between the two countries.

China also played a role as informal meeting point for North and South Korean officials preparing for the inter-Korean summit between Kim Dae Jung and Kim Jong Il in June 2000. South Korean minister of culture Park Chi Won secretly visited Shanghai and Beijing in March and April that year to meet with his counterpart Song Ho Gyong, of North Korea's Asia Pacific Peace Committee, to make arrangements for the summit. In a subsequently more controversial role, the Hyundai Corporation secretly transferred up to US$500 million dollars to the Macao-based company Delto Banco Asia, on the day before the summit; Kim Dae Jung's original departure date was postponed because North Korea required confirmation of the cash before proceeding to welcome him in Pyongyang. In a meeting with the South Korean foreign minister shortly after the announcement of the inter-Korean summit, Chinese foreign minister Tang Jiaxuan issued a statement welcoming the summit and pledging to support both sides in their efforts to achieve conciliation, independence, peace, and unification of the peninsula.[30] The implication seemed to be that direct inter-Korean dialogue at the highest levels would serve to diminish the role of the United States on the Korean peninsula.

On May 29–31, 2000, less than two weeks prior to the inter-Korean summit, Kim Jong Il made his first visit to China as chairman of the Central Defense Commission, putting an end to rumors that he might visit Beijing, which had been circulating since Kim Yong Nam reopened high-level contact with Chinese counterparts in 1999. The discussions were described as "intimate and friendly," with both sides committing to "make joint efforts to carry on the tradition" of Sino–North Korean leadership exchanges. China also committed to providing "free assistance of grain and goods . . . to help the DPRK overcome difficulty."[31] The reconsolidation of Sino–North Korean economic ties was also reflected in the recovery of bilateral trade during this period.

During Kim Jong Il's Beijing visit as well as during his subsequent visit to Shanghai in January 2001, there was considerable speculation, based on his positive references to China's economic development, that the visits were intended to jump-start North Korean economic reforms. As had been the case in Chinese interactions with his father, the Chinese leadership promoted their own reform experience as a model for economic development without ceding political control, but it seemed that North Korean counterparts were slow to get the message. The North Korean leadership showed a burst of enthusiasm for importing reform experiences in 2001, and a formal attempt to institute more market-oriented pricing and wage structures was implemented on July 1, 2002, but neither of these efforts represented the unmitigated embrace of a new direction that Deng Xiaoping was able to initiate at the start of China's reform process in the late 1970s and early 1980s. Specialists continue to debate whether Kim Jong Il is constrained from reform efforts by his symbolic responsibility to uphold his father's legacy, or whether he is nimble enough to redefine that legacy on his own terms to make space for a new direction in North Korean economic policy.

Subsequently, in October 2000, Chinese defense minister Chi Haotian visited Pyongyang to mark the anniversary of Sino–North Korean defense ties, but the visit was overshadowed by the near simultaneous visit of US secretary of state Madeleine Albright to Pyongyang. The international media interpreted the visits as a "diplomatic competition," suggesting that Chinese cadres were unhappy with the relative warmth of the reception given to Secretary Albright compared to reception of their own defense minister to commemorate a critical event in Sino–North Korean relations.[32]

Chinese president Jiang Zemin made a return visit to North Korea on September 2–4, 2001, the first visit by a Chinese president since Yang Shangkun's in 1992, just prior to Beijing's decision to normalize political relations with South Korea. Jiang attempted to restore high-level exchanges and economic cooperation and to promote consultation on regional issues, while Kim Jong Il praised China's economic development under Jiang's leadership.[33] Interestingly, although the visit received less coverage in the international press, given the global focus on the terrorist attack of September 11 and the US response, Jiang was in fact greeted with even more pomp and circumstance than had been afforded to Kim Dae Jung during the historic inter-Korean summit of June 2000. One Korean analyst interpreted the visit as an attempt to restore China's strategic influence on the peninsula following the near breakthrough in US–North Korean relations at the end of the Clinton administration.[34]

As China and North Korea resumed high-level visits, this improvement in political relations was reflected by a further increase in economic relations. In conjunction with Jiang's visit, China was reported to have provided an unspecified package of food and other economic assistance. The linkage between economic assistance and improved political relations was also clear in the dispatch of a Chinese trade delegation to Pyongyang in June 2000, less than one month following Kim Jong Il's visit to Beijing.

On a longer-term basis, the recovery of the bilateral trade relation-ship—and North Korea's increased economic dependency on China—track closely with the gradual improvement in the Sino–North Korean political relationship since 1999. Although this improvement is partially a reflection of North Korea's economic stabilization (commensurate with the end of its so-called arduous march) and political stabilization that resulted from the public emergence of Kim Jong Il as chairman of the National Defense Commission in 1998, the expansion of the Sino–North Korean trade relationship is also a barometer of a gradually recovering political relationship. The political relationship appears to undergo improvement in direct proportion to the level of China's will-ingness to subsidize North Korea's economic recovery, and is clearly "led" by the frequency of high-level political interactions between Beijing and Pyongyang. Although the long-sought objective of putting the Sino–North Korean economic relationship onto a market-basis remains as distant as ever, economic changes in North Korea appear to have stimulated a gradually increasing cross-border barter trade at the local level, in addition to the increased central government assistance China has provided to North Korea.

From "Patron" to "Lifeline": China's Attempts
to Bolster Its Economic Leverage, 2003–2006

China's own economic development gave it the ability to harness new economic instruments to gain political leverage in its relationship with North Korea. The need to have high-level political contacts was directly catalyzed by the outbreak of the second North Korean nuclear crisis, China's realization of the limits of its influence on the one hand and the risks that would accompany a military confrontation between the United States and North Korea on the other, and the perception derived from the Iraq War of an increased likelihood that the George W. Bush admin-istration would use military instruments against North Korea under the doctrine of preemption. Although there was a momentary lull following Jiang Zemin's visit to Pyongyang in September 2001, China has assidu-ously cultivated direct contacts with Kim Jong Il since early 2003, with high-level visits to North Korea happening on an almost quarterly basis. The culmination of this effort was the exchange of visits between Kim Jong Il and Hu Jintao in October 2005 and January 2006. This exchange was accompanied by a commensurate intensification in Sino–North Korean trade relations and economic assistance, and coincided with a significant increase in Chinese investment in North Korea.[35]

As part of its efforts to address the second North Korean nuclear crisis, China became the host and mediator for the six-party talks, which provided Beijing an additional excuse to maintain regular high-level contacts with North Korea, but also required additional use of economic instruments to secure Pyongyang's cooperation and participation in the talks. In some respects, North Korea appeared to approach the six-party dialogue with an attitude similar to that which developed as part of the four-party process during the late 1990s. As long as North Korea was receiving external economic subsidies, it would participate in the talks, but North Korea's participation rarely resulted in concrete progress toward the objective of denuclearization. China is reported to have pledged economic aid and energy assistance worth as much as US$50 million to secure North Korean participation in the second round of six-party talks in February 2004.[36]

China also increased investment in infrastructure projects along the Sino–North Korean border beginning in 2005. Hunchun municipal authorities are reported to have agreed with counterparts in the Rajin-Sonbong special economic zone to upgrade the road between the two cities and to give Hunchun access to docks in the port city of Rajin in 2005, but as of mid-2008 road construction had not yet begun. The bridge from Helong, in China, to Musan, where North Korea's iron mines are located, was reported to have been upgraded to support Chinese investment estimated at about US$500 million. One Chinese researcher said that "the reason why China has chosen the area along its national border with North Korea for investment is that the area is within a visible distance, providing peace of mind. If the projects were successful, China's investments would spread further into the interior region of North Korea, which would be incorporated into China's economic sphere."[37]

According to one Jilin province–based Chinese scholar, "There are two forms of investment. In the agricultural sector, the deals are 100% Chinese investment. In road construction, the DPRK provides the labor and the Chinese company provides the technology and the capital equipment. More and more Chinese enterprises want to invest in the DPRK. I talked to a friend who has already been involved in business in the DPRK. In the coming years, investment will be mainly from China and the ROK. I think this situation will last a long time. . . . [Previously,] the central government decided who could trade and who could not. There were restrictions on border trade and on economic cooperation with the DPRK provinces. The supply of goods from the DPRK was very small, so if the local border trade got too big, then the central government would get nothing back. The situation is different nowadays. Chinese businessmen learned lessons and know that they first have to find contacts at high levels in the DPRK. It is useless to deal with the local authorities."[38]

Coinciding with the culmination of efforts to restore Sino–North Korean high-level political ties, news agency Kyodo reported that during Hu Jintao's visit to Pyongyang in October 2005, Beijing committed to provide as much as US$2 billion in economic assistance pledges to Pyongyang over five years.[39] This comprehensive assistance package was actually part of China's ongoing support to North Korea. It was intended to provide North Korea with assurances of economic stabilization and to bind Kim Jong Il closer to Beijing. China's financing and construction of the Tae'an glass factory in Pyongyang was the highest-profile evidence of its efforts to use politically directed investment as a form of assistance—and as an instrument through which to enhance political leverage and influence on leaders in Pyongyang. This type of investment may be useful as a means of providing assistance to North Korea, and has been used to promote its economic and political stabilization. During discussions between Hu Jintao and Kim Jong Il in Pyongyang, the two men are reported to have discussed putting their economic interactions onto a market economy basis through promotion of expanded relations among private enterprises, but still with strong direction and involvement of the state. The latest bilateral five-year economic cooperation agreement is reported to reflect market principles, rather than solely providing central government–directed subsidies to North Korea in critical sectors. The agreement is "comprehensive," but responds to North Korean needs especially in the energy and transportation sectors.[40]

Chinese scholars report that China has adopted a three-point policy for economic cooperation with North Korea based on an underlying principle of "mutual benefit." These guidelines were discussed during Hu's visit to Pyongyang in October 2005, and again when Kim visited China in January 2006. First is strengthened government-to-government exchanges and cooperation. Second is expanded reliance on market mechanisms. And third is a leading role for enterprises in economic cooperation between the two countries.[41]

In the run-up to Hu Jintao's official visit to Pyongyang, Vice Premier Wu Yi visited Pyongyang, at which time she is reported to have negotiated extensive new economic agreements with Kim Jong Il that would give Chinese firms preferential access and rights to work in North Korea. Among those agreements, China has committed to continue providing materials and economic cooperation in support of the Chinese-built Tae'an glass factory, which opened in October 2005.[42] In addition to infrastructure investments in the Musan iron mine, China is reported to have invested in the Hyesan copper mine, the Manp'o zinc mine, and the Hoeryo'ng gold mine. Chinese businesses have also been active in North Korea's coal sector, including China Minmetals Corporation, which has proposed a joint project with North Pyongan province's Yongtung coal mine to produce 1 million tons of anthracite annually. A number of Chinese real estate investments in North Korea have also been reported, including department stores in Pyongyang, a variety of hotels, a bicycle factory, and a power plant.[43]

Chinese analysts also cite changes in North Korea's economy that have opened up new opportunities for market-based interactions. These changes have made possible expanded Chinese trade and investment in North Korea on a purely private-sector basis, outside government control. However, there is no empirical information available to determine the proportion of Chinese government backing on an informal level in support of such efforts on the part of Chinese private firms. Chinese companies that have engaged in trade with North Korea have long faced substantial risks of nonpayment, but circumstances inside North Korea appear to have improved sufficiently since about 2005 to increase confidence. The risks to individual firms might also be mitigated if government financing becomes available to cover any debts they may incur.[44]

Chinese Views of North Korea's Economic Future

Given the potential ramifications of North Korean economic instability for China's economy, Chinese analysts are closely watching the progress of North Korean economic reforms, the impact of external inputs, prospects for North Korean internal economic stability, and the potential economic and political impact on the provinces in China that border North Korea and on China's capacity to promote economic and political stability in North Korea. Interconnected with this analysis is the question of whether and how China can effectively utilize economic tools to achieve its objectives of ensuring economic and political stability on its periphery by stabilizing North Korea.

China's economic engagement with North Korea might be utilized in various ways to achieve various political objectives. The first objective of China's economic interactions with North Korea is to ensure that North Korea remains economically and politically stable. Put simply,

"The foundation of Chinese policy is to secure stability of North Korea. PRC does not want to see any destabilizing factors that will negatively influence the DPRK government."[45] A stable Sino–North Korean trade and aid relationship is the primary instrument available for achieving that objective.

China has strategic reasons for continuing to grant North Korea special treatment. "The fact is that a collapsing country in chaos and turmoil won't serve Chinese interests. So from that perspective, we won't reduce our assistance to the DPRK. Aid and trade are different from the view of the Chinese government. Different departments are in charge. The aid is not decided by MOFCOM [China's Ministry of Commerce]. It is part of our foreign policy. It is strategic aid. It is provided under the strategic consideration of our external environment. . . . From a geopolitical perspective, China is very close to the DPRK so it is natural that we will take this into consideration."[46]

Although there is frustration among some Chinese analysts about the imbalanced nature of China's economic relations, there is also broad understanding that promoting economic stability in North Korea is a means by which to stabilize China's periphery. Chinese analysts are particularly sensitive about the domestic political impact of North Korean instability on China's northeast, because that region has historically been a source of uprisings that have led to political instability. "The close economic ties are helpful to the DPRK in overcoming its difficulties. Stability in the DPRK is conducive to peace and stability in Northeast Asia. For China, stability in this region is an important external precondition for China's harmonious society."[47] According to a military analyst, "We think that increased bilateral trade will enhance the stability of the DPRK government. Increased trade will provide an improvement in living standards, strengthen stability, and ease the pressures we face in the border areas."[48]

But there is also a critical recognition among many Chinese analysts that North Korea's economy currently cannot stand on its own and that this means that China must continue to provide substantial inputs to ensure stability and avoid political turmoil on its periphery. According to one specialist, "Problems haven't been fundamentally resolved. . . . The people no longer have faith . . . people who used to be unquestioning now feel puzzled. . . . [If] this is improperly handled, then contradictions could result in increased social disorder."[49]

A second school of thought argues that the economic instrument is limited and that China's greatest role in promoting North Korean reforms is as an example of the benefits that come from following the reform path. According to this view, "China does not wish to interfere with the internal affairs of the DPRK and . . . they must decide in what ways they wish to make changes in their own economic system. China sees its role as sharing China's own experience with economic reform and opening up, but not as advising the DPRK on what it should do. . . . If the increased interaction helps the DPRK leaders to open up to the outside world, if it improves the lives of the people, if it changes the thinking of the leadership, then it will add to stability." According to another analyst, "We view Kim's visit to China as a reflection of his commitment to reform. He made the trip [in January 2006] due to the domestic situation, not because of China. China is not trying to be a teacher, but a showcase. The DPRK may seek to learn more from China, but China won't actively teach. It wasn't our suggestion to set up a tour modeled after Deng Xiaoping's southern tour. That was Kim's idea."[50]

A third, albeit minority, view is that the economic tool is most effectively used by pushing to conduct economic relations with North Korea solely on a market basis as a means by which to catalyze necessary reforms. "I don't think that China will increase its aid to the DPRK. We don't want to increase DPRK's dependence on economic aid from China. If Chinese companies are willing to develop ties with the DPRK, then the Chinese government won't oppose it even though there is a risk of widening the trade deficit. . . . The Chinese economy continues to grow, so the burden is not as great as it was in the past."[51]

Chinese analysts broadly encourage North Korean economic reforms, but have differing views regarding how far along the economic reform path North Korea is willing to go, and also regarding the pace of the reform process. Most see North Korea's willingness to pursue reforms as contingent on its external security environment, a consideration that is directly related to the North Korean leadership's overarching concern with maintaining political stability. While accepting that North Korea seeks to forge its own path based on its unique conditions, China's reform process is the benchmark by which Chinese analysts judge North Korean reforms. Despite North Korean protestations, Chinese analysts expect that, eventually, North Koreans will have no choice but to borrow from China's reform experience. "In the DPRK, there is no reform mentality yet. Kim Jong Il's regime lacks the political and economic basis for reform. There is a lack of ideological theory— that is the political context. And there is a lack of capital—that is the economic context. . . . We hope reforms that promote stability will be implemented. We should not treat the DPRK reforms as the same as Chinese reforms. They have a totally different situation. China is a much bigger country. . . . The DPRK is facing a very different international environment than China faced thirty years ago."[52]

Reforms continue to be driven primarily by bottom-up changes as a result of necessity at the grassroots level, rather than being led by central government policy. Changes in the relationship between state and society, between government and enterprises, and between central and local government are occurring, but those changes appear to be resulting in confusion. The key problem is the relationship between regime stability and economic opening.[53] North Korean leaders see stability as the key precondition for economic reform.

North Korea's Attempts to Leverage Its Economic Dependency

The political estrangement between China and North Korea that followed China's decision to normalize diplomatic relations with South Korea clearly correlates with a decline in the volume of Sino–North Korean trade and a lessened North Korean dependence on economic relations with China during the 1990s. The decline in the officially recorded Sino–North Korean trade relationship and in China's share of North Korea's overall trade during that decade is all the more remarkable in light of the fact that, with the loss of the Soviet Union as one of North Korea's major patrons, China became its only remaining great power supporter. But despite North Korea's increased need, officially recorded levels of support and North Korea's level of economic dependency on China (even despite internal economic difficulties) declined in the 1990s as North Korea diversified its external economic relations with Japan. Although South Korea and the United States continued to ask China to weigh in with North Korea during the nuclear crisis of the 1990s, the relative passivity of China's role suggests awareness among Chinese policymakers of the limits of their own political influence with Pyongyang. Nonetheless, Chinese policymakers were clever enough to reap a public relations reward by accepting credit from South Korean and US counterparts for "behind the scenes" diplomacy. In the end, it is more likely that North Korea made its own decision to deal with the United States based on perceptions of its own national interest.

As the Sino–North Korean political relationship showed signs of recovery beginning in 1999, the bilateral trade relationship also recovered, and North Korea's economic dependency on China increased to over 40 percent of North Korea's overall trade by 2004. Chinese policymakers appear to have concluded that increased aid, trade, and investment will work to their advantage by enhancing China's economic leverage over North Korea. The upturn in high-level political interactions was accompanied by substantial improvements in Sino–North Korean trade and investment relations.

Figure 5.1 shows a rough correlation between the Chinese exports to North Korea and the frequency of high-level meetings between North Korean and Chinese leaders (on the latter, see Appendix A). While the economic and political relationship languished through much of the 1990s, there is a clear correlation between the expansion of the Sino–North Korean economic relationship and the frequency of high-level political ties between the two countries from 1999 onward (although there is an unexplained gap in high-level exchanges following Jiang Zemin's visit to Pyongyang in September 2001). The growth in Sino–North Korean bilateral economic exchange correlates closely with the revival of senior-level official ties between the two countries.

Yoichi Funabashi observes that "China is being transformed from a patron of North Korea to its lifeline, which should make it easy for China to exert pressure on North Korea."[54] While China's increasing economic support for North Korea may have promoted North Korea's economic stability, it does not appear to have gained China much politi-

Figure 5.1   China–North Korea High-Level Visits and Exports, 1992–2005

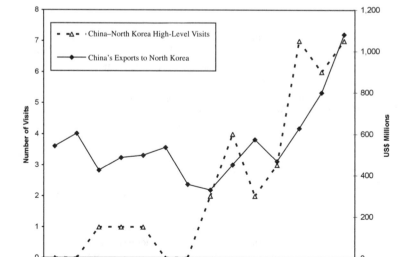

cal leverage to control or influence the North Korean leadership's policy choices. Perhaps Chinese policymakers thought that North Korea's economic dependency on China would impose implicit constraints on the capacity of North Korean leaders to take actions contrary to Chinese interests.

However, North Korean economic dependency on China and greater levels of Chinese trade with and assistance to North Korea do not appear to have enhanced China's political leverage. Instead, North Korean policymakers assume that China's increasing aid, trade, and investment derive from its own economic and political self-interest. This perception has mitigated the ability of China to use economic instruments as leverage against North Korea. In fact, the greater North Korea's economic dependency on China, the greater China's fears that withdrawal of assistance may have negative consequences for North Korea's economic and political stability, which by extension may have negative ramifications for China itself. Thus, China's increased use of aid, trade, and investment as vehicles for enhancing political influence on North Korea has thus far worked in precisely the opposite manner, making China a hostage to and enabler of North Korean provocations. This situation is likely to remain unchanged as long as the frame of reference for China's policymakers is one in which North Korea is regarded as a strategic asset rather than as a strategic liability.

Notes

1. For an economic analysis of China's response to North Korea's food and energy needs, see also Stephan Haggard and Marcus Noland, *Famine in North Korea: Markets, Aid, and Reform* (New York: Columbia University Press, 2007).

2. Institute of Far Eastern Studies, "DPRK Monthly Recap: January 2008," NK Brief no. 08-2-5-1, February 5, 2008, accessed at the North Korea economy watch website, http://www.nkeconwatch.com/2008/02/05/ifes-dprk-monthly-recap-january-2008, on June 13, 2008.

3. "China and North Korea: Comrades Forever?" International Crisis Group, Asia Report no. 112, February 1, 2006, accessed at http://www.crisis-group.org/home/index.cfm?id=3920&l=1 on January 31, 2006.

4. Author conversations with Chinese scholars, Beijing, June 2007.

5. Ibid.

6. All of these channels previously were tightly controlled, but with China's economic reforms, the central planning mechanism also became obsolete. The impact of China's decentralization on its economic relations with North Korea appears to be mixed. North Korea has benefited from increased

opportunities to work with potential donors at the provincial and local levels, but it has also been harder for North Korea to negotiate overall assistance packages with Chinese counterparts. Author conversations with Chinese researchers, April 2006 and June 2007.

7. Author conversation with Chinese researcher, June 2007.

8. United Nations ComTrade Database, DESA/UNSD, UN Commercial Trade Statistics, overall Sino–North Korean trade.

9. See Scott Snyder, *North Korea's Decline and China's Strategic Dilemmas: Report on a June 1997 Research Trip to Beijing, Shenyang, Yanji, and Changchun* (Washington, DC: US Institute of Peace, October 1997).

10. Samuel S. Kim, "The Dialectics of China's North Korea Policy," *Asian Perspective* 18, no. 2 (Fall–Winter 1994): 19.

11. Samuel S. Kim and Tai Hwan Lee, "Chinese–North Korean Relations," in *North Korea and Northeast Asia,* p. 127. See also Marcus Noland, *Avoiding the Apocalypse: The Future of the Two Koreas* (Washington, DC: Institute for International Economics, 2000), p. 100.

12. "N. Korea Agrees Economic Aid by China Based on Market Principles," *Japan Economic Newswire,* February 25, 2006.

13. Nicholas Eberstadt, "North Korea's Interlocked Economic Crises: Some Indications from 'Mirror Statistics,'" *Asian Survey* 38, no. 3 (March 1998): 218.

14. Yuan Pau Woo and Kenny Zhang, "China Goes Global: The Implications of Chinese Outward Direct Investment for Canada," accessed at http://www.asiapacific.ca/analysis/pubs/pdfs/surveys/china_goes_global.pdf on July 25, 2006.

15. "Actual Foreign Investment by Country or Region" at http://www.stats.gov.cn/tjsj/ndsj/2005/html/R18153.htm, accessed on August 14, 2006.

16. See the website of the Chinese embassy in Pyongyang, http://kp.china-embassy.org/eng/zcgx/jmwl/t306852.htm, accessed on August 18, 2007.

17. Kim and Lee, "Chinese–North Korean Relations."

18. Joel S. Wit, Daniel B. Poneman, and Robert L. Gallucci, *Going Critical: The First North Korean Nuclear Crisis* (Washington, DC: Brookings Institution, 2004), pp. 41–42, 154–164, 198.

19. Samuel S. Kim, "The Dialectics of China's North Korea Policy."

20. Ibid., p. 23, as cited in Douglas Jehl, "U.S. Agrees to Discuss Arms Directly with North Korea," *New York Times,* April 23, 1993, p. 10.

21. Larry Niksch, "North Korea's Campaign Against the Korean Armistice," Library of Congress Congressional Research Service Report no. 95-1187, December 11, 1995, accessed at http://www.globalsecurity.org/wmd/library/report/crs/95-1187f.htm on August 12, 2006.

22. You Ji, "China and North Korea: A Fragile Relationship of Strategic Convenience," *Journal of Contemporary China* 10, no. 28 (2001): 387–398.

23. Author interview with Chinese scholar in Washington, DC, December 2005.

24. Andrew Natsios, *The Great North Korean Famine: Famine, Politics, and Foreign Policy* (Washington, DC: US Institute of Peace, 2001); Hazel Smith, *Hungry for Peace: International Security, Humanitarian Assistance, and*

Social Change in North Korea (Washington, DC: US Institute of Peace, 2005); L. Gordon Flake and Scott Snyder, eds., *Paved With Good Intentions: The NGO Experience in North Korea* (Westport, CT: Praeger, 2003).

25. "Security Boosted Around ROK Mission Housing DPRK Defector," *Associated Foreign Press* (Hong Kong), February 14, 1997, accessed at http://www.opensource.gov, doc. no. FTS19970214000098.

26. "DPRK Agents Try to Enter ROK Compound 27 Feb," *Agence France Presse* (Hong Kong), March 5, 1997, accessed at http://www.opensource.gov, doc. no. FTS19970307000962.

27. "Li Peng: Time Almost Ripe for Resolving Hwang Incident," March 14, 1997, accessed at http://www.opensource.gov, doc. no. FTS19970314000273.

28. Qian Tong, "Zhu Rongji, DPRK Foreign Minister Hail Bilateral Relations," *Xinhua Hong Kong Service,* March 20, 2000.

29. Kim and Lee, "Chinese–North Korean Relations."

30. "China Offers Backing for Korean Reconciliation Summit," *Agence France Presse,* April 28, 2000.

31. "More on Kim Jong Il Visits," *Xinhua,* June 1, 2000, accessed at http://www.opensource.gov, doc. no. CPP20000601000132.

32. Patrick Baert, "China a Nervous Spectator of North Korean–US Thaw," *Agence France Presse,* October 26, 2000.

33. Korean Central News Agency, "North Korean Agency Reports on Chinese President's Visit," as reported by *BBC Monitoring Asia Pacific,* September 6, 2001; "Director of the CPC Central Committee's International Liaison Department Talks About Achievements of General Secretary Jiang Zemin's Visit to DPRK," *Xinhua Domestic Service,* in Chinese, accessed at http://www.opensource.gov, doc. no. CPP20010905000123.

34. Park Doo-bok, "Viewpoint: Jiang's Visit to North Opens New Doors," *JoongAng Ilbo,* September 7, 2001.

35. "Chinese President's Pyongyang Visit Successful, Fruitful: Senior CPC Official," *Xinhua,* October 30, 2005, accessed at http://www.opensource.gov, doc. no. CPP20005103005012.

36. Samuel S. Kim, "China's Conflict-Management Approach to the Nuclear Standoff on the Korean Peninsula," *Asian Perspective* 30, no. 1 (2006): 5–38, as cited in Edward Cody and Anthony Faiola, "N. Korea's Kim Reportedly in China for Talks," *Washington Post,* April 20, 2004; Ralph Cossa, "CVID, WMD, and Elections Galore," in Brad Glosserman and Sun Namkung, eds., *Comparative Connections* 6, no. 1 (April 2004): 1–18.

37. Yoji Gomi, "Cities in Northeast China Actively Investing in North Korea, Stepping Up Trade Route Building for Import of Iron Ore and Other Products," *Tokyo Shimbun,* in Japanese, October 5, 2005, p. 2, accessed at http://www.opensource.gov, doc. no. JPP20051011016004.

38. Author interview with Chinese scholar in Changchun, June 2007.

39. Ralph Jennings, "China's Hu Visits Landmark North Korean Factory, Talks Trade," *Kyodo News International,* October 29, 2005.

40. Author conversations and interviews with Chinese North Korea specialists in Beijing, November 2005 and April 2006.

41. Ibid., February 2006.

42. "N. Korea Agrees Economic Aid by China Based on Market Principles," *Japan Economic Newswire,* February 25, 2006.

43. Yukio Hanabusa, "Special Feature: North Korea Turns Into China's Colony; North Korea Becomes Fourth Northeastern Province—Kim Jong Il Surviving with China's Assistance," *Gendai Korea* (Tokyo), in Japanese, July 1, 2006–August 31, 2006, pp. 10–23, accessed at http://www.opensource.gov, doc. no. JPP20060727026002; author interviews with North Korea specialists in Beijing, April 2006.

44. Author conversations and interviews with Chinese researchers in Beijing, November 2005.

45. Ibid., February 2006.

46. Ibid., June 2007.

47. Ibid.

48. Ibid.

49. Ibid., April 2006.

50. Ibid.

51. Ibid.

52. Ibid., in Yanji, June 2007.

53. Ibid., in Beijing, April 2006.

54. Yoichi Funabashi, *The Peninsula Question: A Chronicle of the Second North Korean Nuclear Crisis* (Washington, DC: Brookings Institution, 2007), p. 324.

6
China's Strategic Policy Dilemmas and the Future of North Korea

China's core interest in maintaining a stable relationship with North Korea as a strategic security buffer did not change in light of its normalization with South Korea, but views regarding the importance of the relationship underwent a profound change during the 1990s as common ideology, generational ties, and shared sentiment derived from common experiences during the Korean War were stripped away from Chinese formulations in favor of a core focus on maintaining a peaceful strategic environment as an essential prerequisite for pursuing economic development. Perhaps the most significant implication of Sino–South Korean normalization was that it symbolized a gradual shift in China's perception of its strategic interests from a framework that had previously focused solely on North Korea as a strategic partner with a shared ideology, to one that viewed China's interests in the context of maintaining stability on the Korean peninsula as an instrument for safeguarding China's economic development.[1] As illustrated in the previous chapter, the objective of maintaining stability on the Korean peninsula as a prerequisite for continued economic development became China's core objective in dealing with the first North Korean nuclear crisis, North Korea's leadership transition, and China's response to the North Korean famine, and continues to be China's defining interest as it grapples with the challenge and dilemmas posed by the second North Korean nuclear crisis.

Chinese public writings and comments on Korea-related issues during the 1990s hewed closely to the official government line, with relatively few public signs of debate or difficulty in the Sino–North Korean relationship. Governmental prohibitions on public discussion of Korea and cross-strait issues during this period served to obscure public fissures in internal Chinese policy debates over North Korea, and contributed to confusion among outsiders over the extent and nature China's influence on North Korea through the 1990s. Close observers drew on private conversations with Chinese counterparts to provide general parameters and foundations of Chinese internal analysis of policy toward North Korea, but changes in Chinese policy analysis of the two Koreas were obscured by official desires not to unnecessarily strain already frayed ties with Pyongyang. Even on the basis of these conversations, there emerged persistent differences between China's Korea specialists and Chinese analysts who examined issues surrounding the Korean peninsula in a broader policy context. However, the widely shared consensus in Chinese thinking toward the Korean peninsula reflected China's "overriding interest in maintaining regional stability, especially near Chinese borders."[2]

The late 1990s marked a transition to a new stage in China's conceptualization of its foreign policy priorities. China's "new security concept" and "peaceful rise" were increasingly premised on the idea that continued economic development, external orientation, and integration with the outside world gave it greater responsibility to secure the regional stability necessary to perpetuate economic growth. Another purpose of the new strategy was to mitigate fears among China's neighbors regarding the implications of its rise. But some of the core assumptions underlying China's new thinking on security issues had the effect of marginalizing relations with North Korea and diluting any form of ideologically based special relationship with Pyongyang as a central component of China's foreign policy. The "new security concept" and "peaceful rise" brought into relief contradictions with long-standing core elements of China's foreign policy, such as the "five principles of peaceful coexistence" and revealed contradictions between the premises underlying China's grand strategy and its fundamental interests in North Korea.

Bates Gill describes changes in Chinese policies regarding the role of alliances and expanded support for confidence- and security-building mechanisms, higher priority on nonproliferation and arms control, and greater flexibility on issues related to sovereignty, intervention, and use of force,[3] but changes in each of these areas posed practical challenges for China's management of its relationship with North Korea, putting China's "new thinking" in each of these areas at odds with foreign policy traditionalists and Chinese "Korea hands" who continued to manage the day-to-day relationship with North Korea. These contradictions derived primarily from the gap between China and North Korea that opened as a result of China's economic development and North Korea's economic policy stagnation and failure to adapt to a post–Cold War world. China's overall objectives did not diminish its fundamental interest in promoting regional stability, including the desire to perpetuate stability in North Korea and to maintain the status quo on the Korean peninsula, but North Korea's accumulated failures made the task of promoting regional stability increasingly costly to China in both political and financial terms, raising new questions among Chinese analysts about how China should position itself vis-à-vis the two Koreas and what measures China should take to protect its core interest in stability. In conjunction with China's new formulation of its foreign policy interests, an increasingly transparent and fractious specialist debate has emerged through Chinese media outlets on how to deal with North Korea.

Coinciding with developments in China's vision of its regional aspirations and responsibilities, North Korea's continued economic decline and the contradictions between its internal political system and the external environment increasingly posed a challenge to China's fundamental objectives on the Korean peninsula. North Korea's systemic economic difficulties and renewed political and security tensions with the United States increasingly forced China to confront undesirable policy dilemmas in managing relations with Pyongyang. North Korea's economic decline—both during the famine of the mid-1990s and in the context of growing political tensions surrounding the second North Korean nuclear crisis beginning in 2003—forced Chinese policy analysts to consider the hard strategic choices that China would face in the context of the possible unraveling of the North Korean system.

This chapter examines China's emerging new formulations regarding its role in regional security and analyzes the accompanying challenges for China's diplomatic relations with North Korea, the implications of China's expanded regional capabilities and objectives for the Korean peninsula, the thinking of Chinese policymakers regarding new economic tools and how they might be used to influence North Korea's reforms, and the fundamental policy dilemmas North Korea poses in light of "new thinking" on regional security. The core dilemmas for Chinese policy analysts derive primarily from the gradual and continuous deterioration of North Korea's economic stability; North Korea's continued strategic isolation vis-à-vis the United States and the rest of the world; Pyongyang's tactical tendencies toward brinkmanship and unilateral, uncompromising approaches to international issues; and the uncertain prospects for North Korea's long-term political stability given the predominant role of Kim Jong Il under North Korea's unique "military-first politics" *(sungun ch'ongch'i)*. All of these developments constitute trends in North Korea that run contrary to China's objective of maintaining regional stability. The specter of North Korea's economic stagnation, strategic miscalculation, political isolation, and possibly even regime failure have progressively become sources of concern to Chinese analysts as significant obstacles to China's pursuit of its core interest in stability.

China's Rising Regional Role and the Korean Peninsula

China's focus on sustaining the conditions necessary to ensure its own economic development, perceived lessening of prospects for great power confrontation in the post–Cold War era, and the development of a broader concept of security have had widespread implications for how China pursues its national security objectives. Among the themes that Wu Baiyi describes as part of China's "new security concept" (and further developed as part of China's "peaceful rise" and "harmonious world" concepts) is a "security of sustained development" that accepts globalization as "inevitable and indispensable for the country's modernization." The new security concept is based on three principles of Chinese foreign policy: (1) "sovereignty and the political, economic, and cultural pluralism of all nations must be respected," (2) national economic development requires "mutual interest and common prosperity," and (3) "all parties must promote mutual trust and understanding while opposing any hegemonic behavior and avoiding the use of force in international affairs."[4] These fundamental premises have resulted in a more flexible, integrative, and interactive Chinese approach to international affairs that emphasizes cooperation with near neighbors, but also focuses on the task of sustainable economic growth as the key to expanding "comprehensive national power [strength]" and influence at regional and global levels.

Another formulation of China's emerging interests and needs has been presented by Wang Yizhou. Wang describes three primary interests and needs as China faces the twenty-first century: (1) the development interest and need—that is, serving the goal of domestic economic construction and seeking a relatively stable external environment conducive to reform and development; (2) the sovereignty interest and need—that is, protecting the territory, borders, and basic sovereignty from encroachment; and (3) the responsibility need and interest—that is, exercising positive and increasingly dominant influence in the Asia

Pacific region and working to become a globally influential country that is generally recognized as playing a constructive role.[5]

A more recent elaboration of new diplomatic initiative that has accompanied China's rise is the idea of the "harmonious world" elaborated by Hu Jintao in a September 15, 2005, address to the United Nations. Hu proposed "respecting the right of all countries to choose their own social system and development road, strengthening dialogue and exchanges between different civilizations, upholding the diversity of civilizations, promoting democratization of international relations, and making concerted efforts to build a harmonious world incorporating civilizations of a diverse nature." Subsequent efforts by Chinese policy analysts to further define the "harmonious world" idea emphasize the replacement of "struggle" with "harmony" in management of China's international relations; the importance of "getting some things done" in accordance with China's major national interests; an emphasis on "balanced diplomacy," including acceptance of "stakeholder" responsibilities; and a focus on national interests rather than ideology as core principles underlying China's diplomacy.[6]

China's expanded capabilities and stature as a rising power have stimulated adjustments in foreign policy interests that reflect its broadened interest in promoting regional stability. In a broader formulation of China's regional security priorities that has as its foundation the core principles of the new security concept outlined above, Zhang Yunling and Tang Shiping identify six core ideas underpinning China's regional strategy: (1) seek comprehensive cooperation with regional states, (2) demonstrate benign intentions through the exercise of self-restraint, (3) demonstrate the ability to live with a United States that does not threaten its core interests, (4) pursue its regional economic development strategy in an open way, (5) embrace regional multilateralism, and (6) shape the regional environment in ways that allow enhanced stature on the global stage.[7] However, China's relations on the Korean peninsula, with North Korea in particular, are contradictory and pose major practical challenges to its aspirations.

Chinese Strategic Dilemmas in Managing Policy Toward North Korea

North Korea's increasing isolation and weakness have raised fundamental contradictions between implementation of China's "new thinking" and the legacy of China's traditional policies toward the Korean peninsula. China's hallmark "five principles of peaceful coexistence" are no longer practical as means for protecting its interests, given the greater regional responsibility and investment required to ensure its regional stability. The fraternal relationship between China and North Korea that grew from common ideological roots is increasingly frayed by challenges resulting from China's adjustment of its own perceived security needs. China must grapple with at least six fundamental contradictions between its long-standing policies toward North Korea and the new parameters and premises that shape its regional strategy. These contradictions are at the root of recent Chinese debates over how to deal with North Korea.

First, China's need for a peaceful regional environment conducive to its own continued development has required it to take a more active stance in management of tensions between the United States and North Korea since the second North Korean nuclear crisis. In the words of one Chinese analyst, "The DPRK nuclear issue has brought China's diplomacy to face a vital juncture, the essence of which is how to choose the appropriate stand between traditional alliance relations and great power relations. From the 1894–95 war to the Korean war, the Korean peninsula twice landed China in a 'strategic trap,' and the strategic interests that China has gained from ensuring the peninsula's denuclearization and its peace and stability are no smaller than those of any other country (including the United States). It is also necessary to see that the negative impact on the regional security situation of having the DPRK nuclear issue drag on unresolved is very evident, and will at the least trigger mutual escalation of the level of regional armament and deterioration of the security environment."[8] This need has increasingly required China to take a more activist role in shaping the regional security environment on the Korean peninsula, through direct diplomatic mediation efforts designed to prevent escalation of tensions between the United States and North Korea. China's involvement in diplomatic mediation requires that it choose between two priorities in its foreign policy: the objective of maintaining positive relations among the major powers (especially the United States) and the objective of maintaining North Korea as a strategic buffer. This contradiction also brings into play, on the one hand, China's worry about US dominance in a reunified Korean peninsula, and on the other hand, China's opportunity to expand its sphere of influence over the peninsula and rid it of a US security presence.

In the early 1990s, China avoided taking an active role in the first North Korean nuclear crisis, in recognition of the limits of its influence with both the United States and North Korea, as a reflection of the relative economic isolation and lack of integration of its northeastern provinces with the international economy, and based on the principle of nonintervention in the affairs of other countries. But following the development in the 1990s of a "new security concept" that articulated its direct economic and strategic interests in the maintenance of regional stability, China could not help but take a more active role as a mediator between the United States and North Korea, engaging in shuttle diplomacy to promote diplomatic communication, hosting the six-party talks as a regional diplomatic forum dedicated to keeping tensions from escalating, and utilizing economic tools in a direct attempt to influence the quality of North Korea's participation in the talks and in an attempt to impose limits on actions by North Korea that contradicted its own national interests.

China's need to maintain regional stability on the Korean peninsula must compete with policy priorities to prevent nuclear proliferation. To the extent that North Korea pursues actions that risk or have negative ramifications for regional stability, China must use the instruments at its disposal to constrain such actions, even if such actions contradict the principle of nonintervention in the sovereign affairs of another state. But China's desire for regional stability also requires that it oppose nuclear development and proliferation activities that could incite tensions and compromise its core national security interests, not the least by inviting pressure and even possible military retaliation from the United States. China thus faces a dilemma between avoiding an escalation of military tensions, which could jeopardize regional stability, and preventing nuclear development, which could stimulate a regional nuclear arms race, heighten prospects for retaliation, and thereby also undermine regional stability. China's approach to balancing these two competing objectives since early in the crisis has been to insist on North Korea's peaceful denuclearization while also insisting that North Korea's justifiable security concerns be satisfactorily addressed.[9]

Second, North Korea's relative isolation and failure to come to terms with the post–Cold War international environment challenge China's vision for multilateral economic and security cooperation based on "mutual interest and common prosperity." North Korea's unilateralist tendency to reject cooperation in favor of satisfying its own paramount interests directly contradicts China's focus on multilateral cooperation. North Korea's failure to fully embrace economic reforms contradicts the premise that an open regional economic strategy will serve both China's interests and the interests of China's neighbors. Thus, China's interest in promotion of economic reforms in North Korea is clear. But China's efforts to promote reform in North Korea may be seen by North Korea's leaders as threatening to their own political stability, and North Korea's insistence on centrally led government-directed economic interactions lays bare for China fundamental contradictions between the desire to move to a market economy and North Korea's continued economic dependency (requiring ever-increasing Chinese economic investments to maintain North Korea's stability).

North Korea's economic stagnation and isolation-driven poverty deprive China's northeastern provinces of a strong cross-border partner for exchange of goods and promotion of economic prosperity. Instead, many of China's cross-border interactions with North Korea are either driven by humanitarian motives or conducted at great economic risk for Chinese business partners, given the lack of regulatory protections. The spread of markets into North Korea in recent years has begun to have an impact, but Chinese traders will continue to face considerable risks until North Korea's central government officially welcomes and endorses such cross-border trade.

Although Chinese authorities have tried to lead North Korean counterparts to consider economic reforms while maintaining political control by following the Chinese economic reform model, North Korean authorities have not yet embraced such a course. For over a decade, Chinese authorities have attempted to put the economic relationship with North Korea on a market basis by reducing the amount of subsidies provided to North Korea from China's central, provincial, and local governments. Instead, North Korea's leaders prefer to live primarily on subsidies rather than take the inherent political risks attached to economic opening. North Korea's hesitancy to open economically poses a direct challenge to China's vision for regional economic cooperation, and continues to drain Chinese resources. On the one hand, Chinese analysts recognize that North Korea's economy is not sustainable without economic "transfusions" from the outside world, but on the other hand, China will not risk the potential economic and political instability along its borders that might be created by cutting back subsidies to North Korea. The latter's isolation remains an obstacle to development of cooperative regional economic and security relations, ensuring a continued US security presence on the Korean peninsula.

Third, the prospect of instability deriving from North Korea's character as a "failed state," the spillover effects of which threaten instability on China's borders, poses a serious contradiction for Chinese policymakers in confronting the question of intervention. On the one hand, the "five principles of peaceful coexistence" are often invoked to underscore

China's unflinching commitment to recognize the sovereignty of North Korea, but the need to minimize direct damage to Chinese national interests in the event of economic or political instability in North Korea requires China to make hard choices about the parameters and limits of its nonintervention doctrine.

The Chinese government also has to cope with an evolving international debate over the limits of sovereignty for failed states as well as for states that do not meet international standards of governance sufficient to guarantee minimum human rights standards. Thus far, China has stood together with North Korea on many such challenges by honoring commitments to repatriate North Koreans residing in China, casting them as illegal immigrants rather than political refugees, and preventing interviews by international authorities such as the UN High Commission for Refugees.

North Korea's own weakness, including its inability to control population movements into China, challenges China's evolving commitment to noninterference, and by extension, its willingness to exercise "benign intentions" through guarantees of North Korea's sovereignty versus the temptation to violate North Korea's sovereignty or intimidate, or "rein in" North Korea's leadership to secure fundamental interests and influence.

Fourth, China faces contradictions between the impulse to secure traditional relations with North Korea as the buffer that provides it with an economic and political foothold on the Korean peninsula, and a peninsular policy that rhetorically supports the independent efforts of the two Koreas to achieve unification. "The key lies in all-around development of friendly and cooperative relations with both north and south. As relations between north and south improve and develop in the process of the peninsula's move out of the Cold War, China can simultaneously develop friendly and cooperative relations with the DPRK and the ROK, and can also provide more help for economic reform and opening up in the DPRK; this not only means China achieving common development and prosperity with the peninsula through economic cooperation, but also means greater security and stability."[10]

In this respect, the triangular relationship imposes peculiar opportunities and constraints on China's diplomatic interactions as it manages relations with the two Koreas. On the one hand, China remains the great power that has the best relationship and most effective communication with both Koreas at high levels. Through consolidation of political ties, regular exchange visits, and meetings at regional multilateral forums, China has developed a comprehensive partnership with South Korea. At the same time, the Chinese leadership has cultivated regular visits with Kim Jong Il and others to maintain its influence with North Korea.

China has sought to improve its relationship with South Korea both to take advantage of the economic complementarities between the two countries and to "lock in" a favorable relationship with Seoul. In this respect, Chinese leaders understand that the future policy orientation of a unified Korean peninsula is most likely to be determined in Seoul rather than Pyongyang, and have devised policies accordingly.

However, China has faced some setbacks in its relationship with both North and South Korea as a result of perceptions on the peninsula that Chinese influence is too heavy-handed or self-interested. During meetings in New York in March 2007, Vice Minister Kim Kye Gwan's striking public comments about China revealed tensions in the Sino–North Korean relationship, while also revealing Pyongyang's hopes that normalization of relations with the United States could serve as a strategic counterweight to Chinese dominance and Pyongyang's extraordinary economic dependence on Beijing. Likewise, South Korean leaders continue to worry quietly over Chinese economic influence inside North Korea, revealing their own anxieties about the possibility that China might either become a dominant political influence in North Korea or completely exhaust its resources, leaving South Korea with all the problems of resuscitating a poverty-ridden state.

Fifth, China must manage relations with the two Koreas in such a way as to prevent the United States from enhancing its strategic position on the peninsula and in Northeast Asia. Chinese analysts continue to express their concern that expansion of US influence on the Korean peninsula, for instance through a rapid US–North Korean rapprochement (as was feared in the aftermath of Chris Hill's sudden visit to Pyongyang in late June 2007),[11] could be the leading edge of a broader US strategy to encircle China. The dilemma is that China's attempts to play the role of responsible stakeholder through cooperation with the United States might result in an enhanced US role in promoting regional stability; on the other hand, China's lack of cooperation with US-led efforts to stem regional proliferation might leave the Korean peninsula issue to fester, tying down the United States and limiting an expansion of interest while preserving a relatively stable status quo.

At least one Chinese analyst has argued that, on balance, China's primary task is that of "curbing U.S. strategic expansion in Korea while maintaining overall stability of Sino-U.S. strategic relations," and that, "viewed from the overall pattern of China's foreign relations, especially from its impact on the Sino-U.S. strategic relationship, the Korean peninsula is very likely to be the only important platform at a global level that China can use to effectively contend with the United States and also . . . engage in substantive cooperation with it." In this view, North Korea remains a "strategic resource" rather than a "strategic burden" for China.[12]

On the one hand, China's interests lie with denuclearization of the Korean peninsula, but presumably not in a fashion that strengthens the strategic position of the United States. Communist Party School professor Zhang Liangui expressed his support for US efforts to uphold the international norm of nonproliferation, but expressed suspicions that the United States could utilize its efforts to secure a nuclear-free Korean peninsula for its own purposes: "In fact, the pursuit of hegemony by the United States and the destruction of a nuclear-free Korean peninsula are all contrary to the interests of China. They also endanger the security of China. Hence, these two will be opposed by China."[13] One way that China could secure its influence on the Korean peninsula (and in the process thwart possible US hegemony) would be to promote trilateral Sino–North Korean–South Korean cooperation. Such cooperation would reduce North Korean suspicions about South Korean aid and lighten and divide China's and South Korea's respective economic burdens in aiding North Korea, eventually leading to "the establishment of a northeast Asia collective security mechanism."[14]

China's ambivalence can be seen in an article by Chinese North Korea specialist Yu Meihua in the days following the inter-Korean summit in June 2000. Yu predicted, "First, the pressure for the withdrawal of troops will grow. If the 'North Korean threat' no longer exists, the United States will find no convincing reason to keep its troops in the ROK or even in the East Asia as a whole. Second, the pressure for readjusting the unsymmetrical ROK-US military relations will grow. The ROK hopes that the United States will return . . . the combat command power taken from it some 50 years ago. Third, a sense of self-determination between the north and the south will pound at the US 'guiding role.'"[15]

Sixth, the intractability of the Korean conflict and the difficulty of promoting mediation have challenged China's ability to shape the regional environment in ways that enhance its stature on the global stage. China has consistently taken credit for its role in promoting the six-party talks by maintaining active diplomatic channels with both the United States and North Korea, and for attempting to facilitate communication through shuttle diplomacy. China has also benefited from the deepening of the multilateral approach as a means to ensure that any process for addressing issues on the Korean peninsula will require its acquiescence if not its support. But China's diplomacy has also revealed clearly the limits of its capacity to bring the North Korean nuclear issue to a comprehensive resolution.

Though China remains dependent on its ability to cooperate with and coax the United States into a more conciliatory approach, it has little leverage by which to urge a change in US policy. Zhu Feng described China's dilemma as follows: "As a hegemonist state, the United States welcomes China playing a leading role in the six party talks. However, because China lacks sufficient 'leverage' to force the Bush administration into changing its current hard-line policy on the DPRK, the mediation diplomacy of China cannot substantively 'manipulate' the process of the six party talks, and naturally, the realization of nuclear abandonment through mediation is quite limited."[16] Chinese Korea specialist Yang Xiyu suggested that the solution to the North Korean nuclear issue is not in the hands of the Chinese people. "This is our difficulty. We can only play the role of mediator in urging peace and promoting talks. Our aim is to make the United States and DPRK hand over the key to the solution of this issue."[17] Although China recognizes the need to take a more active role in the talks, that role also forces China to confront the limits of its influence and leverage over both the United States and North Korea.

To the extent that Chinese diplomatic efforts through the six-party talks have failed, US intransigence is as much an object of frustration as North Korean obstinacy. Chinese policy analysts argue that US flexibility would increase the chances that reform might succeed in North Korea, since a diminished external security threat would help promote an environment conducive to economic reform. The Chinese increasingly question whether the United States really wants to resolve the North Korean nuclear issue and suggest that until Washington demonstrates that a diplomatic solution is a top priority for the administration, there is little that China can do to facilitate further negotiations.

Perhaps because of this recognition that the six-party talks are a limited tool, Chinese analysts also believe that a multilateral, more permanent mechanism for dialogue will ultimately be necessary to manage regional relations. They still believe that the Asian alliances of the United States are in contradiction with the fundamental premises underlying a cooperative approach to managing regional security, characterizing those alliances as "Cold War thinking." The Chinese ask how a multilateral dialogue mechanism can be compatible with US alliances and how those frameworks would have to be adjusted to accommodate a cooperative security framework. Aside from raising questions and suggesting that alliances and cooperative security mechanisms may be incompatible, however, Chinese analysts are waiting for the United States (and North Korea) to make strategic decisions about how to approach the nuclear issue and how to more constructively build the foundations for peace and prosperity in Northeast Asia.

Ultimately, China's capacity to push the diplomatic process forward depends as much on its ability to exercise leverage with the United States as on its ability to influence the direction of North Korea's policy. Prior to the North Korean nuclear test, China's achievements in moving the process forward though attempts to soften US policy and bring Washington and Pyongyang into direct dialogue were hard-won. Ironically, at the same time that North Korea's nuclear test also clearly demonstrated the limits of China's influence on Pyongyang, the test also brought about tactical changes in the US approach and moved it into closer alignment with China's approach. Despite China's manifest frustration with North Korea's willingness to flout its benefactor, Fudan University's Shen Dingli has expressed begrudging admiration that North Korea's stubbornness eventually caused the United States to bend to its demands for direct dialogue, praising North Korea's "strategic judgment" as "circumspect and far-sighted" and noting that, previously, the George W. Bush administration had always demanded that North Korea act first, but "now the United States is always acting ahead."[18]

The Second North Korean Nuclear Crisis

The second North Korean nuclear crisis has served as an important catalyst for an evolution of views among Chinese analysts regarding China's strategic interests on the Korean peninsula, the nature of the Sino–North Korean relationship, and China's views on the extent to which it is possible to cooperate with or oppose the United States to achieve a nonnuclear peninsula without compromising its own long-standing interests in regional stability and the maintenance of a China-friendly peninsula. As the crisis has worn on, the specter of North Korea's economic stagnation, strategic miscalculation, political isolation, and possibly even regime failure have progressively become sources of concern to Chinese analysts as significant obstacles to China's pursuit of its core interest in stability.

The heightening tensions surrounding North Korea's covert uranium-enrichment program became public just prior to the October 25–26, 2002, visit of Chinese president Jiang Zemin to Crawford, Texas, for his last meeting with President George W. Bush before stepping down from office. At that meeting, Bush raised questions about the North Korean regime and asked Jiang if the North Koreans could be trusted, only to receive an equivocal response. Without directly requesting Chinese assistance, Bush's questions to Jiang constituted an early warning of the seriousness of the issue to the United States and framed it as a focal point for potential US-Chinese cooperation. The dialogue also laid the foundations for the "Crawford consensus," a common understanding that North Korea's denuclearization should be pursued through peaceful means, and marked the beginning of a productive, high-level collaboration between the United States and China to achieve that goal.[19]

Shortly after that meeting, US–North Korean tensions rapidly escalated as the Geneva agreed framework began to fail and the situation reverted to that which existed in the early 1990s. The United States stopped supplying heavy fuel oil to North Korea, under the Korean Peninsula Energy Development Organization, on the grounds that North Korea was in breach of its framework obligations in November 2002. North Korea's rapid response, in December 2002 and early January 2003, was to evict International Atomic Energy Association inspectors from the Yongbyon site, announce its withdrawal from the Nuclear Nonproliferation Treaty, and reload and resume operation of its five-megawatt reactor at Yongbyon. In addition, North Korea began reprocessing operations, using fuel rods that had been placed in storage after having been removed from North Korea's reactor in 1994, to produce weapons-grade plutonium that could be used in nuclear bombs. Freed from the restraints of the agreed framework, North Korea pursued production of new nuclear materials as rapidly as it was able, escalating the crisis and causing concerns in the region that the United States might respond with military escalation.

In light of these events, Chinese analysts became particularly concerned about the ramifications of a military confrontation between the United States and North Korea over the nuclear issue, attributing the standoff to an extreme lack of trust. In March 2003, a series of articles appeared in the journal *Shijie Zhishi* debating whether the United States would take military action against North Korea in response to the latter's escalation measures.

Chinese Japan specialist Jin Xide judged that the United States was constrained by a more complex geopolitical environment than in Iraq, and that US desires to maintain hegemony in Northeast Asia would override any specific concern about North Korea as a primary objective of foreign policy.[20] Communist Party School professor Zhang Liangui judged that UN resolutions condemning North Korea, its reprocessing of fissile materials, or its self-declaration as a nuclear state would result in military conflict, and argued that the most serious issue was the lack of trust between the United States and North Korea. Presciently, he also advocated the establishment of a multiparty dialogue to address the issue.[21]

The dominant tone of Chinese commentary in the initial stages of the crisis, from 2003 to 2005, was to view the crisis dispassionately as a struggle between the United States and North Korea driven by extreme mutual mistrust. But Chinese analysts were concerned that the crisis could escalate and drag China into a Cold War state of confrontation with the United States and Japan.[22] According to some analysts, China would be placed in a difficult position by US expectations that it pressure North Korea: "As hostility between the United States and the DPRK is very deep, and as the United States, to a very large extent, held talks with the DPRK only when push came to shove, it is still very difficult to say whether it sincerely wants to settle the issue through dialogues. Because both the United States and the DPRK pin great hope on China, they may harbor grievances against China once the six-way talk fails, and our policy will face a very difficult choice."[23]

At this relatively early stage in the crisis, Renmin University professor Shi Yinhong identified North Korea's pursuit of nuclear weapons as an issue that directly affects China's strategic interests and as a top priority for China's foreign policy. "In reality, the DPRK has consistently adopted an attitude of resistance to China's diplomatic persuasion. . . . No matter how complex the DPRK nuclear crisis is or even how complex the whole DPRK issue is, and no matter what cautious and careful thinking and policy are required to deal with these issues, China's highest strategic interest or primary strategic objective during the DPRK nuclear crisis lies in firmly urging the DPRK to stay clear of nuclear weapons."[24] Shi also believes that "China's participation in the Korean War was clearly a mistake" and that "if North Korea's nuclear development causes a war on the Korean peninsula, China should not intervene."[25]

Through shuttle diplomacy between Pyongyang and Washington and continuing efforts to develop momentum in the dialogue in the early rounds of the six-party talks, Chinese officials tried to cajole North Korea and the United States to overcome their deep mutual distrust and to show flexibility. While North Korea insisted on direct talks with the United States, the George W. Bush administration appeared to insist on multilateral talks only, and put forward as its objective an uncompromising formulation—"comprehensive, verifiable, irreversible dismantle-ment"—which came to be known as CVID. Despite China's roles as host and mediator at each of the first three rounds of six-party talks, held in August 2003, February 2004, and June 2004, the only outcome China was able to achieve was a series of "chairman's statements" that continuously urged the participants to settle their differences over North Korea's nuclear program through peaceful dialogue. Although China's role as host was played up for domestic audiences as an example of its rising importance in international relations, public criticism occasional-ly emerged, primarily directed toward the United States. Chinese chief negotiator Wang Yi revealed his frustration following the first round of six-party talks, saying that "America's policy toward the DPRK—that is the main problem we are facing."[26]

By early 2005, Shanghai Academy of Social Sciences researcher Liu Ming assessed that the gap between the United States and North Korea was too great for China to bridge by siding with the United States, and that cornering North Korea over its nuclear weapons program would result in refugee flows and a loss of influence that would be counterpro-ductive to Chinese policy interests; instead he advocated that China's only realistic option to help bridge the gap was the continuation of "shut-tle diplomacy."[27] Following North Korea's self-declaration on February 10, 2005, as a nuclear weapons state, however, Liu's colleague Zhang Zuqian made precisely the opposite argument in Singapore's *Straits Times,* arguing that the message to North Korea should be that its nuclear activities "compromise China's vital interests, including China's securi-ty." Zhang argued that the political, military, and economic risks attached to instability in North Korea were short-term compared to the benefits that would accrue from finally resolving the issue in a clear-cut way.[28]

North Korea's self-declaration as a nuclear weapons state apparent-ly pushed Chinese policy further toward support for the US emphasis on denuclearization. Shen Dingli claimed that this is the message that was conveyed from Hu Jintao to Kim Jong Il during Wang Jiarui's visit to Pyongyang immediately following North Korea's February 10, 2005, announcement. According to Shen, China's message that "resolving the nuclear issue through the six party talks and the DPRK side's reasonable concerns is in accord with China's fundamental interests" may have marked the first time that China linked its fundamental interests with another country's foreign policy, a notable public departure from the tra-ditional principle of noninterference in the affairs of other countries.[29]

Later that year, in October 2005, China and North Korea reached an apparent high point in their interactions through a leadership exchange visit, followed by a second in January 2006. These exchanges generated optimism about the potential for North Korean economic reforms, but it was tempered by an underlying realism regarding the difficulties China faced in effectively curbing North Korean escalation without damaging its own vital national security interests. One analyst concluded, "The focal content and substantive significance of Hu Jintao's visit to the DPRK do not lie in whether or not impetus can be given to the Korean nuclear issue negotiations, and still less in how to recall past friendship, but in whether or not China's successful development experiences can convince and cause the Kim Jong Il authorities to truly get out of their self-enclosed state. . . . As a neighbor, China has the responsibility to help Pyongyang to extricate itself from its ossified political mentality and replace the 'traditional friendship,' which has become a historical burden, with new-style mutually beneficial cooperation relations."[30]

Kim Jong Il organized an elaborate welcome for Hu Jintao that was even more impressive than the reception given to Kim Dae Jung in June 2000. With great pomp and ceremony, Hu and Kim paid tribute to the "traditional friendship," the historical ties between forerunners, and the geographically close nature of the relationship, but also discussed four broad areas of cooperation in greater detail: (1) forging closer high-level contacts and exchanges, (2) extending the scope of exchanges and enriching the substance of cooperation, (3) promoting economic and trade cooperation for common development, and (4) actively coordinating to promote national interests. China's Xinhua news service reported Kim's response: "Regardless of changes in the international situation, the DPRK will proceed from the strategic height in taking an effective grasp of DPRK-China friendship and making the development of DPRK-China friendship the unswerving strategic principle."[31]

In January 2006, Kim Jong Il visited Beijing and undertook a "southern tour" of China along many points of the route that Deng Xiaoping had followed in 1992 to signal China's affirmation of economic reforms. Senior Chinese party officials accompanied Kim throughout the tour, promising economic and moral support for North Korea in following China's economic reform path while maintaining political control. Hong Kong media sources reported that Kim was deeply moved by China's development; he hoped that North Korea could "introduce the vitality of the market economy under the premise of maintaining a planned economy" and that North Korea could learn from China's experience. Kim also affirmed that North Korea would continue to pursue the goal of a nuclear-free peninsula, adhere to the September 19, 2005, joint statement, and continue to promote the six-party talks. Kim's visit was also important as a way of affirming China's continued oil and food subsidies to North Korea, despite China's desire to put the relationship on a "market basis."[32]

The optimism that followed this leadership exchange led some Chinese analysts to hope that North Korea was indeed prepared to follow China's reform path, and that the North Korean nuclear issue was under control. While reform is indeed under way in North Korea, it is distorted and incomplete. At least one Chinese expert has argued that fundamental changes are occurring in North Korea at three levels: the relationship between the state and the public, the relationship between the state and the enterprises, and the relationship between the central government and the local government. However, these changes have been imposed by circumstance, rather than being state-led. The failure of the North Korean central government to provide policy leadership, combined with increased information flows resulting from bottom-up market-based interactions, is promoting greater levels of political disaffection inside the country, revealing the depth of the dilemma and the political risks accompanying North Korea's reform.[33]

Most Chinese analysts note that a prerequisite for pursuit of China's economic reforms was a peaceful environment, a condition that Kim Jong Il himself has reportedly noted as being absent in the case of North Korea. For this reason, a primary objective among many Chinese analysts has been the softening of US policy toward North Korea.[34] But there are also reports that Kim's "southern tour" was undertaken not to promote economic reform in North Korea, but rather to seek a doubling of Chinese economic assistance. Perhaps Kim interpreted China's lack of response to these requests as further evidence that Chinese assistance serves China's own interests in stability; thus there was no need for Kim to offer a quid pro quo.[35]

The North Korean missile and nuclear tests in July and October 2006 "angered," "shocked," and "humiliated" China and catalyzed the internal debate over dilemmas posed by its ongoing relationship with North Korea,[36] especially given the lengths to which China had gone to deter the North Korean leadership from testing a nuclear device. In addition, the challenge of how to lead North Korea to accept gradual economic reforms while maintaining political control had beset Chinese analysts since the 1990s, but the nuclear test threw into relief the question of the extent to which North Korea, once considered a strategic asset to China, may have become a strategic liability.

North Korea's nuclear test heightened Chinese concerns that the test would be a catalyst for regional proliferation in South Korea, Japan, and

Taiwan, and stimulated further scrutiny of every aspect of the Sino–North Korean relationship given that China's core security interests had already been damaged. One unnamed analyst stated, "This nuclear test and subsequent nuclear tests will surely exert impacts on both the soft and hard environments of China's three Northeast provinces; it is only that we are unable to tell what the exact impacts will be at this moment. Kim Jong-il has not only deceived the whole world, but has all the more fooled China. People would say: What has China done (to solve the DPRK nuclear crisis)? What role has it played? Worst of all, it turns out in the end that the nuclear arms in the hands of the DPRK are actually directed at China."[37] Some analysts sought to "turn strength into power" in management of policy toward the Korean peninsula by strengthening military deployments in the Sino–North Korean border area, participating in international diplomacy through cooperation with UN resolutions, and attempting to "resolve the Korean peninsula nuclear issue in a peaceful fashion through dialogue and consultation." China's policy toward North Korea would be based squarely on "realistic options based on seeking to maximize national interests . . . discarding ideology, and establishing normal state relations with the DPRK."[38]

The nuclear test unleashed active debate over the extent to which China should cooperate with the United States in response to North Korea's escalation. Some analysts argued that cooperation with the United States would cost China the influence it needed in order to prevent worsening of Sino–North Korean relations, which would trigger additional political and economic problems in North Korea that could spill over into China's border areas. Qinghua University scholar Liu Jiangyong stated, "I believe that we cannot slap the DPRK down just because it has conducted a nuclear test; this is not the way to resolve the problem, and in the long term it may pose a still greater threat to us."[39] From this perspective, the greatest concern following North Korea's nuclear test was the possibility that the United States might respond militarily, not any further threat of escalation by North Korea. According to this line of thinking, North Korea had played into the hands of the United States: as a result of its nuclear test, several countries joined together to impose sanctions on North Korea within the multilateral framework of the United Nations, thereby undermining China's influence over North Korea and giving the United States the upper hand in reshaping North Korea's foreign policy.[40]

A third school of thought argued that China's core interests in nonproliferation aligned it with the United States and the international community in ways that required China to use all available means to maintain a nonnuclear Korean peninsula, including pressuring North Korea to its prior denuclearization commitments as part of the September 19, 2005, joint statement. China and the United States are not only "interested parties," but also constructive "collaborators." Any future process to resolve the Korean nuclear issue will require maintenance of Sino-US cooperation, which cannot occur without mutual strategic trust. "A nuclear-armed DPRK is a burden that East Asia cannot absorb"; China and the United States must cooperate on the Korean peninsula and in North Korea in ways that promote stability.[41] Along similar lines, one analyst suggests that China's interests would best be served if it were to abandon its efforts to maintain a failing status quo and refashion its policy to account for the interests of the Korean peninsula as a whole, by promoting North Korea's reform and opening up, supporting Korean reunification, and promoting Korean prosperity and stability. This approach emphasizes that a strategy designed to counter the prospect of a xenophobic nuclear North Korea would serve not only China's interests, but also the interests of other major powers and of the international community. Such a strategy would also have the virtue of "untying the fast knot" by which North Korea is currently leading China.[42]

The specter of North Korea's economic stagnation, strategic miscalculation, political isolation, and possibly even regime failure have become significant obstacles to China's pursuit of its core interest in stability. Chinese analysts assert that it is increasingly clear (even to Kim Jong Il) that, without economic reforms, North Korea's political leadership cannot survive. However, the path of economic reform for such a small country, facing a hostile international environment (compared to the benign international environment of the Chinese reform experience), may entail fatal political risks to North Korea if it opens itself to the outside world, which it must if it is to achieve the full benefits of its economic reform.[43]

The Chinese military has given serious consideration to the ramifications of regime failure in North Korea, and admits that there are circumstances under which military intervention might be necessary. It is no accident that Chinese forces have moved closer to the North Korean border in recent years. Military analysts assert that Chinese contingency plans are in place to intervene, on grounds of "environmental control," in order to secure North Korea's nuclear weapons and fissile materials in the event of regime instability. But the immediate concern for China is to secure potential threats along its border with North Korea, presumably including management of potential refugee flows that could result from a collapse of political control.[44]

A recent quantitative analysis of interactions in the Sino–North Korean relationship concludes the following: that Beijing's efforts to intensify regular high-level visits with Pyongyang have had positive results in easing nuclear tensions; that without Chinese pressure on North Korea, the situation would likely deteriorate, but that China does not have the capacity to fundamentally resolve the North Korean nuclear crisis; and that US policies toward North Korea are the primary limiting factor affecting China's influence on the Korean peninsula. China is playing the role of coordinator and rescuer in giving impetus to a solution for the North Korean nuclear crisis, but the final solution will still be mainly determined by the United States and North Korea itself. One implication of this conclusion is that US attempts to push China to put greater pressure on North Korea are counterproductive to China's interests and should be resisted.[45]

China's Economic Leverage: Instrument for Influence in North Korea?

Given North Korea's economic dependency, China has many economic tools that should enhance its leverage, but it is not clear that China can effectively utilize those tools without endangering fundamental interests in stability. After the North Korean nuclear test, the purposes and rationales for China's continued economic assistance to North Korea came under serious scrutiny, and the debate over whether economic instruments were best used as inducements or for coercion was joined anew. On the one hand, China had forsworn the use of economic tools to enhance political leverage over North Korea, claiming that such pressure would ultimately prove counterproductive to its own national interests, while at the same time ramping up economic assistance to regain political influence in Pyongyang. On the other hand, Chinese economic inputs had clearly failed to achieve their objective of stabilizing North Korea, and promoting regional stability in general, given the latter's nuclear test.[46]

While China has been reluctant to use sticks, it has tried to use carrots to influence North Korea's economic opening and to promote reforms. China has attempted to show North Korea the benefits of economic reform by example, and by encouraging the North Korean leadership that it would be possible to utilize market mechanisms while still retaining political control. North Korea has traditionally borrowed many lessons from the Chinese experience, and China's economic and social example has been at least partially accepted in Pyongyang, according to some Chinese reports. North Korea has sent officials to China to learn from its economic and technological development.[47]

Since North Korea's nuclear test, China has attempted to utilize the promise of economic benefits to influence North Korea's direction, conditional on the latter's performance. This approach appears to have yielded the most tangible results. The Chinese government initially seemed wary of pursuing coercive tactics to force North Korea to cooperate with the international community, but more recently has quietly pursued its own retaliatory measures targeting North Korean financial accounts alleged to have been used in illegal counterfeiting and money-laundering activities.[48]

Despite the fact that China has attempted to utilize increased economic interaction to gain political leverage over and restrain North Korea, many Chinese specialists on Korean affairs continue to express skepticism that increased coercive measures against North Korea are likely to yield the desired effect. Instead, they worry that such measures will further diminish Beijing's leverage, which they tend to see as limited despite North Korea's considerable economic dependence on China and in light of China's overarching policy objective of avoiding instability on the peninsula. At the same time, frustration with North Korea's hesitancy to pursue bolder reform measures, its crisis escalation tactics, and its reluctance to participate in the six-party talks has grown. Most Chinese analysts also hold to the view that the United States remains the party with the greatest leverage to induce North Korea to pursue a path of economic reform.

Notes

1. See Hong Liu, "The Sino–South Korean Normalization: A Triangular Explanation," *Asian Survey* 33, no. 11 (November 1993): 1086–1088; Jia Hao and Zhuang Qubing, "China's Policy Toward the Korean Peninsula," *Asian Survey* 32, no. 12 (December 1992): 1137–1156.

2. For instance, see Banning Garrett and Bonnie Glaser, "Looking Across the Yalu: Chinese Assessments of North Korea," *Asian Survey* 35, no. 6 (June 1995): 528.

3. See Bates Gill, *Rising Star: China's New Security Diplomacy* (Washington, DC: Brookings Institution, 2007), pp. 4–10.

4. Wu Baiyi, "The Chinese Security Concept and its Historical Evolution," *Journal of Contemporary China* 10, no. 27 (2001): 275–283.

5. Wang Yizhou, "Chinese Diplomacy Oriented Toward the 21st Century:

Pursuing and Balancing Three Needs," *Zhanlue Yu Guanli* (Beijing), December 30, 1999, pp. 18–27, accessed at http://www.opensource.gov, doc. no. CPP20000215000115.

6. Yuan Peng, "'Harmonious World' and China's 'New Diplomacy,'" *Xiandai Guoji Guanxi* (Beijing), in Chinese, April 20, 2007, pp. 1–8, accessed at http://www.opensource.gov, doc. no. CPP20070511455001.

7. Zhang Yunling and Tang Shiping, "China's Regional Strategy," in David Shambaugh, ed., *Power Shift: China and Asia's New Dynamics* (Berkeley: University of California Press, 2005), pp. 48–49.

8. Yang Bojiang, "Changes in and Status of the Northeast Asian Security Situation," *Xiandai Guoji Guanxi* (Beijing), in Chinese, April 20, 2003, pp. 12–14, accessed at http://www.opensource.gov, doc. no. CPP20030512000264.

9. See Shi Yinhong, "The DPRK Nuclear Crisis: New Turn for the Better and the Still Existing Dangers," *Ta Kung Pao* (Hong Kong), in Chinese, August 1, 2003, p. A12, accessed at http://www.opensource.gov, doc. no. CPP20030801000038.

10. Xu Weidi, "Resolving the Korean Peninsula Nuclear Crisis and Moving the Korean Peninsula out of the Cold War," *Shijie Jingji Yu Zhengzhi* (Beijing), in Chinese, September 14, 2003, pp. 59–64, accessed at http://www.opensource.gov, doc. no. CPP20030925000192.

11. Author interviews with Chinese analysts in Beijing, June 2007; Lu Chao, "Ideal and Reality in Establishment of U.S.-DPRK Diplomatic Relations," August 1, 2007, accessed at http://www.opensource.gov, doc. no. CPP20070806455002.

12. Xu, "Resolving the Korean Peninsula Nuclear Crisis."

13. Zhang Liangui, "Re-understanding the Six-Party Talks on the Korean Nuclear Issue," *Shijie Zhishi,* in Chinese, October 16, 2005, accessed at http://www.opensource.gov, doc. no. CPP20051028329001.

14. Zhang Liangui, "Four Topics Regarding the Korean Peninsula Issue," *Shijie Zhishi,* in Chinese, July 16, 2006, accessed at http://www.opensource.gov, doc. no. CPP20060726329002.

15. Yu Meihua, "Ice-Breaking Trip Takes Place After Being Expected for Half Century: On Successful DPRK-ROK Summit," *Shijie Zhishi* (Beijing), July 1, 2000, pp. 8–9, accessed at http://www.opensource.gov, doc. no. CPP20000712000051.

16. Zhu Feng, "China's Diplomatic Mediation and the Six Party Talks on the Korean Nuclear Issue: Why Is the Diplomatic Resolution of the Korean Nuclear Issue So Difficult?" *Waijiao Pinglun,* April 25, 2006, accessed at http://www.opensource.gov, doc. no. CPP20060713455001.

17. "China Tries to Force the United States to Hand Over the Key to the Solution of the DPRK Nuclear Crisis," *Hsiang Kang Shang Pao* (Hong Kong), in Chinese, August 15, 2004, p. B3, accessed at http://www.opensource.gov, doc. no. CPP20040816000036.

18. Shen Dingli, "Initial Results of DPRK Nuclear Politics," *Guoji Zhanwang* (Shanghai), in Chinese, August 1, 2007, pp. 10–13, accessed at http://www.opensource.gov, doc. no. CPP20070830329001.

19. Bonnie S. Glaser and Wang Liang, "North Korea: The Beginning of a China-U.S. Partnership?" *Washington Quarterly* 31, no. 3 (2008): 165–180.

20. Jin Xide, "Will the United States Launch a War for the Sake of a Grudge?" *Shijie Zhishi* (Beijing), March 16, 2003, accessed at http://www.opensource.gov, doc. no. CPP20030331000173.

21. Zhang Liangui and Jin Xide, "Under What Circumstances Will the United States Take Action?" *Shijie Zhishi* (Beijing), March 16, 2003, accessed at http://www.opensource.gov, doc. no. CPP2030331000173.

22. Wang Yong, "Northeast Asia Faces a New 'Cold War,'" *Zhongguo Jingying Bao* (Beijing), April 28, 2003, accessed at http://www.opensource.gov, doc. no. CPP20030428000270.

23. Zhang Tuosheng and Ruan Zongze, "Lurking Challenges," *Shijie Zhishi* (Beijing), in Chinese, December 16, 2003, pp. 25–26, accessed at http://www.opensource.gov, doc. no. CPP20040108000207.

24. Wang Te-chun, "The DPRK Nuclear Crisis Puts China's Security to the Test," *Ta Kung Pao* (Hong Kong), January 14, 2003, accessed at http://www.opensource.gov, doc. no. CPP20030114000038.

25. Yoichi Funabashi, *The Peninsula Question: A Chronicle of the Second North Korean Nuclear Crisis* (Washington, DC: Brookings Institution, 2007), pp. 296–299.

26. Joseph Kahn, "Chinese Aide Says U.S. Is Obstacle in Korean Talks," *New York Times,* September 2, 2003, p. 3.

27. Liang Rong, "Negotiation over the DPRK Nuclear Crisis Relies Heavily on the 'China Card,'" *Wen Wei Po* (Hong Kong), in Chinese, March 20, 2005, accessed at http://www.opensource.gov, doc. no. CPP20050321000115.

28. Zhang Zuqian, "Beijing Can Make Pyongyang Toe the Line," *Straits Times* (Singapore), February 25, 2005, accessed at http://www.opensource.gov, doc. no. CPP20050225000073.

29. Shen Dingli, "New 'DPRK Nuclear Diplomacy' Sees Results," *Wen Hui Bao* (Shanghai), in Chinese, February 23, 2005, accessed at http://www.opensource.gov, doc. no. CPP20050226000001.

30. Du Ping, "PRC-DPRK 'Traditional Friendship' Is No Longer Traditional," *Lianhe Zaobao* (Singapore), October 28, 2005, accessed at http://www.opensource.gov, doc. no. CPP20051028071005.

31. Chen Hegao, Luo Hui, and Ji Xinlong, "Hu Jintao Holds Talks with Kim Jong Il," *Beijing Xinhua Domestic Service,* in Chinese, October 28, 2005, accessed at http://www.opensource.gov, doc. no. CPP20051028053057.

32. "Beijing Source Reveals, Kim Jong Il Shaken by Tremendous Changes in China, 'Could Hardly Sleep,'" *Zhongguo Tongxun She* (Hong Kong), in Chinese, January 23, 2006, accessed at http://www.opensource.gov, doc. no. CPP20060123029009.

33. Author interviews in Beijing, November 2005 and February 2006.

34. Funabashi, *The Peninsula Question,* pp. 449–457; Bonnie Glaser, Scott Snyder, and John Park, *Keeping an Eye on an Unruly Neighbor: Chinese Views of Economic Reform and Stability in North Korea* (Washington, DC: US Institute of Peace, 2008), accessed at http://www.usip.org/pubs/working_papers/wp6_china_northkorea.pdf on January 4, 2008.

35. The report claims that Kim requested 30 billion yuan to cover food, energy supplies, foreign currency, and goods, to be chosen according to North Korea's need. Satoshi Tomisaka, ed., *Taikitachosen Chugoku Kimitsu Fairu (China's Secret File on Relations with North Korea)*, in Japanese, September 15, 2007, accessed at http://www.opensource.gov, doc. no. JPP20070919026005.

36. Wang Jianmin, "Story Behind Beijing's Emergency Measures in the Face of the DPRK's Nuclear Test," *Yazhou Zhoukan* (Hong Kong), in Chinese, October 22, 2006, accessed at http://www.opensource.gov, doc. no. CPP200610177100007.

37. Ibid.

38. Hu Mingyuan and Yu Jie, "An Analysis of the North Korean Nuclear Test and China's Countermeasures," *Donbeiya Yanjiu* (Changchun), in Chinese, December 25, 2006, pp. 33–35, accessed at http://www.opensource.gov, doc. no. CPP20070601329001.

39. Shijie Zhishi press forum held on October 24, 2006: "After the DPRK Nuclear Test, What Can the World Do?" *Shijie Zhishi* (Beijing), in Chinese, November 16, 2006, accessed at http://www.opensource.gov, doc. no. CPP20061129455001.

40. Shen Dingli, "United States Uses DPRK Nuclear Test to Gain Initiative," *Huanqiu Shibao* (Beijing), in Chinese, October 24, 2006, accessed at http://www.opensource.gov, doc. no. CPP20061031455001.

41. Zhu Feng, "Sino-U.S. Cooperation Will Have to Surmount Bumpy Road of Korean Nuclear Issue," *Huanqiu Shibao* (Beijing), in Chinese, November 9, 2006, accessed at http://www.opensource.gov, doc. no. CPP20061115455001.

42. Xue Li, "A Comprehensive Strategic Framework for China's Response to the DPRK Nuclear Issue," *Zhongguo Pinglun* (Hong Kong), in Chinese, February 1, 2007, accessed at http://www.opensource.gov, doc. no. CPP20070201309201.

43. Author interviews with Chinese scholars in Beijing, February and April 2006.

44. Ibid., April 2006.

45. Li Kaisheng, "Quantitative Analysis of Chinese Influence over the DPRK Nuclear Issue," *Shijie Yu Zhengzhi* (Beijing), in Chinese, April 14, 2007, accessed at http://www.opensource.gov, doc. no. CPP20070427455001.

46. Hu Mingyua and Yu Jie, "An Analysis of the North Korean Nuclear Test and China's Countermeasures," *Dongbeiya Yanjiu* (Changchun), December 25, 2006, pp. 33–35, accessed at http://www.opensource.gov, doc. no. CPP20070601329001.

47. Li Dunqiu, "China–North Korea: From Friendly Neighboring Countries to Friendly Cooperative Partners," *Shijie Zhishi* (Beijing), in Chinese, November 16, 2005, accessed at http://www.opensource.gov, doc. no. CPP20051129329001.

48. Gordon Fairclough, "China Banks to Halt Dealings with North Korea," *Wall Street Journal,* October 20, 2006, p. 3.

7

The China–
South Korea–United States
Security Triangle

The previous four chapters have explored in detail the practical economic and political challenges of the triangular relationship among China, North Korea, and South Korea that developed as a result of Sino–South Korean diplomatic normalization in 1992. This triangular relationship has presented political challenges for China in simultaneously managing rapidly expanding economic and political relations with Seoul while maintaining an increasingly tense political and one-sided economic relationship with Pyongyang. Though China's interests have increasingly coincided with those of South Korea, strategic considerations have prevented it from completely abandoning its relationship with North Korea. China's relationship with South Korea has benefited from a mutual improvement in economic and political spheres, while its relationship with North Korea has become increasingly strained; its efforts to utilize economic ties to influence North Korea's political choices have achieved limited success. Although China maintains security obligations with North Korea according to its 1961 friendship treaty, in practice the Sino–North Korean alliance relationship is virtually dormant.

Until the normalization of relations between China and South Korea in 1992, following the end of the Cold War, there was no need to consider a China–South Korea–United States triangular relationship. This triangle had not yet emerged in the 1990s, when the focal point for strategic maneuvering remained on China's triangular relationship with the two Koreas. But by the late 1990s, it had become apparent to Chinese leaders that despite the unresolved confrontation on the Korean peninsula, Seoul would become the dominant strategic partner following the end of inter-Korean confrontation; China shifted the focal point of its policy from maintaining formal equidistance in its respective relations with North and South Korea, to ensuring regional stability, and protecting its own stake in that stability, even at the expense of traditional relations with North Korea.

As the Sino–South Korean economic relationship has grown, and as South Korea has sought greater latitude in the context of its security alliance with the United States, a new triangular relationship has developed among China, South Korea, and the United States. This triangle arguably has become increasingly salient in two respects. First, South Korea increasingly depends on China for economic growth, while continuing to depend on the United States to meet its security needs. Second, triangular cooperation has become important in the context of the six-party talks, because it is only when the policies of China, South Korea, and the United States are sufficiently aligned that North Korea loses its freedom to play these three parties against one another.

China's normalization with South Korea, South Korea's emergence as the key variable likely to shape the future direction of the Korean peninsula, and the escalation of the North Korean nuclear crisis have heightened the relevance of the China–South Korea–United States triangular relationship.[1] The triangle has so far existed only to the extent that critical decisions related to the future of the Korean peninsula require the involvement of these three parties—the future direction of the Sino–North Korean relationship and the prospects for the US–South Korean alliance regarding settlement of the North Korean nuclear issue, whether resulting in inter-Korean reconciliation and peaceful coexistence, or unification of the Korean peninsula. Thus far the triangle has not been relevant to consideration of non–North Korea issues. The respective strategies of each of the three countries as they relate to the North Korean nuclear issue have increasingly involved tactical maneuvering to influence North Korea's policy options.

South Korea has not yet had to make a strategic choice between China and the United States, but China's economic influence in South Korea has arguably influenced South Korean attitudes in ways that challenge US–South Korean political and security coordination. For instance, on the day that Lee Myung Bak arrived in Beijing to establish a Sino–South Korean "strategic partnership," the spokesman for the Chinese foreign ministry remarked, "The Korean-U.S. alliance is a historical relic. . . . We should not approach current security issues with military alliances left over from the past Cold War era."[2] How to deal with China is a newly emerging issue in the US–South Korean alliance relationship, especially because the economic and security benefits of the alliance, which had been closely aligned during the Cold War, are now potentially at cross-purposes. During the Cold War, not only was South Korea dependent on the United States for security, but the United States was the primary consumer of South Korean goods. Today, the establishment of a multilateral framework for addressing the North Korean nuclear issue and the economic role of China as South Korea's most important economic partner constitute new developments that may influence the nature and limits of cooperation in South Korea's security relationship with the United States.

Dynamics of the Triangular Relationship

The security triangle concept has been used as an analytical tool for understanding aspects of political rivalry, confrontation, and strategic maneuvering in the international system. Security triangle theories have primarily been developed as vehicles for understanding the dynamics of strategic alignments and formation of coalitions, with the expectation being that coalitions among the weaker members of a triangle will be used as a means to balance against the most powerful member of the triangle. The most actively studied example has been the China–United States–Soviet Union rivalry during the Cold War period. Lowell Dittmer has analyzed three primary variations in relationships among members of strategic triangles: the "ménage à trois," in which the power relationships among all three members of a triangle are roughly equal; the "romantic triangle," consisting of a single "pivot" player and two "wing" players; and the "stable marriage," consisting of a positive relationship between two players and enmity with a third player.[3]

The security triangle concept has been applied to a wide range of cases, and appears to have become more relevant in an Asian context as a vehicle for addressing regional security dilemmas and interactions following the end of the Cold War. Analyses of this sort have included the United States–China–Taiwan triangle, the China–Vietnam–United States triangle, and the United States–Japan–China triangle, the latter of which has been touted as the critical triangular security relationship likely to define prospects for Asian security relations in the future.[4] With partial cross-recognition of Chinese and Russian relations with South Korea at the end of the Cold War, and of the dilemmas accompanying continued tension in US relations with North Korea, there has been a focus on emerging triangles involving the two Koreas and the United States, as well as the two Koreas and China.[5]

There is also the perception that the long-standing stalemate on the Korean peninsula is undergirded by opposition between two security triangles, involving the United States, Japan, and South Korea on the one side, and China, Russia, and North Korea on the other. As part of his emphasis on inter-Korean rapprochement, former South Korean president Kim Dae Jung often emphasized the "dismantling of the Cold War structure" on the Korean peninsula, a phrase that some in Seoul appear to interpret as the breakdown of opposing security triangles focused on the Korean peninsula, or at least the need to take steps to prevent these triangles from hardening to such an extent that the environment would presage a "new Cold War" in Asia.[6]

The China–South Korea–United States security triangle has arguably only become relevant within the past decade, following China's normalization with South Korea and in the context of a South Korean foreign policy (especially toward North Korea) that exhibits greater independence from the US–South Korean security alliance. These developments mark a transition from what Dittmer calls a "stable marriage," in which the United States and South Korea are allies and China remains on the outside of the relationship, to a "romantic triangle," a more dynamic interaction in which "wing" players compete for attention from the "pivot" player. One puzzle is that while the United States may be considered the "pivot" player in aggregate power terms, South Korea, as the weakest actor, is likely to be the independent variable in the triangular relationship, while China might be viewed as the most influential "pivot" player in issue-specific terms, involving questions of how to deal with North Korea, with the United States and South Korea's competing to influence China's position. The ambiguity regarding which party is the "pivot" player in the romantic triangle introduces greater complexity regarding the dynamics of interaction among the three members.

Another complicating factor in the triangular relationship is that South Korea, especially during the Roh Moo Hyun administration, appeared to anticipate a transition by which China would become the strongest power in Asia, replacing the role of the United States and further introducing instability into the interaction among the three players. According to the transactional logic underlying security triangle theory, such a power transition from the United States to China as the leading actor might be accompanied by a corresponding strategic realignment of the position and preferences of the weakest actor South Korea. But leading South Korean analysts, such as Chung Jae Ho of Seoul National University, regard such a strategic realignment as highly unlikely, at least in the near term.[7]

Second, China–South Korea–United States triangular relations have become visible in the tactics of the respective countries in pursuing a satisfactory resolution to the North Korean nuclear crisis. As North Korea seeks room for maneuver as part of the diplomatic process surrounding the six-party talks, a key variable in determining its scope for action is the extent to which the United States, South Korea, and China hold similar views. Where differences among these three parties remain, North Korea seeks opportunities to exploit those differences. At the same time, there are clear security incentives for all the members of the triangle to cooperate with one another to solve a common security threat.

North Korea's scope of action is dependent on the ability of China, South Korea, and the United States to effectively manage long-term strategic anxieties for the sake of pursuing short-term cooperation. The opportunity for and experience of near-term, practical cooperation to address the North Korean nuclear issue might also reduce the likelihood and severity of longer-term strategic mistrust among the key actors in ways that could ameliorate the geostrategic security concerns that constitute the most intractable sources of instability in triangular relations. The imperative of avoiding nuclear proliferation by North Korea, as a "higher" threat to the security of all three countries concerned, would in this case drive triangular cooperation and diminish prospects that strategic rivalries would remain as the core focus of regional relations, at least in the near to middle term.

Third, with greater prospects for inter-Korean reconciliation and peaceful coexistence since the end of the Cold War, external parties have increasingly perceived Seoul as the critical actor in determining the future strategic orientation of the Korean peninsula, while Pyongyang's influence has continued to wane. Regional security relations on the Korean peninsula are no longer a subset of the Cold War, but the security structures that do exist on the peninsula to regulate the possibility of war, including the Military Armistice Commission, the UN Command, and the US–South Korean alliance, remain as defining characteristics of the Korean security environment. What sort of shifts might occur as part of a transition to a fully post–Cold War regional security interaction? An analysis of the China–South Korea–United States triangular interaction may provide some partial answers to that question, although the China–Japan–United States triangle and the future of the South Korean–Japan bilateral relationship are other factors that may also influence the orientation of a South Korea no longer preoccupied by inter-Korean confrontation as its primary security concern. The security triangle concept might be particularly useful in examining possible strategic realignment of South Korea in relation to the United States and China. It is worthwhile to examine whether current developments in that triangle presage any significant adjustments in the China–South Korea–United States relationship and the implications of such adjustments for regional security relations in Northeast Asia.

Relevance of the Strategic Triangle Concept

Frictions in the US–South Korean alliance during the Roh administration highlighted the prospects for change in the nature of triangular relations among China, South Korea, and the United States from that of a "stable marriage" between the United States and South Korea as long-standing alliance partners, to that of a "romantic triangle" among the three players, with South Korea seeking greater scope of action to develop new relations and China seeking to secure its economic and strategic interests through enhanced cooperation with South Korea. The establishment of such a relationship in diplomatic terms is illustrated in the establishment of a "comprehensive cooperative partnership" during former Chinese premier Zhu Rongji's summit meeting with then–South Korean president Kim Dae Jung in Seoul in 2000, and it is notable that even a conservative Lee Myung Bak administration accepted the upgrading of the relationship to the level of a "strategic partnership." While the nature of interaction among the three players appears to approximate that of a "romantic triangle," it is important to recall that the United States and South Korea are still in a "marriage," even if it might not always seem so stable.[8]

One complicating factor in analyzing the China–South Korea–United States relationship is the ambiguity concerning which is the "pivot" and which are the "wing" actors in the "romantic triangle." In aggregate power terms, the United States is the "pivot," and China and South Korea are the "wing" actors, but under current circumstances it is hard to envision a competition between China and South Korea for the attention and protection of a dominant United States. Instead, both countries appear to be alternately skeptical and desirous of the future role and influence of the United States. Within the framework of the US–South Korean alliance, South Korea has sought greater scope for independent action, or "voice" (and has independently pursued an enhanced relationship with China in many areas). However, South Korea has not sought to exit the alliance,[9] while China alternately cooperates with the United States and shows concern that the United States seeks to hem it in strategically and block recovery of its historical role as the regional "center" of East Asia.

In traditional balance-of-power terms, the Korean peninsula has historically held geostrategic importance. Especially since the late nineteenth century, it has been the battleground and object of strategic rivalry among larger neighbors including China, Japan, the Soviet Union, and the United States. Thus, the future orientation of the Korean peninsula remains a matter of interest and concern for both China and Japan, each of which seeks a strategic buffer to enhance its own security. Although the China–Japan–United States triangle has its own dynamics and influence on the Korean peninsula (to be considered in Chapter 8), the US security interest in the context of the China–South Korea–United States triangle is buttressed by US alliances with both Japan and South Korea. It is arguable that there is significant strategic value for the United States (and Japan) to keep South Korea as a traditional component in its strategy of utilizing alliances with Japan and South Korea as a fundamental tool for ensuring stability in Asia. China's strategic stake in the Korean peninsula and its commitment to maintain a friendly buffer state on the peninsula are best illustrated in Mao Zedong's decision to intervene on behalf of North Korea during the Korean War, despite China's own domestic circumstances and unfinished reunification objectives vis-à-vis Taiwan. From this point of view, South Korea, the weakest party, would nonetheless have the deciding influence as the "pivot" player and object of strategic rivalry, while China and the United States would woo South Korea as "wing" players in the "romantic triangle."

In the context of diplomacy surrounding the North Korean nuclear issue, a third pattern is evident in which China is the "pivot" player and the United States and South Korea act as "wing" players. In this circumstance, China is viewed as the external actor likely to have the greatest influence and leverage with the North Korean leadership, and the one who holds the key to resolving the nuclear crisis. In light of the pre–nuclear test divergences in South Korean and US preferences for bringing the North Korean nuclear crisis to a resolution, there has been an element of competition between the United States and South Korea to influence China's positions in managing the crisis in the early rounds of the six-party talks.

As convener and host of the six-party talks, China has taken a position of responsibility in facilitating diplomacy to bring the crisis to resolution, but clearly prefers the crisis to be resolved via negotiation rather than pressure. Chinese views also attribute responsibility for the crisis as much to the United States for failure to overcome mistrust in its relations with North Korea, as to North Korea for pursuing asymmetric methods to ensure its own security. South Korean interests also lie in pursuing a negotiated settlement to the issue that will avoid heightened tensions, instability, or military conflict. Despite the existence of US–South Korean coordination in pursuit of the shared objective of a denuclearized North Korea, South Korean prioritization of maintaining stability on the Korean peninsula regardless of North Korea's nuclear status overlaps with China's preferred priorities. There is a clearly discernible triangular pattern by which China takes the "pivot" position as the convener of the six-party talks and as the party with the greatest apparent leverage over North Korea, while the United States and South Korea compete as "wing" players for China's favor in a "romantic triangle" relationship.

Under current circumstances, another factor for consideration is the existence of a common security problem—North Korea—that can serve as a driver for joint cooperation among all three members of the triangle, and the possibility that the experience of practical cooperation might serve as a foundation for lessening, at least temporarily, the strategic rivalries that otherwise might naturally occur among the three parties. Although the three parties are unequal in terms of power, this type of joint coordination on North Korean issues, to the extent that it might be possible to organize, would conform most closely to the "ménage à trois" relationship, in which China, the United States, and South Korea would work together to achieve the same overriding objective of denuclearizing North Korea. Given the rhetorical support that all the parties have provided for the idea of an eventual cooperative security framework as an endpoint for managing long-term regional security concerns beyond the North Korean nuclear crisis, there is the possibility that such cooperation might serve to abate or ameliorate security competition among states. But such cooperation would only be possible in the context of proper management of the strategic rivalries inherent in the China–South Korea–United States triangular relationship, which could also emerge as primary obstacles to the effective management of the North Korean nuclear issue. Therefore, it is necessary to analyze the interaction of the three parties in the context of recent diplomatic developments in the six-party talks.

Triangular Relations and the North Korean Nuclear Issue

The North Korean nuclear issue has stimulated a mixture of cooperation, competition, and negotiation among all the negotiating parties, including members of the triangle. The common problem of North Korea's nuclear program both complicates the triangular relationship and offers prospects for triangular cooperation. The six-party dialogue for addressing the North Korean nuclear issue serves as the context through which day-to-day interactions of the China–South Korea–United States triangle are being played out. This framework is the primary window through which tactical decisions concerning the North Korean nuclear crisis have been framed. In this context, the strategic aspects of the triangular relationship are accompanied, and perhaps occasionally overshadowed by, a tactical diplomatic dimension: how to respond to specific diplomatic and operational needs as part of the challenge posed by North Korea's ongoing effort to develop nuclear weapons.

In recent years, both unilateral actions by all parties and the triangular interaction among the United States, South Korea, and China have intensified as each party weighs short-term tactical efforts to promote a satisfactory resolution to the North Korean nuclear issue against longer-term national security objectives as they relate to Northeast Asia's future. To understand these interactions, it is necessary to examine each party's response to the North Korean nuclear crisis as they relate to the interests and approaches of the other members of the China–South Korea–United States strategic triangle.

US Strategy Toward North Korea

There have been two distinct phases in US policy toward North Korea during the second North Korean nuclear crisis. During the first phase, which lasted until the North Korean nuclear test, the United States pursued coercive diplomacy toward North Korea while simultaneously pursuing multilateral negotiations. In the second phase, since the North Korean nuclear test, the United States has pursued direct negotiations with North Korea. The Chinese and South Korean responses were shaped by the nature of the US policy approach. Regardless of whether the United States pursued coercion or negotiation, a critical prerequisite for successful implementation of US policy objectives has been cooperation with China and South Korea.

US coercive diplomacy posed special challenges for triangular security relations among China, South Korea, and the United States during the first phase of US policy toward North Korea, not least because such efforts required cooperation from China or South Korea, or both, to be effective. But neither China nor South Korea was comfortable with an approach that emphasized coercion alone, without serious efforts to engage North Korea in negotiation and dialogue. The United States pursued broad coercive diplomacy to counter North Korea's illegal or destabilizing actions, such as drug and cigarette smuggling, counterfeiting, and missile sales, while devoting relatively less energy to promoting an environment for give-and-take negotiations. Although such efforts may have been necessary and justifiable instruments for ensuring that North Korea adhered to international norms, they also contributed to a diplomatic stalemate to the extent that other parties, including South Korea and China, perceived that the United States was more interested in destabilizing North Korea than in pursuing a negotiated solution to the North Korean nuclear crisis. Such efforts initially contributed to skepticism about US intentions among observers in both Beijing and Seoul, while also providing North Korean authorities with a convenient pretext for contributing to the stalemate.

The main thrust of US coercive diplomacy to stem North Korea's illegal activities has involved formation of "coalitions of the willing" in support of practical efforts to halt North Korean missile sales, possible transfer of fissile materials, and drug-smuggling efforts. One instrument through which these efforts have been pursued is the Proliferation Security Initiative, established by President George W. Bush on May 31, 2003, to strengthen interdiction of materials that could be used to support proliferation of weapons of mass destruction.[10] This initiative seeks to build a coalition among partner countries that are willing to actively investigate illegal commercial activities, including possible worldwide transfer of fissile materials and dual-use components that might be used to build an active nuclear program. While neither South Korea nor China has yet formally joined the program, South Korea announced in January 2006 that it was considering participation in the program as an observer.[11] The greatest concern among those in South Korea who are opposed to participation in the initiative is alienation of North Korea.[12] Sanctions constitute another coercive instrument that the United States has used. For example, on September 15, 2005, the US Treasury announced sanctions against eight North Korean companies alleged to have participated in illegal economic activities, and cited the Macao-based Banco Delta Asia as a primary money-launderer that had actively facilitated financing for North Korea's illegal activities, thus requiring cooperation with Chinese authorities in Beijing and Macao to address the concern.[13]

Perhaps the most interesting effect of US financial warnings against Banco Delta Asia in the triangular context is that they capitalized on a growing debate within China over policy toward North Korea. The United States attempted to frame Chinese policy choices toward North Korea in terms of China's own commitments to globalization and global responsibility, China's need for continued regional stability in the context of the existing international system, and China's need to maintain a good relationship with the United States as a necessary precondition for achieving continued peaceful development. One side-effect of the US Treasury's designation of Banco Delta Asia as a money-launderer is that it forced China to make a clear policy choice regarding whether North Korean illegal activities were tolerable and whether North Korean actions should remain beyond international legal norms. For China, the decision of whether to support global financial regulations or instead to shelter possible criminal activities by allowing North Koreans access to the international financial system was not a difficult one to make.

North Korea's nuclear test provided a stark demonstration that the mix of US coercive and diplomatic measures pursued to that point had failed. But the failure to stop North Korea's nuclear test was also a collective one, since the existence of a nuclear North Korea ran counter to the interests of all the country's Northeast Asian neighbors. The immediate response to the nuclear test took the form of UN Security Council Resolution 1718, which condemned the test and recommended stiff international sanctions against North Korea.[14] Enhanced promotion of regional cooperative and collective action was the only option available to the Bush administration. However, the only means to pursue collective action in the aftermath of the nuclear test was through more active negotiation forged through the six-party talks. That approach resulted in the February 13, 2007, statement on initial actions to be taken regarding a prior agreement that had bound North Korea to shut down and disable its core nuclear facilities in return for economic and political benefits from the parties to the agreement, including China and South Korea.

The February 13 statement came about in the context of North Korea's isolation and lack of alternatives, given North Korea's diplomatic isolation. For the first time in the wake of North Korea's nuclear test, all parties were willing to recognize their common strategic interest in maintaining a nonnuclear Korean peninsula and to subordinate lesser (bilateral) interests to a common objective. A major concession in the wake of the nuclear test was the willingness of the United States to engage in bilateral dialogue with North Korea on steps toward normalization of relations in return for denuclearization. But these steps, too, could only succeed through collective coordination and action. To the extent that the US–North Korean bilateral negotiations were not coordinated with other parties, such as China, South Korea, and Japan, there was risk that North Korea could exploit any differences among those parties. Achieving the shared objective of denuclearizing the Korean peninsula will depend on whether or not all parties hold firm to policies that place all collective interests, including normalization, economic development, and peace, above perceived bilateral strategic interests vis-à-vis other parties in the region.[15]

Chinese Strategy Toward North Korea

The Chinese diplomatic strategy toward the Korean peninsula has utilized co-optation and persuasion alongside pursuit of negotiations through the six-party talks, with inducements' playing the primary attractive role in China's approach toward North Korea. China's high-level diplomacy with North Korea underscores its fundamental interest in stability, while recognizing that stability may not be sustainable in the absence of Chinese-style reforms. But the North Korean nuclear test caused a shift in Chinese views, toward willingness to publicly condemn as well as coerce North Korea. China went along with a stronger-than-anticipated UN Security Council resolution condemning the nuclear test and began using sticks in dealing with North Korea, mainly in the form of withholding cooperation above and beyond items that are necessary to ensure North Korea's stability.

The primary objective of China's efforts to promote stability and encourage Chinese-style economic reforms in North Korea is to enhance its leverage. The Chinese leadership believes that stability and reform are necessarily linked. While China is rumored to have demanded that Kim Jong Il halt North Korea's illicit activities, it simultaneously enhanced its financial assistance to North Korea through a variety of channels. Some sources report Chinese pledges of assistance to North Korea of as much as US$2 billion per year, a figure indirectly confirmed by Chinese researchers who note that China's annual assistance to North Korea is higher than the annual bilateral trade volume (over US$1.6 billion in 2005) of the two countries.[16]

Enhanced US-Chinese cooperation and the resulting increase in China's leverage over North Korea have also had the side-effect of inducing strategic anxieties in South Korea over the possibility that China could use its leverage to obstruct Korean reunification or impinge on what many South Koreans see as their sphere of influence on the Korean peninsula. One potential result of such a development would be to stimulate South Korean competition vis-à-vis China to promote economic ties and enhance leverage and influence in North Korea. The creation of a competitive development assistance pattern in China's and South Korea's respective policies toward North Korea would ultimately not serve US interests if such assistance were to allow North Korea sufficient flexibility and freedom to avoid or delay denuclearization.

Although South Korea has recently become unnerved by China's increased economic leverage over North Korea outside the six-party talks, China's overall diplomatic objectives during the second North Korean nuclear crisis have overlapped considerably with those of South Korea, including an emphasis on peaceful resolution of the crisis, gradual change, maintaining stability in North Korea regardless of nonproliferation, and encouragement of reform. China has played a relatively passive role within the six-party dialogue, preferring to allow South Korea to make the direct case to North Korea and preferring to essentially allow South Korea to set the "lowest common denominator" among the parties regarding the necessity of North Korea's denuclearization. This strategy has several residual benefits for China: it avoids direct confrontation with North Korea in the multilateral context; it preserves the perception that China is an even-handed or "neutral" convener; and it allows space for South Korea to play an important role as a broker between the United States and North Korea in addition to China's mediating roles as the convener of the six-party talks.

Overall, Chinese analysts are aware of difficulties in the US–South Korean alliance and the contested nature of that alliance in South Korea's domestic politics.[17] Some Chinese analysts may have concluded that a passive stance toward security on the peninsula is sufficient for China to achieve its own strategic objectives, in that a nationalist reunified Korea would likely rid itself of the US–South Korean security alliance and could eventually be restored to its traditional place in the Chinese economic and political sphere. The rapid growth in bilateral Sino–South Korean economic relations in recent years serves to buttress such a view. The Chinese leadership has tried to cultivate a positive bilateral relationship with South Korea, but cites possible economic conflicts, historical and territorial issues, and the US–South Korean alliance as three factors that restrain the potential development of the Sino–South Korean relationship. It has become standard practice for China to characterize the concept of alliance as a legacy of the Cold War, and to underscore the need to abandon alliance thinking in favor of cooperative multilateralism as a more suitable model for preserving cooperation among states in the future.[18]

The election of Lee Myung Bak and his desire to revitalize the

US–South Korean "strategic alliance for the twenty-first century" may have come as a surprise to some in China who had seen South Korea as low-hanging fruit ripened by Sino–South Korean trade. However, anxieties in the context of China's continuing economic rise already suggest the likelihood that South Korea will pursue a hedging strategy that involves strengthening both its political and its economic relations with the United States, through a revitalized security alliance and a free trade agreement, respectively.[19]

South Korean Strategy Toward North Korea

South Korea has sought to deal with the simultaneous effects on North Korea of US coercion and then diplomacy, and Chinese co-optation, by stepping up its own independent bilateral engagement. The objective of this strategy is to preserve South Korea's maneuverability and expand its scope of action and influence toward North Korea. Under Roh Moo Hyun, South Korea sought to expand its influence within the six-party dialogue by seeking a role as an "independent" broker or mediator between the United States and North Korea. South Korea has also been motivated by a sense of competition and fear that China will become an overly dominant influence in North Korea, possibly denying Korean unification or taking advantage of North Korea's weakness to extract resources regarded as "Korean" in the South.

Any effort by South Korea to ease strategic tensions independent of the US–South Korean alliance requires North Korea's cooperation. Dissatisfied with US attempts to squeeze North Korea and distrustful of China's expanded economic influence as part of its efforts to stabilize and promote reforms in North Korea, South Korea has been eager to promote inter-Korean cooperation in pursuit of a dual hedging strategy in reaction against the policies of both China and the United States. Resentful of US coercive diplomacy and discomfited by North Korea's overdependence on China to meet its economic needs, South Korea has sought to promote the Kaesong economic zone as an opportunity for inter-Korean cooperation under the mantra of teaching economic skills and promoting North Korean reform. However, the failure on the part of South Korea to insist on critical market efficiencies as part of the Kaesong project belies South Korea's fundamental desire to enhance its leverage with North Korea, and by so doing expand its freedom of action vis-à-vis both China and the United States. South Korea's need to enhance the relative importance of inter-Korean economic relations in order to demonstrate political relevance and independence of action from both the United States and China runs counter to US and Chinese interests, ironically making South Korea the odd man out in the China–South Korea–United States triangle that surrounds North Korea. These motives explain continuing South Korean efforts, despite the ongoing threat from the North Korean nuclear crisis, to expand inter-Korean economic exchanges through the Mount Kumgang project, the Kaesong economic zone, and the inter-Korean railway project. But South Korea has also been frustrated by the slow pace of efforts to expand inter-Korean economic relations, especially in view of the perceived expansion of Chinese dominance in North Korea. For instance, the inter-Korean economic agreements in July 2005 included a pledge to cooperate in the area of natural resource development, but there has been no progress in the ensuing months, despite reports of China's apparent progress in pursuing several joint mining ventures. South Korea has big plans to expand the Kaesong project, but this project is limited to a single area of North Korea, while Chinese firms appear to operate on preferential terms throughout the rest of the country. Moreover, difficult inter-Korean negotiations have led South Koreans to make numerous concessions to North Korean counterparts that in part undermine the viability of Kaesong as a model for promoting market-based economic reforms in North Korea. The infrastructure of Kaesong is primarily "made in South Korea," and the economic zone itself lies in North Korean territory, but is an extension of South Korea's economy. North Koreans have been reluctant to provide the numbers of workers necessary to fuel expansion, while the South Korean government has provided all the infrastructure and guarantees to South Korean companies that might normally be provided by a host government in an overseas special economic zone. North Korean workers themselves may receive a healthy South Korean–made lunch, but their salaries are still paid from Hyundai Asan to the North Korean government, not to the workers themselves. South Korean government guarantees to South Korean companies within the zone have mitigated the risks of failure, since corporate debts due to economic failure are absorbed by the South Korean government's inter-Korean economic cooperation fund. Many of these concessions on the part of the South Korean government are a reflection of South Korean anxieties about being left out of the North Korean game, and they are exacerbated by discomfort over the direction of US and Chinese policies.[20]

The dilemma for South Korea is how to assert itself as a "pivot" player while China and the United States, as larger players, mete out a mixture of confrontation and cooperation. While the second inter-

Korean summit, in October 2007, emphasized surprisingly detailed areas for cooperation that represented a potential advance toward reconciliation and economic integration, many of these economic projects were motivated by South Korean concerns regarding China's dominant economic influence in the North, a factor that Kim Jong Il no doubt also sought to use to his advantage in an attempt to diminish the level of North Korea's economic dependence on China. The October 4, 2007, joint statement between the two Koreas also contained language that was annoying to China regarding whether "three" or "four" parties would be involved in negotiation of peace arrangements. Although there are differences in point of view regarding which of the "three parties" North Korea might consider to be legitimate participants in such discussions, the wording of the declaration set off alarms among Chinese analysts, who expressed concern that the two Koreas might be seeking to exclude China from such talks.[21] Even if a conservative Lee Myung Bak administration brings South Korea's policies toward the North more in line with those of the United States, there will still be substantial pressures within South Korea to pursue a blended approach that attempts to pivot in response to China and the United States and to maximize South Korea's independent influence on the North.

Alliance Reaffirmation, Separation, or Stable Tripartite Cooperation?

Aside from short-term positioning over how to deal with North Korea, the China–South Korea–United States triangular relationship may play an important role in influencing regional relations in Northeast Asia. The levels of competition and cooperation within the triangular relationship will also be key factors in determining the extent to which regional relations are driven by rivalry or characterized by mutual "win-win" collaboration. China's economic rise and South Korea's likely critical role in shaping the future orientation of foreign policy on the Korean peninsula are new factors that may also influence the effectiveness and longevity of the US–South Korean security alliance. The days of a "stable marriage" between the United States and South Korea to the exclusion of or in opposition to China have certainly passed, but the nature and level of competition among the three parties are yet to be determined. At this stage, the coexistence of the security alliance with the United States and enhanced economic and political cooperation with China works well for South Korea; to the extent that strategic choices can be avoided—for instance, in the context of a relatively harmonious US-Chinese relationship—this is the best scenario for South Korea. One option for South Korea would be to switch allegiances within the triangle by enhancing cooperation with China to pursue a truly "regional solution"—a settlement of the nuclear issue between North Korea and its neighbors independent of the United States. Despite highly complementary Chinese and South Korean views on the North Korean nuclear crisis, North Korea's focus on bilateral talks with the United States makes such an approach unlikely to succeed. North Korea's consistent approach for the past decade has been to link willingness to abandon its nuclear development efforts to normalization of diplomatic relations with the United States, something that only the United States can provide. Sino–South Korean coordination to balance against the United States would promote a settlement at the expense of the US–South Korean alliance and appears to be a relatively risky strategy for South Korea at this stage. As long as South Korea remains in an alliance "marriage" with the United States, no matter how active the "romantic triangle," the penalty for infidelity could remain quite severe for South Korea, but less severe for the United States.

Progress toward addressing the North Korean nuclear issue will also raise questions for members of the six-party talks about how a resolution of the problem might influence the respective longer-term strategic objectives of each party in the region. How would this process influence the strategic orientation of the Korean peninsula? Would a reunified Korea be possible, and if so, would it be more likely to "tilt" toward China, the United States, or Japan, or be neutral? Although the North Korean nuclear issue is far from being settled, it has become clear that geostrategic interests of neighbors to the Korean peninsula are likely to be influenced by the shape of any resolution of the nuclear issue. As the concerned parties attempt to address the North Korean nuclear issue, they are increasingly influenced by the question of how longer-term geostrategic interests that might surface in the process will affect their relative influence on a Korean peninsula no longer beset by confrontation. However, despite the increasing relevance of geostrategic concerns, the process of moving toward resolution of the North Korean nuclear issue demands increasing cooperation and consensus, especially among the United States, China, and South Korea, as a prerequisite for moving forward in negotiations with North Korea.

To the extent that cooperation among concerned parties is possible, North Korea will be more constrained in its available options and more likely to find that the only way out is a path of cooperation. However, to the extent that strategic differences among those parties remain, North Korea would have more room to maneuver and be more likely to avoid the most onerous demands of its neighbors as part of a resolution of the nuclear issue. Given the impact of solidarity among the six parties on North Korea's possible room for diplomatic maneuver, the relative positions and interests of the neighboring parties have become a critical factor in determining prospects for a negotiated settlement of the nuclear issue. The primary tactical maneuvering in this respect lies with the China–South Korea–United States strategic triangle, with marginal contributing roles for Japan and Russia.

The most desirable scenario both for South Korea and for a resolution of the North Korean nuclear issue would be for South Korea, China, and the United States to reach a comprehensive consensus on the priorities for North Korea's denuclearization and the means by which these objectives would be accomplished. This would involve mutual efforts by the three parties to reach a full consensus on the mixture of coercion and incentives that should be used and on the steps that North Korea must take to resolve the crisis. Within the China–South Korea–United States strategic triangle, achieving this level of coordination would be like opening a combination lock; only when all three positions are aligned perfectly would it be possible to expect progress or to ensure a satisfactory response from North Korea.

Notes

1. Chung Jae Ho has analyzed the prospects for South Korea's strategic realignment in light of the importance that Seoul has given to cooperation with China in recent years. See Chung Jae Ho, "China's Ascendancy and the Korean Peninsula: From Interest Reevaluation to Strategic Realignment?" in David Shambaugh, ed., *Power Shift: China and Asia's New Dynamics* (Berkeley: University of California Press, 2005), pp. 151–169.

2. Michael Ha, "Chinese Official Calls Korea-U.S. Alliance 'Historical Relic,'" *Korea Times,* May 28, 2008.

3. See Lowell Dittmer, "The Strategic Triangle: An Elementary Game-Theoretical Analysis," *World Politics* 33, no. 4 (July 1981): 485–515.

4. For a literature review on the concept and utility of strategic triangles, see Seungji Woo, "Triangle Research and Understanding Northeast Asian Politics," *Asian Perspective* 27, no. 2 (2003): 33–63. A sampling of regional analyses that make use of the security triangle concept include Andrew J. Nathan and Robert R. Ross, *Great Wall and Empty Fortress: China's Search for Security* (New York: Norton, 1997); Xiaobing Li, Xiaobo Hu, and Yang Zhong, eds., *Interpreting U.S.-China-Taiwan Relations: China in the Post–Cold War*

Era (New York: University Press of America, 1998); John W. Garver, "Sino-Vietnamese Conflict and the Sino-American Rapprochement," *Political Science Quarterly* 96, no. 3 (Fall 1981): 445–446; Thomas J. Christensen, "China, the U.S.-Japan Alliance, and the Security Dilemma in East Asia," *International Security* 23, no. 4 (Spring 1999): 49–80.

5. Hong Liu, "Sino–South Korean Normalization: A Triangular Explanation," *Asian Survey* (April 1993): 1083–1094.

6. "Roh Hints at New East Asian Order," *Chosun Ilbo,* March 23, 2005, accessed at http://www.opensource.gov, doc. no. KPP20050322000143.

7. See Chung, "China's Ascendancy and the Korean Peninsula."

8. See ibid.

9. Ibid.

10. US Department of State, "Multinational Proliferation Security Initiative Now Two Years Old," May 25, 2005, accessed at http://usinfo.state.gov/xarchives/display.html?p=washfile-english&y=2005m:may&x=20050527144216sjhtrop0.420849&t:xarchives/xarchitem.html on February 21, 2006.

11. Park Song-wu, "South Korea to Observe PSI Exercise," *Korea Times,* January 25, 2006.

12. Kwon Hyok-bom, "The ROK Government's De Facto Surrender to U.S. Pressure," *Hanguk Ilbo,* in Korean, January 25, 2006, accessed at http://www.opensource.gov, doc. no. KPP20060125033003).

13. US Department of Treasury, "Treasury Designates Banco Delta Asia As Primary Money Laundering Concern Under USA PATRIOT Act," press release, September 15, 2005, accessed at http://ustreas.gov/press/releases/js2720.htm on February 21, 2006.

14. UN Security Council S/RES/1718 (1718), October 14, 2006, accessed at http://daccessdds.un.org/doc/undoc/gen/n06/572/07/pdf/n0657207.pdf?openelement on May 22, 2007.

15. See Scott Snyder, "Responses to North Korea's Nuclear Test: Capitulation or Collective Action?" *Washington Quarterly* 30, no. 4 (Autumn 2007): 33–43.

16. Author conversations with Chinese researchers in Beijing, February 2006; "Trade Between North Korea and China Hits Record High in 2005," *Yonhap News Agency,* February 5, 2006; International Crisis Group, "China and North Korea: Comrades Forever?" *Asia Report* no. 112 (February 1, 2006): 1–30.

17. Author conversation with Chinese scholar in Beijing, February 2006.

18. For instance, see Tang Shiping, "China and Korea in East Asia: Possibility for Collective Actions?" paper presented to the Korean Association of International Studies conference "China and Korea in the 21st Century," Seoul, August 23–24, 2002. See also Liu Jiangyong, "Creating a Peace Regime in Northeast Asia," presentation at Hankyoreh-Busan International Symposium "After 2007 Inter-Korean Summit: The Role of Two Koreas for Peace in Northeast Asia," November 13–15, 2007, pp. 223–240.

19. Scott Snyder, "Lee Myung Bak Era: Mixed Picture for China

Relations," in Brad Glosserman and Carl Baker, eds., *Comparative Connections* 10, no. 1 (April 2008): 99–107.

20. For more analysis of South Korea's strategic choices, see Scott Snyder, "South Korea's Squeeze Play," *Washington Quarterly* 28, no. 4 (Autumn 2005): 93–106.

21. Author conversation with scholars in Beijing, October 2007.

8

The Korean Peninsula and Sino-Japanese Rivalry

The Korean peninsula has been an object of past competition for influence and control between China and Japan. Not only did China and Japan historically play critical roles in influencing Korea's internal rivalries for power at various stages in the peninsula's dynastic history, but intensifying Sino-Japanese rivalry over Korea also coincided with the modern concept of the nation-state in East Asia, a set of developments that ultimately led to the loss of Korea's nationhood. The adoption by Korea of its first international treaty signifying a formal relationship between modern nation-states in 1876, a treaty of amity and cooperation with Japan, marked the initial phase of rising tensions between China and Japan over the Korean peninsula. By coaxing Korea into a treaty that introduced modern nation-state diplomacy, Japan both challenged Korea's tributary role and, by extension, China's dominance on the peninsula. At the time, China's leading foreign policy thinker, Li Hung Chang, considered whether to annex the Korean peninsula in response to Japanese maneuvers. An ongoing competition for influence over the Korean peninsula between China and Japan led to military conflict in the mid-1890s, and the eventual annexation of Korea by Japan in 1910.

Although over a century has passed since the Sino-Japanese war of 1894–1895, memories of the lost nationhood that resulted from this earlier period of confrontation between China and Japan are fresh enough for South Koreans to be distinctly uncomfortable with the reemergence of contemporary Sino-Japanese rivalry. Likewise, China's increasing economic influence on the Korean peninsula is a development that has not gone unnoticed in Japan. The idea of a unified Korean peninsula under the control of Japan is a matter of concern among regional and Korean peninsula specialists in Tokyo.[1]

This chapter reviews contending responses in South Korea to the prospect of renewed rivalry between China and Japan, with special reference to the implications of China's rising economic influence on the Korean peninsula for Japan's security and for the US-Japanese security alliance. First, the chapter recaps the recent rise in tensions between China and Japan, and South Korea's responses. The range of Korean responses provides useful background for measuring the extent to which China's economic and political influence on the Korean peninsula poses challenges for Japan and for security cooperation with South Korea in the context of the US-Japanese security alliance. This chapter also examines how changes on the Korean peninsula might stimulate or mitigate Sino-Japanese rivalry, depending on future developments. South Koreans cannot ignore the prospect of heightened Sino-Japanese rivalry that might derive from inter-Korean reconciliation. Successful steps toward inter-Korean reconciliation and eventual reunification will require development and implementation of a strategy that simultaneously manages adjustments in the inter-Korean relationship while also managing Chinese, Japanese, and other external interests in the Korean peninsula as a strategic buffer to mitigate fundamental security dilemmas in Sino-Japanese relations that might be exacerbated by any change in the status quo on the peninsula.

Historical Korean Responses to Rising Sino-Japanese Tensions

The South Korean government has had a quasi-alliance relationship with Japan by virtue of the fact that both South Korea and Japan are allies with the United States.[2] South Korea is tied to Japan in the security sphere given Japan's role as a rear base through which US forces would flow in order to ensure security in the event of a threat to South Korea from the North. However, South Korea's views on Japan's management of historical issues have always been more complementary with those of China. Following South Korea's normalization of diplomatic relations with China in 1992, the height of commonality in Sino–South Korean views regarding Japan's handling of history-related issues came at the time of Chinese president Jiang Zemin's first visit to Seoul, for meetings with South Korean president Kim Young Sam, in November 1995, at which time both leaders criticized Japan for failing to more directly acknowledge and apologize for its imperialist legacy.[3]

Despite such a clear expression of complementary views on Japan's unwillingness to sufficiently acknowledge its historical mistakes, Chinese and South Korean diplomatic paths diverged in the fall of 1998 as a result of a change in South Korea's policy under newly elected president Kim Dae Jung, whose new policies toward Japan enabled a historic breakthrough in South Korean–Japanese relations. During Kim Dae Jung's September 1998 visit to Tokyo for a summit with Prime Minister Keizo Obuchi, the two leaders agreed to put their historical differences behind them in favor of future-oriented relations, creating the basis for a less antagonistic and more cooperative diplomatic relationship. Kim Dae Jung also allowed a gradual lifting of domestic restrictions on Japanese cultural products in the Korean peninsula in return for a more forward-leaning formal acknowledgment and written statement by Obuchi expressing regret for the unfortunate historical entanglements of the past.

When Jiang Zemin visited Japan in November 1998 (a visit that had unfortunately been postponed from August due to severe flooding in China), he was unable to procure a similar statement of regret from Obuchi or to give up the rhetorical club of demands for an apology that China had used for diplomatic purposes in the past. This diplomatic failure frustrated President Jiang, who gave several harsh public speeches in Japan during his trip, adding to the negativity surrounding the Sino-Japanese relationship and putting Korean-Japanese relations and Chinese-Japanese relations on different diplomatic tracks.

The divergence in South Korean and Chinese approaches to Japan over historical issues began with the different treatment that Jiang and Kim received in 1998, but there have been other structural factors that contributed to differences in Japan's handling of China and South Korea. Most important is the fact that both Japan and South Korea are allies of the United States. In addition, the effects of South Korean democratization, its stage of development as a fellow Organization for Economic Cooperation and Development country, greater self-assurance vis-à-vis Japan, positive experience in cultural and sports exchanges (including the cohosting of the 2002 World Cup), and most importantly, the extensive two-way grassroots exchanges and cultural cross-fertilization over the course of the past two decades, are important factors that have mitigated political conflict in the Japanese–South Korean relationship.

On the other hand, Chinese public sentiment toward Japan has remained overwhelmingly negative, and that sentiment has been subject to manipulation by Chinese authorities through controlled messages delivered via the Chinese educational curriculum and media. In addition, the experience of Chinese students in Japan has generally not been very positive, as these students have been blamed for a rising crime rate. Meanwhile, some ugly incidents involving untoward Japanese behavior in China, including a mass orgy and Japanese expressions of disrespect for China, have drawn widespread negative public attention in China. Other negative factors that have influenced Japanese public sentiment include poor Chinese sportsmanship at a soccer match between China and Japan in August 2004 and Chinese street demonstrations and damage to the Japanese embassy in April 2005 in protest of Japanese textbooks and Prime Minister Koizumi's continued visits to the Yasukuni shrine.

Despite these structural differences that have led to divergences in the Sino-Japanese and South Korean–Japanese political relationships, Japan's handling of events since early 2005 has served to alienate South Korea and to stimulate shared reactions from Chinese and South Koreans over historical issues. Prime Minister Koizumi's visits to the Yasukuni shrine, the reemergence of the history textbook issue, and provocative statements by Japanese foreign minister Taro Aso have provoked similar reactions from both China and South Korea, including the refusal of both South Korean and Chinese leaders to participate in bilateral summit meetings with Prime Minister Koizumi since Koizumi's visit to Yasukuni in October 2005. (There is an additional dispute, between South Korea and Japan but not involving China, that flared up simultaneously to the history-related issues in March 2005: the territorial dispute over the disposition of Tokdo/Takeshima island.) Despite rapidly growing economic interdependence with China, South Korea has not shown an interest in directly collaborating with China on this set of issues, despite the similarities in the responses of the two countries.

South Korea's Dilemma: Preservation of Its Pivotal Role Between China and Japan

As tensions between China and Japan arose in early 2005, South Korean president Roh Moo Hyun gave a speech at a military graduation in March of that year that referred to the idea of South Korea as a "balancer" in Asia.[4] This statement was widely interpreted as an attempt to weaken the US–South Korea alliance or as an attempt to move closer to China. (Shortly following President Roh's speech, the South Korean defense minister returned from Beijing with an announcement that South Korea would bring its military exchanges with China up to the same level as its military exchanges with Japan.)[5] However, Roh's original statement dealt specifically with how a regional dispute between its larger neighbors, China and Japan, might affect South Korea, and an assumption that South Korea needed to take preventive measures at its disposal to avoid such a scenario.

Given South Korea's alliance relationship with the United States— and by extension South Korea's quasi-alliance relationship with Japan— such an equidistant or "even-handed" approach clearly has implications for the US–South Korea alliance. In fact, the misunderstandings that resulted from Roh's statement resulted both in strenuous criticism of the new concept and in a major effort by the Roh administration to clarify to the Korean public and the US government the implications of the statement for the US–South Korean alliance. Although the controversy appears to have been inadvertent, Roh's balancing statements created an additional area of sensitivity in an already strained alliance relationship. The controversy also reveals the extent to which it is difficult for South Koreans to consider responses to emerging Sino-Japanese rivalry without considering the role of the United States.

Roh's original statement hinted that South Korea should take diplomatic initiatives to prevent rising tensions in Sino-Japanese relations, or at least to seek ways to remain neutral amid such rising tensions. Several weeks following the speech, the South Korean National Security Council issued a lengthy explanatory document stating, "The theory on the balancer in Northeast Asia has been put forth with the understanding of the issue that geopolitically, the Korean peninsula, China and Japan form predestined partnerships, and that [we must] squarely look at the reality in which they can always become the concerned parties of a potential conflict in the future because of this [geopolitical factor], and that it is necessary to establish a strategy to prevent it."[6]

The National Security Council document further laid out several principles that reveal its thinking about South Korea's role vis-à-vis larger regional powers, including (1) that South Korea is a "major actor, not a subordinate variable" in Asia, (2) that South Korea can be trusted in the region since it has no history of hegemonism, (3) that, as a "balancer for peace," South Korea can play the roles of mediator, harmonizer, facilitator, and initiator, and (4) that, through "hard power plus soft power," South Korea can maintain existing alliances while also promoting establishment of regional cooperative security institutions.[7] The former chairman of the South Korean Presidential Committee on Northeast Asian Cooperation, Moon Chung-in, stated in an opinion column that "the essence of the idea of a balancer role is to mediate the chronic feuds and dissonance that have plagued this region through open diplomacy, and to establish there a new order of cooperation and integration."[8] The "balancer" theory is based on a sense of Korean nationalism that recognizes itself as an actor, no longer as an object, and attempts to utilize promotion of regional cooperation as the vehicle by which to serve national interests.[9]

The rise in Sino-Japanese tensions along with Roh's "balancer" theory stimulated a wide range of reactions among the Korean public. Some opposition critics immediately interpreted the "balancer" theory as an attempt to move away from the US–South Korean alliance and closer to China. The first response, led primarily by opposition conservatives, was to call for continued reliance on the alliance with the United States as the key to balancing and stabilizing incipient Sino-Japanese rivalry. A *JoongAng Ilbo* editorial expressed the critique as follows: "The notion of being a regional balancer is unrealistic, given our current military capabilities. That is why we have been putting so much emphasis on the alliance with the United States."[10] Others lamented tensions in the US–South Korean security relationship and used the "balancer" theory as an opportunity to blame President Roh for a weakened relationship with the United States.

Even former president Kim Dae Jung provided an indirect critique of Roh's "balancer" theory in a meeting with Uri Party leaders, advising that South Korean diplomatic relations would be most successful if they attempted to maintain a strong South Korea–US alliance, a tripartite alliance with Japan, and cooperation with the region's four great powers. He argued that these structural constraints were permanent features of South Korea's security environment that South Koreans had to "accept fatalistically [as] destiny."[11]

A second response, also considered within the context of a continuing US–South Korean alliance relationship, emphasized the pursuit of neutrality as a means to avoid possible negative effects of Sino-Japanese tensions. This perspective was expressed by Kim Soung-chul of the Sejong Institute: "Open neutrality means that we show balanced diplomacy to all countries. This goes for the South Korea–US alliance, and also for our relationships with China and Japan. Strengthening our alliance with the United States and having a neutral diplomatic strategy are not contradictory to each other. In that respect, Korea maintaining an alliance with the United States while refusing to participate in any Northeast Asian disputes is an example of proclaiming diplomatic neutrality."[12]

A third response, advocated by the progressive newspaper *Hangyore,* was to express emotional nationalism, take the moral high ground, and continue to build international pressure on Japan to step back from destabilizing behavior and come to terms with its historical legacy: "There is now only one approach left to take. If Japan is not going to wake up to its own shame, then it should be made to do so by being thoroughly shamed in the international community."[13]

The theory and the various responses illustrate the range of plausible options that South Koreans see for handling the rise of Sino-Japanese rivalry. The "balancer" theory combines self-confidence based on nationalism, with a desire to promote greater regionalism, as a way of managing Sino-Japanese tensions. A second approach attempts to draw in the United States as an actor that has the capacity to restrain Japan and keep China in check, so as to maintain regional stability, while minimizing South Korean exposure and limiting risks by maintaining neutrality in the dispute. A third approach utilizes emotional nationalism to mobilize a response to Japan in an all-out effort—possibly in combination with China—to reject Japan's "immoral" actions.

It is interesting that despite the growth of Sino–South Korean economic relations, issues related to South Korea's economic dependence on China did not arise at this time as part of the discussion of how South Korea should position itself vis-à-vis China and Japan. There were no political arguments in South Korea suggesting that China would side with South Korea, nor was there even serious consideration of the option that Kim Young Sam had chosen a decade earlier, when the Sino–South Korean economic relationship was less developed. This situation illustrates the extent to which the Sino–South Korean economic relationship has grown without consideration for regional politics. Likewise, in the context of rising Sino-Japanese tension in 2005, China did not attempt to leverage its relationship with South Korea, either through offering economic inducements to South Korean companies that might have otherwise gone to Japanese firms in China, or through withholding economic benefits in order to influence South Korea to join with China against Japan.

Avoiding Regional Polarization: Can South Korea Stop a "New Cold War" in Asia?

Another theme of South Korean concern related to the rise of Sino-Japanese rivalry has been the rise of tensions involving the United States and Japan on one side, and China, Russia, and North Korea on the other, which could lead to renewed regional tensions and ruin the atmosphere and prospects for improved relations with North Korea. Given the incomplete nature of the inter-Korean reconciliation process and its prioritization as part of South Korean national policy objectives, the idea of a "new Cold War" in Asia is a highly negative scenario that has been greeted with anxiety in South Korea.[14] Derivative of this set of concerns, South Korea has shown great sensitivity to the upgrading of cooperation within the US-Japanese alliance as well as to the issue of "strategic flexibility," which would allow US forces in South Korea to deploy for regional stability missions off the peninsula.

Although the South Korean National Security Council worked hard to justify Roh's "balancer" theory as not being directed at weakening the US–South Korean alliance, the justification shows a strong belief that South Korea's national interests are most effectively pursued through a policy stance that assumes greater independent action, with less regard for the United States. President Roh clearly desires to maintain good relations with the United States, but he has expressed concern about how South Korea can assert itself within the context of the alliance to take a more independent role where the national interest might demand it, or how South Korea can mitigate the perceived negative effects of US policy trends on the Korean peninsula. In an interview with a progressive website, Roh stated,

> One of the biggest pending issues for both the ROK and the United States is ultimately the strategic planning for Northeast Asia. If the strategic planning for Northeast Asia is based on the premise of a confrontational order, in short, if the United States regards a future confrontational front between the United States and Japan and China and Russia as a premise and manages its strategy accordingly, tension will always prevail in Northeast Asia and an unfortunate incident could take place under some circumstances. . . . We cannot play a balancing role in this if we unilaterally rely on the United States. We can play a positive role in formulating the order in Northeast Asia only when we have relative independence from the United States. Another important point in this process is that such a strategy cannot work properly unless the people also share the same perception.[15]

To the extent that a strengthened US-Japanese alliance appears designed to balance China or may heighten Chinese anxieties about US policy, Roh perceives such developments as having negative implications for South Korea. This statement clearly reveals Roh's discomfort with South Korea's position in relation with the United States and Japan, a point of controversy that has also invited opposition criticism. For instance, Yonsei professor Kim Woosang has argued that, "by stating that Korea will no longer be confined to the 'southern tripartite alliance,' it has effectively downgraded the significance of the Korea-U.S. relationship."[16]

At the same time, there is no indication in Roh Moo Hyun's statement that moving closer to China would be in South Korea's interest, despite the fact that China had become South Korea's largest trade partner. Instead, Roh's vision is of a South Korea capable of independently managing its own security relations and not caught up in alliance partnerships that might enhance the security dilemmas of others. Roh's statement attempts to transcend security dilemmas by focusing on cooperation as a vehicle that could secure South Korea's independence and give it an equal seat at the table with Northeast Asian neighbors.

Balancing Against China: US–Japanese–South Korean Trilateral Coordination

The Roh administration is wary of the idea of a trilateral US–Japanese–South Korean regional alliance in the context of the tense South Korean–Japanese bilateral relationship, despite the fact that both South Korea and Japan are democracies, that both share alliance relations with the United States, and that the United States has persuaded Japan and South Korea separately to sign up to similar rhetorical templates that envisage joint cooperation in promoting democratic values and human rights, and to view their respective alliances as tools for promoting global stability.[17]

Some of the progress that the United States has facilitated in Japanese–South Korean defense cooperation over the past decade has been set aside with the return of Japanese-South Korean tensions over historical issues. These tensions have also inhibited additional three-way cooperation over common security issues. For instance, the trilateral coordination meetings on North Korea that had once taken place among the United States, South Korea, and Japan have fallen by the wayside partly due to these frictions. Although a trilateral consultation meeting took place in early April 2006 under the cover of a track-two academic gathering held in Tokyo, the fact that cover was necessary illustrates the level of sensitivity that has developed in Seoul concerning such trilateral coordination.[18]

South Korean defense planners have become increasingly uncomfortable with Japan's expanded role, but have been reticent to express that discomfort to the United States as the beneficiary of a more robust level of cooperation and assistance from Japan.[19] Because of a recognition that the United States welcomed Japan's enhanced contributions to the Iraq War, South Korean planners had little opportunity or recourse to express such concerns or to make this issue a subject of broader public debate, as such an issue would only add to an already troubled political relationship between the United States and South Korea. The outbreak of tensions over Tokdo/Takeshima, Japan's textbook revision, and Koizumi's continued visits to Yasukuni finally led top South Korean political leaders to blow off emotional steam about these issues in ways that generally engendered surprise, dismay, and further doubts about South Korea's reliability as an ally among US counterparts.[20]

The idea of an enhanced strategic posture for Japan as part of a broader US security strategy has been greeted in Seoul with anxiety. Mixed emotions in South Korea underscore South Korean fears and ambivalence that are tied both to Japan's enhanced role in relation to US security strategy, and to uncertainty over the future of the US–South Korean relationship. South Koreans have been particularly active in expressing concern about China's response to these developments—for instance, in the context of US–South Korean discussions over the strategic flexibility of US forces in South Korea—and the dangers of an emerging Sino-Japanese strategic rivalry for Asian leadership, possibly abetted (intentionally or unintentionally) by US policy choices.

In fact, the worst of all worlds for South Korea is to be forced to make a choice between the security benefits it derives from its security alliance with the United States and the economic opportunities its firms are experiencing as a result of China's economic growth. The considerable economic interdependence that has developed between China and South Korea since the early 1990s requires South Korea to pursue an interesting balancing act that seeks to avoid regional divisions that might jeopardize those economic interests. China is South Korea's largest economic partner and a key player whose support is essential to Korean unification. Thus, South Korea has no interest in renewed great power confrontation between China and Japan or between China and the United States.

South Korea's growing economic interdependence with China and the Roh administration's concerns with the ways in which a "new Cold War" in Asia would limit South Korea's diplomatic independence, flexibility, and opportunities for prosperity are primary reasons why there has been such great sensitivity in South Korea regarding the issue of strategic flexibility for US forces in Korea. In relation to the latter, President Roh stated in a speech at the Korea Air Force Academy in March 2005 that "we will not be embroiled in any conflict in Northeast Asia against our will. This is an absolutely firm principle we cannot yield under any circumstance."[21] The reason for the sensitivity is that strategic flexibility has been framed as an issue that requires South Korea to make a choice between China on the one hand and the United States (and by extension, Japan) on the other. The concern has been that US force deployments off the Korean peninsula might enmesh South Korea in a regional conflict—for instance, in the event of a cross-strait conflict, in which the United States might intervene in defense of Taiwan.

Although the two governments eventually formed an understanding on the concept of strategic flexibility at the first round of the Security Consultations for Alliance Partnership in January 2006, the issue has been subject to an active public debate that once again illustrates South Korean sensitivities to the prospect of US-Chinese confrontation and the dominance of the United States as a factor in South Korean thinking about security issues that almost automatically frames all choices in terms of independence from or reliance on the US–South Korean alliance and, by extension, on the "tripartite framework" of alliances with Japan and South Korea which could increasingly be used to balance against a rising China.

Korean Reunification and Its
Implications for Sino-Japanese Rivalry

The Korean peninsula remains a strategic security concern and an object of competition for influence for both China and Japan. The division of the Korean peninsula into two separate spheres of influence, one dominated by China, the other secure from Chinese influence and under US domination, which itself serves as an effective surrogate for ensuring Japan's security interests, has been a stable and probably mutually satisfactory scenario in terms of managing China's and Japan's security concerns. These concerns will be heightened in both Beijing and Tokyo only if there is a change in the status quo that has persisted on the Korean peninsula since the armistice brought a halt to military conflict. Stability between China and Japan as it relates to the Korean peninsula has come at a high price for South Koreans, who have continuously sought national reunification and restoration of the peninsula as their highest priority. However, Korean reunification would likely heighten tensions and exacerbate the security dilemma between China and Japan. Both parties may feel a need to compete to preserve influence on the Korean peninsula as a strategic buffer for enhancing their own security.

South Korea is the twelfth largest economic power in the world, while North Korea ranks near the bottom in almost every development category. The status quo internal to the Korean peninsula is unsustainable, yet the future strategic orientation, economic capacity, and resources for protecting a reunified Korean peninsula within East Asia remain question marks in the broader context of Sino-Japanese relations. The dilemma for Korea is how to accommodate Korean aspirations for unification, and the nationalism that is likely to accompany reunification, while also accommodating Chinese and Japanese national security needs. This means that South Korean leaders must find the tools and build the capacities to manage two simultaneous tasks: promoting stability on the Korean peninsula while reassuring Japan and China. *Hangyore* newspaper columnist Jang Jungsoo has characterized this challenge in the following way: "Another source of tension in the Korean peninsula is the Sino-Japan rivalry in East Asia. Mindful of the rapid rise of China's influence in the region, Japan has been building up its military power. Japan may justify its military buildup as self-defense against North Korea's nuclear weapons and long-range missiles. Japan has been exploiting North Korea's nuclear threat as a pretext for rearming itself as well as pushing for a revision of Article 9 of its constitution to allow it the right to wage war and maintain legitimately armed forces. But it is widely believed that Japan's military buildup is aimed at its archrival China."[22] Despite the reality that Korean unification may actually be a catalyst for heightened Sino-Japanese rivalry, the task of how to achieve it absorbs so much time and energy that there is little left for considering how to manage the possibility of renewed Sino-Japanese rivalry.

There is an apparent conflict between South Korean nationalist impulses, which often manifest themselves in a preoccupation with achieving reunification to the apparent exclusion of its influence on the security interests of Korea's neighbors, and regionalist writings, which often concern themselves with how to pursue lasting peace, stability, and reunification in a way that positively affects not only the peninsula but also the East Asian region. Though Korean "nationalist" preoccupation with reunification is often so strong that consideration of the regional environment seems an afterthought, aligning nationalist aims with regional aspirations will be critical if Korea is to avoid its past path of confrontation in reaction to Sino-Japanese rivalry. The most attractive way of solving this problem lies in Korean visions of economic integration of the peninsula as the first step toward economic integration of the region, which would lay the foundations for a Northeast Asian security community for which mutual economic interests would alleviate security dilemmas and make the costs of military conflict unthinkable. But it is not clear that this long-term regionalist vision will overcome the near-term realities of nationalist sentiment, which are a critical component of domestic politics not only in the two Koreas, but also in every other country in Northeast Asia.

Economic Interdependence and South Korean Hopes for Security Cooperation

South Korea has played a leading role in developing and promoting a functionalist vision for East Asian cooperation on the premise that enhanced regional integration and economic interdependence will mitigate strategic rivalries. In this vision, cooperative institutional arrangements should take root as a basis for overcoming regional security tensions.[23] It is a naturally appealing vision for South Korea, geographically surrounded by major powers that have fought past strategic rivalries on Korean soil, to promote structures for cooperation that emphasize equality of participation, minimize prospects for rivalry, and in the process give South Korea a place at the table on the basis of equality and mutual respect.

Despite South Korean apprehensions about a more "normal" Japan and strategic anxieties about China's enhanced economic leverage in North Korea, the dominant vision of South Korea's national security and economic strategies is multilateral in nature and anticipates that the thickening of cross-border relationships of all sorts will promote security and prosperity. It melds Korean nationalism and regionalism by positively applying a vision of a newly capable South Korea in the service of a cooperative regionalism that would promote prosperity and prevent war. This vision first took shape in the latter part of Kim Dae Jung's administration, but has been carried forward in the form of the Roh Moo Hyun administration's interest in promoting Northeast Asian cooperation and advertising Korean aspirations for the peninsula to become a regional financial hub.

For South Koreans, such a vision begins at home. The first step is to mobilize and institutionalize inter-Korean cooperation. A second step is to mobilize and institutionalize regional political support, via the six-party talks, for resolution of tensions related to North Korea.

Beyond the Korean Conflict: Rising Great Power Rivalry?

Steady progress toward establishment of a regional cooperative dialogue on how to deal with the shared problem of North Korea coexists with security dilemmas that participants in the six-party talks face as they deal with both the near-term tactics of moving toward denuclearization of the Korean peninsula and the long-term challenges of imagining the strategic ramifications of Korean reunification. But there are also other emerging forms of multilateral cooperation in the region driven by the motivation to hedge against China's rise. Most notably, the strengthening of the US-Japanese and US-Australian security alliances, and the signing of a new security declaration between Japan and Australia, have enabled the establishment of regular trilateral security coordination dialogue among the three parties. In addition, the United States and Japan have strengthened their respective relationships with India as means by which to hedge against China's rise.

South Korea's growing economic interdependence with China, and South Korea's concerns with the ways in which a "new Cold War" in Asia would limit its independence, flexibility, and opportunities for prosperity, are primary challenges for South Korean diplomacy. South Korea's rapidly growing economic relationship with China, together with China's rising political influence, now requires South Korean strategists to think twice about whether China will view South Korean involvement in multilateral security arrangements as threatening. Even South Korean conservatives think twice about Chinese perceptions before considering a return to the type of "minilateral" security cooperation signified by the Trilateral Coordination and Oversight Group of the 1990s.[24]

The de facto consolidation of power on the peninsula in the hands of Seoul, combined with North Korea's continued decline, pose internal challenges in managing any possible Korean reunification and complicate regional relations to the extent that the buffer provided by the previous rough balance between North and South is no longer sustainable. Korean reunification would likely heighten tensions and exacerbate the security dilemma between China and Japan. Both parties might compete to preserve influence on the Korean peninsula as a means to enhance their own security. If a regional security mechanism in Northeast Asia is to succeed, the litmus test for such an effort will be whether it is able to manage or prevent regional rivalry among the region's great powers.

Notes

An earlier version of this chapter appeared as "The China-Japan Rivalry: Korea's Pivotal Position?" in Shin Gi-wook and Dan Sneider, eds., *Cross Currents: Regionalism and Nationalism in Northeast Asia* (Stanford: Shorenstein Asia Pacific Research Center, Stanford University, 2007).

1. Author conversations with Japanese analysts in Tokyo, February 2006.

2. Victor D. Cha, *Alliance Despite Antagonism: The United States–Korea–Japan Security Triangle* (Stanford: Stanford University Press, 2000).

3. Cameron Barr, "A 'Whale' and a 'Shrimp' Gang Up on Japanese," *Christian Science Monitor,* November 15, 1995, p. 6.

4. Address at the Fortieth Commencement and Commissioning Ceremony of the Korea Third Military Academy, March 22, 2005, accessed at http://english.president.go.kr.

5. "Defense Minister Stresses 'Power Balancer' Role," *Korea Times,* April 8, 2005.

6. Secretariat of the National Security Council, "Theory on Balancer in Northeast Asia: A Strategy to Become a Respected State in International Cooperation," April 27, 2005, accessed at http://www.opensource.gov, doc. no. KPP20050428000225.

7. Ibid.

8. Moon Chung-in, "Theory of Balancing Role in Northeast Asia," *Chosun Ilbo,* April 12, 2005, accessed at http://www.opensource.gov, doc. no. KPP20050412000011.

9. Although a lot of energy has been put into developing and articulating the "balancer" theory, it appears that concept has had little impact thus far in practice, other than to stir up a vigorous debate during the spring of 2005 over South Korea's diplomatic orientation and capabilities. Since that debate, the concept appears to have been quietly set aside, with no additional explanation of whether and how it might be applied.

10. "A Military Isn't a 'Balancer,'" *JoongAng Ilbo,* April 9, 2005, accessed at www.opensource.gov, doc. no. KPP20050408000167.

11. "Will Roh Take Kim Dae Jung's Advice?" *Chosun Ilbo,* April 11, 2005, accessed at http://www.opensource.gov, doc. no. KPP20050410000100.

12. Kim Soung-chul, "Forge Alliance with U.S., China," *JoongAng Ilbo,* March 18, 2005, accessed at http://www.opensource.gov, doc. no. KPP20050317000198.

13. "Let's Shame Japan on the International Stage," *Hangyore Shinmun,* April 5, 2005, accessed at http://www.opensource.gov, doc. no. KPP20050407000214.

14. "Roh Hints at New East Asian Order," *Chosun Ilbo,* March 23, 2005, accessed at http://www.opensource.gov, doc. no. KPP20050322000143.

15. Yi Ki-ho, "Full Text of ROK President Roh Moo-hyun's Answers to Questions in an Interview to Mark the First Anniversary of Daily Seoprise," October 21, 2005, accessed at http://www.opensource.gov, doc. no. KPP20051021053002.

16. Kim Woosang, "Breakup of Triangular Alliance Will Only Lead to Isolation," *Chosun Ilbo,* March 23, 2005, as published in *Korea Focus* 13, no. 3 (May–June 2005), accessed at http://www.koreafocus.or.kr.

17. For a recasting of those relationships in ways that promote global stability, see the US–South Korean joint statement issued by Presidents Roh Moo Hyun and George W. Bush at Kyongju on November 16, 2006, "Joint Declaration on the US-ROK Alliance and Peace on the Korean Peninsula," at

http://www.whitehouse.gov/news/releases/2005/11/20051117-6.html, accessed on September 25, 2008; and the US-Japanese "2+2" statement issued in March 2005, Joint Statement, US-Japan Security Consultative Committee, at http://www.mofa.go.jp/region/n-america/us/security/scc/joint0502.html, accessed on September 25, 2008.

18. Private author conversation with a Bush administration official, Washington, DC, March 2006.

19. A representative expression of South Korean concerns about Japan as a "normal" nation is Nam Ki-jeong, "Dealing with a Different Japan," *JoongAng Ilbo*, August 6, 2005, accessed at http://www.opensource.gov, doc. no. KPP20050805000134: "If a Japan that has been born again as a 'traditional security country' were to decide to do something unexpected beyond the current system of checks and balances, the resulting situation could develop most unfavorably for South Korea."

20. Author conversations with US administration officials, Washington, DC, April and June 2005.

21. Address at the Fifty-third Commencement and Commissioning Ceremony of the Korea Air Force Academy, March 8, 2005, accessed at http://english.president.go.kr.

22. Jang Jungsoo, "How Can Peace Be Realized on the Korean Peninsula?" *Hangyore Sinmun*, May 10, 2007, accessed at http://english.hani.co.kr/arti/english_edition/e_opinion/208361.html on September 16, 2007.

23. *National Security Strategy of the Republic of Korea*, 2003. For further analysis and comparison of key points of the US and South Korean national security strategies, see Scott Snyder, "A Comparison of the U.S. and ROK National Security Strategies: Implications for Alliance Coordination Toward North Korea," in Philip W. Yun and Shin Gi-wook, eds., *North Korea: 2005 and Beyond* (Stanford: Walter A. Shorenstein Asia Pacific Research Center, 2006), pp. 149–166.

24. Author conversations with South Korean analysts on Jeju Island, October 2007.

9

The New Sino-Korean Economic Relationship: Implications for Northeast Asian Security

China's economic influence in Northeast Asia has grown dramatically in the past three decades. China has effectively utilized its rapid economic development and growing economic interdependence with its Asian neighbors, including the two Koreas, as a centripetal force of attraction, drawing the Korean peninsula closer to China economically as well as politically. But it remains to be seen whether China has the right combination of attraction and leverage to draw the Korean peninsula completely within its orbit. Sustained economic growth has enabled China to expand its regional aspirations in an attempt to safeguard its own prosperity and to promote regional stability on its periphery. By utilizing its economic development to burnish its credentials with its neighbors, China has also sought to enhance its political image and prevent economic instability as a means by which to preserve its own economic development and shape its own regional environment in order to enhance its economic and political influence. China has set records in trade growth with economically vibrant neighbors while utilizing aid and investment instruments as vehicles for preventing economic or political instability in weaker states on its periphery. All of these broader trends are also apparent in China's dealings with the two Koreas.

The rapid growth in Sino–South Korean economic relations has not yet directly threatened the US position, but it has served to create ambivalence in South Korea about how best to ensure its own security needs while taking advantage of new economic opportunities with China. Utilizing rising economic interdependence as a vehicle for promoting positive-sum cooperation, China has promoted the idea that such interdependence is sufficient to ensure regional stability, a proposition that if taken to its logical conclusion would mean that China-centered economic ties could eventually fulfill the role that the US forces in Korea have traditionally played by military means through deterrence and the prevention of conflict. Moreover, the US security role in Korea had dual benefits during the Cold War: prevention of war and the accompanying economic opportunity of being able to produce goods for consumption in US markets. But the end of the Cold War and China's remarkable economic development have enabled South Korea to take advantage of economic interdependence with China while continuing to enjoy security benefits from the United States.

South Korea is likely to continue to reap the advantages of expanded trade and investment in China while also maintaining security ties with the United States. But the level of South Korea's perceived economic and political interdependence with China may also raise questions about the future of the US–South Korean security alliance. Is there a point at which South Korea may eventually determine that its economic and political ties with China are sufficient that it no longer needs to maintain a security relationship with the United States? Although the final answer to this question is still to be determined, I have argued in this study that China's expanded economic influence is ultimately unlikely to be translated into strategic gains with South Korea at the expense of the United States, given South Korean concerns about being "swallowed" by China.

The second North Korean nuclear crisis has provided a new backdrop for assessing the development of China's relations with the two Koreas and their implications for the future regional security order. Although the George W. Bush administration has focused primarily on cooperation with China as a way of harnessing the latter's leverage in the service of denuclearizing North Korea, China for the first time has taken the initiative to shape the environment and context in which the North Korean nuclear issue is addressed. The transformed economic relationship between South Korea and China indirectly influences the range of perceived options and potential futures for the Korean peninsula. Although there is a clear need for short-term cooperation in managing the North Korean nuclear crisis through the six-party talks, it seems likely that the respective long-term visions and priorities of China, South Korea, and the United States for the future of the region will come into contradiction. China's near-term objectives (no nuclear weapons, no war, no North Korean regime collapse) and motivations for taking a strikingly more active role in mediating the second North

Korean nuclear crisis are all focused on how to maintain regional stability, but longer-term, the Chinese strategy has been described as "concealing strength and waiting for opportunities *(taoguang yanghui).*"[1] China may hope to reap political gains from the success of its relationship with South Korea while managing improved relations with the United States as part of its emergence as an indispensable player in the region and as a key player on the global diplomatic stage.[2]

Economic Interdependence and China's Relationship with the Korean Peninsula

This study began by reviewing the role that expectations for mutual economic benefit played in laying the foundations for normalization of relations between China and South Korea despite the political objections of North Korea. Although Chinese and South Korean leaders also identified short-term political objectives as reasons motivating Sino–South Korean diplomatic normalization, the lure of economic opportunity between South Korea and China and the continued economic stagnation that characterized the Sino–North Korean relationship were primary factors that led to the normalization. Sino–South Korean normalization also marked China's transition to an official "two Koreas" policy and marked the formal beginning of the Sino–North Korean–South Korean triangular relationship. Sino–South Korean economic relations initially evolved with little regard for political considerations; China sought to maximize its economic gains while maintaining influence with both Koreas. These opportunities came faster than anyone might have expected, as a result of China's sustained high growth rates. Economic interdependence both outstripped expectations and stimulated opportunities for closer political relations between China and South Korea. But recent structural obstacles and outstanding security concerns, including China's relationship with North Korea and South Korea's security alliance with the United States, have inhibited the full maturation of the Sino–South Korean political relationship.

Limitations of China's Economic Leverage and Political Influence over North Korea

China's attempts to wean North Korea from its economic dependency on major energy and grain subsidies were forestalled by North Korea's famine in the mid-1990s. Since 2000, China has used expanded economic relations with North Korea as a means to reinforce simultaneous improvements in political relations, but China's generosity in promoting economic relations with North Korea has not been reciprocated by Pyongyang. Although China enjoys considerable economic influence with North Korea, utilizing economic incentives in an attempt to influence North Korea's political choices and to prevent North Korean leaders from taking actions contrary to China's national interests (such as conducting a nuclear test), there is little evidence that China has been able to convert its considerable economic leverage over North Korea into political gains. Instead, North Korea has shown that it has a "rubber stomach," absorbing whatever aid China is willing to provide and coming back for more.[3]

China's expanded economic relations with North Korea have served both as an insurance policy for preserving influence in North Korea and as a vehicle for safeguarding North Korea's economic stability, but North Korea regards Chinese economic assistance as serving China's own self-interest and therefore sees no need to reciprocate by exercising political self-restraint.

Although reluctant to utilize sanctions against North Korea, China has at critical moments withheld promised benefits or frozen expansion of economic cooperation as a form of leverage and signal of displeasure intended to discipline North Korea. But the nature of the Sino–North Korean relationship is in transition. Given a change of attitude among Chinese policymakers regarding the effectiveness of economic incentives and sanctions as tools for influencing North Korea, China has increasingly acted to reinforce the concerns of the international community at the expense of supporting North Korea. There is also a greater willingness in Beijing to utilize economic tools as coercive instruments against Pyongyang. However, China still prefers the withholding of promised benefits resulting from cooperation in critical areas, rather than the imposition of sanctions, as the instrument likely to be most effective and least likely to have a negative impact on stability in North Korea.

Even more complicated for Chinese policymakers are North Korea's attempts to diminish China's economic and political influence in Pyongyang, either by seeking a strategic relationship with the United States or by enhancing economic cooperation with South Korea. At the same time, North Korea has taken advantage of South Korean fears that China's economic domination of the North will have negative consequences for Korean reunification. Moreover, given North Korea's inability to compete with the South, the future of the Korean peninsula will likely be determined in Seoul, not Pyongyang. If the United States and China want to sustain their influence on the Korean peninsula in the long run, the key will be which party is able to maintain favorable relations with Seoul. Nonetheless, management of the North Korean nuclear issue is the primary means by which strategic considerations on the part of all parties have come to the fore. How the United States and China pursue their policies toward North Korea is a critical litmus test for South Korea in its evaluation of their respective intentions.

From Command Economy to Market Economy in North Korea

China's efforts to promote economic reform in North Korea have primarily consisted of subtly and directly encouraging North Korea to follow the Chinese model. The most powerful tool by which to promote economic reforms inside North Korea has been cross-border trade, much of which has taken place on a private basis outside of state control. As markets develop inside North Korea, there have been expanded opportunities for Chinese trading companies to work with North Korean counterparts on a market basis. However, larger projects involving Chinese joint ventures with North Korean counterparts require some level of cooperation among governments. A fundamental dilemma that China has faced in managing its economic relationship with North Korea is how to find the right balance between encouraging private activity that can promote economic reform in North Korea, but may weaken the role of the central government, and the desire to ensure stability in North Korea through economic cooperation projects that help to strengthen the capacity of North Korean leadership institutions, but at the cost of pursuing reforms.

From "Special" to "Normal" Relations with North Korea

China has made serious efforts in recent years to transition its relationship with North Korea from "special" to "normal." Evidence of China's desires to move in this direction includes efforts to place economic interaction with North Korea on a market basis, the absence of special consideration for North Korea in symbolic aspects of diplomacy and appointments of officials to serve in North Korea, and an increasing level of transparency in China's management of its relationship with North Korea. But to the extent that China expects to influence North Korean behavior, play an influential role in managing

North Korea's nuclear crisis, or satisfy its own expectations and concerns about the longer-term future of the Korean peninsula, it is impossible for Chinese leaders to set aside the traditional tools that have made the relationship with North Korea "special" rather than "normal." A "normal" relationship with North Korea can be pursued only if China's strategic anxieties regarding South Korea and the United States are fully assuaged, and only if North Korea is effectively integrated into the Northeast Asian political system. Likewise, it remains to be seen how China will settle the political challenges and contradictions that North Korea poses to the broader principles and objectives guiding its overall foreign policy.

From Buffer to Buyout:
North Korea as a Hedge Against Instability

China is casting aside its concept of North Korea as a "strategic buffer" in favor of the idea that economic interdependence with the Korean peninsula will mitigate the possibility of threat to its own interests. Increased economic "investment" in North Korea can also serve as a hedge against the type of instability that accompanies failed states. China's economic relationship with North Korea has been characterized by stagnation in transitioning from one based on aid to one based on markets. North Korea has been an economic burden to China and has successfully resisted periodic Chinese efforts to place the overall economic relationship on a market basis. Moreover, China's desire for stability on its borders means that much of its economic assistance to North Korea remains "strategic." Such strategic considerations have prevented China from making this transition, given that its economic influence in North Korea can serve both as a hedge against the spillover effects of economic instability in North Korea and as a means to preserve some measure of influence on the Korean peninsula in the event of regime transition in the North or sudden Korean reunification. North Korea's economic dependency appears to provide one means by which China can preserve some influence, even if this does not allow China sufficient leverage to control North Korea's political choices.

North Korea's economic dependency on China is double-edged. On the one hand, dependency has not prevented North Korea from acting contrary to Chinese policy interests, especially since North Korean leaders already presume that China is acting solely in its own interests and therefore do not feel a need to reciprocate. On the other hand, China's predominant economic influence in North Korea has stimulated South

Korean anxieties that China might utilize its influence either to unfairly exploit North Korea's economic resources or to deny South Korea the rightful political influence that it should exercise in the contest for Korean reunification.

Economic Dependency on China as a Growing Political Issue in South Korea

South Korea has become concerned about its own economic dependency on China. This discomfort can be seen in recent South Korean investment trends, which no longer focus so heavily on China after having peaked at 43 percent of South Korea's overall investment in 2006, but instead have become more diversified. South Korean businesses no longer want to put all their eggs in the China basket.

China has yet to utilize economic tools explicitly for political purposes with South Korea, but the growth of the overall economic relationship has clearly enhanced China's relative political importance and profile in Seoul. As China has begun to close its production gap with South Korea and compete for global market share, South Koreans have perceived their potential economic vulnerability to competition from China. This has induced a political response, with South Korea's seeking to diversify and reduce its dependence on the Chinese market out of fear of the consequences.

Moreover, shifting terms of trade and the decline of South Korea's trade surplus with China have stimulated a sense of vulnerability that is likely to limit China from continuing to gain leverage from South Korean economic dependency. Finally, South Korea's decision to pursue a free trade agreement with the United States appears to have had both strategic and economic motivations, suggesting South Korean discomfort with overreliance on a nonally and a desire to strengthen economic relations in ways that reinforce the security relationship and enhance prospects for comprehensive cooperation between South Korea and the United States, in part as a response to concerns about China's economic rise. All of these developments suggest that South Korea's own concerns that excessive economic dependency on China might eventually impose constraints on its own political and strategic choices have already catalyzed a correction, in the process reinforcing relations with the United States as a means by which to maintain freedom of action.

As Chinese local companies close the technology gap with South Korean counterparts and gain labor and management skills, Chinese companies are increasingly able to compete with South Korean firms for access to third-country markets; at the same time, South Korean firms must learn how to compete with Chinese counterparts in China's domestic market. Moreover, there is a risk that too much technology transfer, resulting from South Korean firms doing business in China, will erode South Korean market share; there have already been cases of industrial espionage involving South Korean workers selling critical information to Chinese competitors.

Future Challenges in Sino–South Korean Political Relations

On the basis of rapid economic growth, China and South Korea have continuously experienced improvement in their political relationship, and both sides have gained practical experience in the course of managing contentious issues. During the first ten years following diplomatic normalization, it seemed that the imperative of good economic relations overshadowed most major political problems in the bilateral relationship, but since 2004, several chronic issues have emerged that require more active management by both sides, including the dispute over the historical origins of the Koguryo kingdom, management of issues involving North Korean refugees and cross-strait relations, and South Korean anxieties over whether China's economic influence in North Korea might be used in ways that deny Korean reunification. In addition, a looming issue of difference between South Korea and China is the role of the United States and the future of the US–South Korean security alliance. In no case, however, have political disputes risen to the point of negatively impacting Sino–South Korean economic relations.

The future of North Korea is the single issue that has the greatest potential to bring China and South Korea into conflict, yet South Korea's policies have been based on the assumption that China's cooperation is vital if it is to achieve its own objectives in relations with North Korea. Although South Korean and Chinese strategic interests in maintenance of stability have converged, there are still conflicts over the intent and significance of their respective economic roles with North Korea. While South Korea's strategic anxieties have focused on China's intentions vis-à-vis Korean reunification, China's concerns have focused on the future role and influence of the United States on the peninsula in the context of Korean reunification. One result is the growing strategic importance of the China–South Korea–United States triangular relationship as it relates to North Korea.

Sino-Korean Economic Interdependence:
Implications for the Alliance

The main political and security challenge to the United States that is posed by China's economic interdependence with the Korean peninsula is the question of whether China will be able to leverage South Korea's economic dependency in ways that will allow it to enhance its own regional political or security role at Washington's expense. China has sought to utilize growing economic interdependence to secure regional economic stability, to promote cooperation with its neighbors on a "win-win" basis, and to improve its image and diminish any sense of threat that its neighbors might feel as a result of its rapid economic growth and accompanying growth of political influence. Chinese analysts have identified economic growth as an element of China's "comprehensive national power," or capacity to translate economic influence into political leverage. China has indeed enhanced its political and economic profile in South Korea, to the extent that South Korean leaders now give special consideration to whether their words and actions might generate disfavor from China. As explored in Chapter 4, the South Korean government has been particularly cautious to avoid conflicts with China on sensitive issues such as cross-strait relations (for instance, in the form of the US–South Korean discussions regarding "strategic flexibility" of US forces in Korea) and cooperation with the United States and Japan on development of missile defense.

But there have also been countervailing political and economic factors that have pushed South Korea away from China and back into the arms of the United States. For instance, the Koguryo history dispute has had a major impact on South Korean views of China's intentions; South Koreans worry about China's strategic intentions vis-à-vis North Korea and prospects for Korean reunification; and South Koreans have increasingly expressed anxiety about becoming overly economically dependent on China in the trade and investment sphere. In the economic sector, South Korea's decision to pursue negotiation of a free trade agreement with the United States prior to pursuing negotiation of such an agreement with China represented a clear strategic choice that was motivated mostly by South Korea's desire to counterbalance its economic reliance on an increasingly competitive China. This decision is particularly interesting given that it was made by the Roh Moo Hyun administration, which arguably had pursued an independent posture vis-à-vis the United States to a greater extent than any other administration in modern South Korean history.

If the Korean-US free trade agreement negotiated under Presidents Roh and Bush is ratified by the South Korean National Assembly and the US Congress, its strategic significance will exceed any economic value it may have. The reestablishment of a structure whereby economic benefits flow parallel to security commitments under the US–South Korean alliance can only serve to strengthen the relationship in ways that limit China's ability to convert economic influence on the peninsula into political and security gains.

Antihegemonism and Korea's Foreign Policy Orientation

South Korea's geography—as a small country surrounded by larger neighbors—continues to define its strategic choices. Despite South Korea's emergence as a global economic leader, the core principle underlying its management of relations with the United States and China is *antihegemonism*. For the United States, this means that any strategy to maintain US influence on the Korean peninsula must treat South Koreans with respect, with sparing use of coercive tools or unilateralism in managing relations with South Korea. Given South Korean sensitivities in this area, China's size and relative proximity to the Korean peninsula are natural disadvantages, since China's continued growth may result in South Korea's desire to enlist the aid of a distant, powerful counterweight—a strategic need and role that the United States is naturally well-suited to play.

In the near term, it is certainly possible that the United States will forfeit the advantage of being a *distant* power—for instance, by managing its relationship with South Korea in ways that emphasize US hegemony or show disregard for South Korea's core interests. This is arguably the situation that developed in 2001–2003, when South Koreans responded negatively to how the United States was handling the North Korean nuclear issue, including President Bush's inclusion of North Korea in the "axis of evil." South Koreans perceived their own security to be at threat, a mood exacerbated by the perceived impunity of US forces in South Korea as a result of lax punishment for an accident in which two schoolgirls had been killed by a US military vehicle. These incidents were symbolic to South Koreans of US "arrogance" and took their toll on public support for South Korea's relationship with the United States.

South Korean responses to Chinese forms of hegemony are equally emotional and deep-seated, but show themselves in different forms. Widespread public outrage about the Chinese foreign ministry's decision in 2004 to "erase" the history of Korea prior to 1948 from its website evoked a strong public reaction in South Korea, but it did not incite South Koreans to take to the streets. Rather, a spate of Korean historical dramas were produced for television to raise public consciousness of Koguryo as an essential part of Korean history. Likewise, the South Korean public responded strongly to incidents of violence by Chinese students against anti-China protesters during the staging of the Olympic torch run in Seoul in April 2008. As China's regional and global influence rises, there may be more cases in which the South Korean public responds to "arrogant" Chinese actions, especially if there are collateral effects on the Korean peninsula.

In the middle to long term, a more complicated issue may arise: What if China's relative economic importance continues to rise, or if South Korea's economic dependence on China indeed becomes great enough that it constrains South Korean policy choices and inhibits South Korean willingness to support alliance-based security cooperation? Thus far, only two alliance issues (missile defense and strategic flexibility) have evoked South Korean concerns about China's response; both of these issues have arisen as a result of South Korean anticipation of objections that China might raise, rather than as a result of actual expressed concern by China. But these issues may only be the tip of the iceberg in terms of potential future challenges that China-related issues might pose to US–South Korean security cooperation under the alliance.

China has thus far treated South Korea's decision to pursue an alliance with the United States as a sovereign decision, but it is imaginable that China might begin to formally weigh in on operational aspects of the alliance if it were to feel its interests were threatened, even if China were not specifically targeted by those aspects of the alliance. China is already criticizing aspects of the US-Japanese security alliance, especially where it perceives that alliance cooperation might be applied in a cross-strait scenario. Even the knowledge that China opposes military alliances in principle could become an issue within South Korea if the latter were to feel that China has the capacity to impose a tangible cost for its continuing participation in the alliance. Moreover, if South Korea were to perceive China as more powerful in aggregate terms than the United States, it would be an open question whether South Korea might abandon its alliance with the United States and seek a strategic realignment with China, to promote good relations with a more powerful protector.

Given the rising sensitivity of South Korean security planners to the effects of China's economic rise, the United States should seek to pursue a much more active dialogue about China's political strategies and military capacities and their implications for the future of the security alliance. Such a discussion should also address whether South Korean and other civilian production capacities now based in China might be used to strengthen China militarily, and whether China's increasing influence on the Korean peninsula has implications for the pursuit of alliance coordination between the United States and South Korea.

Nuclear North Korea, Korean Unification, and China: Implications for the United States

As outlined in Chapter 6, China faces serious contradictions in managing policy toward North Korea: the desire to promote regional economic integration versus North Korea's economic isolation; the principle of noninterference versus the imperative of maintaining regional economic and political stability; the desire to promote and benefit from market economic principles versus North Korea's continuous need for subsidies if it is to avoid becoming an unstable, failed state; and finally, the need to cooperate with the United States to manage the North Korean situation versus the desire for a Korean peninsula free of US influence.

The second North Korean nuclear crisis has provided China with an opportunity to more actively promote regional stability through its roles as convener, mediator, and promoter of shuttle diplomacy between Washington and Pyongyang. The Chinese government spent three rounds of the six-party talks tirelessly promoting opportunities for direct dialogue between the United States and North Korea, and criticized both sides for their failure to cooperate. But ultimately, China did not have the tools at its disposal to persuade or compel either the United States or North Korea to change its position or attitude. Instead, the North Korean nuclear test further underscored the limits of China's diplomatic capacity to keep the crisis from escalating, as well as illustrated China's failure to prevent North Korea from taking an action that was directly opposed to China's own vital national interests. North Korea's nuclear test succeeded in catalyzing China's willingness to consider coercion along with persuasion as part of its diplomatic toolbox, but there was nothing that China could fundamentally do to close the gap between the United States and North Korea.

The limits of China's diplomatic capacity have been further emphasized in the events following the nuclear test, as the United States has changed its policy and engaged in direct talks with North Korea in the context of the six-party talks. China has had to endure Kim Kye Gwan's public criticism of the United States for depending on China as an agent for carrying out US policy toward North Korea (a criticism that probably hurt more in Beijing than in Washington), and has been sidelined as the United States and North Korea have initiated negotiations and cut deals that have subsequently been taken to the six parties for ratification and implementation. Even the inter-Korean summit declaration in October 2007 contained a fillip for China in the form of references to "three or four parties" that might be involved with peace talks on the Korean peninsula, as Pyongyang once again attempted to keep Beijing on the outside, just as it had done in 1996 following the Bill Clinton–Kim Young Sam proposal for four-party talks on the Korean peninsula.

By taking these actions, North Korea has played on Chinese worries that the United States may cut a separate deal on the Korean peninsula that might achieve North Korea's denuclearization, but might also place the Korean peninsula under greater US influence than before. The result of a US-led process would be the establishment of a unified, democratic Korea on China's border, which would become a constant irritant to China's broader regional objectives and development—an outcome that Chinese strategists clearly prefer to avoid. Chinese strategic preferences as they relate to North Korea remain ambivalent: there is still a clear hesitancy to let go of the status quo on the Korean peninsula, despite the fact that North Korea's weakness has undermined China's traditional role as strategic buffer and has been a drain on China's overall objectives. At the same time, China recognizes that the currently existing status quo is artificially maintained and has become unsustainable. In that context, China has shown an increasing willingness to adopt new policies that would promote reform in North Korea and closer economic ties with South Korea. But the political role of China in its relationship with the Korean peninsula remains clouded by Chinese doubts about US intentions, the likely nature and political orientation of South Korea or a unified Korea, and an awareness that the tools available to China for influencing the future direction of the peninsula in its favor remain limited.

On the necessity of the denuclearization of the Korean peninsula, the second North Korean nuclear crisis has on balance brought China and the United States closer together.[4] Chinese specialists have taken to heart the opportunities and benefits that might accrue from active cooperation to achieve North Korea's denuclearization. However, there is still a temptation among Chinese analysts to distinguish between the priorities of maintaining stability on the peninsula versus denuclearization, while the United States continues to press its case that to distinguish between stability and the nuclear issue is a false choice, because a nuclear North Korea is inherently destabilizing.

China has long advocated normalization of US–North Korean relations, but the initial steps in the warming of that relationship have also meant that China no longer plays a central mediating role and thus has less ability to influence the pace or level of US–North Korean cooperation. Normalization of the US–North Korean relationship might indirectly be another obstacle to Korean reunification, to the extent that it affirms the political status quo on the Korean peninsula. At the same time, the subject of Korean reunification is one that appears to stimulate Chinese distrust regarding US intentions. On the one hand, Chinese analysts see fissures in the US–South Korean security alliance and presume that in the event of Korean reunification, a US troop presence in Korea will be unjustifiable to Koreans and unsustainable. On the other hand, conspiracy theories continue to persist in Beijing regarding US intentions and capacities to manipulate the strategic situation on the Korean peninsula in ways that will ultimately be detrimental to China's interests.[5]

Korean Reunification and Prospects for Regional Rivalry

A central paradox that has beset security relations in Northeast Asia is that, since the end of the Korean War, the outcome of a divided Korea has been stable, and that this division has also ironically contributed to strategic stability both between the Soviet Union and the United States and between China and Japan. A major concern associated with South Korea's economic rise and North Korea's stagnation is that Korean reunification could be accompanied by a tilt in the orientation of the Korean peninsula that might exacerbate security dilemmas for its immediate neighbors, China and Japan. The stakes associated with either a negotiated Korean reunification or a German-style reunification through absorption are magnified when one considers that both China and Japan see the Korean peninsula as threatening if Korean leaders fail to maintain friendly relations with both sides or choose to align with one neighbor at the expense of the other.

Regardless of the future of the US–South Korean security alliance or questions about the continued deployment of US forces on the Korean peninsula, the US-Japanese security alliance and Japan's special historical sensitivities to the possibility of hostility emanating from the Korean peninsula will inevitably require the United States to be involved in securing the stability of the peninsula if the US-Japanese alliance is to thrive. Without a US security role on the Korean peninsula, the prospect for Japan to seek self-defense measures is high. Likewise,

China remains concerned about the prospect of a Korean leadership that might be overly influenced by the United States or could be used as a tool to undermine stability in China. A continued US role in maintaining stability, even following Korean reunification, would probably be desirable, especially when one considers the possibility of renewed regional rivalry for influence on the Korean peninsula that might develop between China and Japan. However, the United States will weigh military, budgetary, and other factors, as well as levels of domestic public and congressional support, in the event that sudden changes on the Korean peninsula raise the costs of continued US military involvement in a reunified Korea.

North Korea's Pursuit of Strategic Realignment, and the US Response

North Korea has long sought its own strategic realignment and normalization of relations with the United States. But when North Koreans seek to end the "hostile policy" of the United States, there are rarely indications that they themselves are prepared to change in order to gain the benefits of improved relations. North Korea's definition of "strategic," when dealing with great powers, defines the situation in terms of benefits that North Korea can extract without having to provide concessions.

The prospect of a move toward a more normal relationship between the United States and North Korea was a major background consideration even as China and South Korea began to move toward diplomatic normalization. A centerpiece of China's policy toward the Korean peninsula in the early 1990s was "cross-recognition," whereby the United States and Japan would normalize relations with North Korea while China would normalize relations with South Korea. Deng Xiaoping reportedly urged Kim Il Sung to improve relations with the United States as early as the mid-1980s. Likewise, South Korean leaders fretted over whether the United States might interpret their normalization of relations with the Soviet Union and China as a betrayal, even despite the fact that the United States had already normalized relations with China over a decade earlier than normalization between China and South Korea.

The prospect of the United States normalizing relations with North Korea has the potential to catalyze North Korea's transformation and integration into the region. Chinese analysts have consistently viewed the improvement of US–North Korean political relations as a development that would reduce tensions on the Korean peninsula. But such a development has also been viewed with suspicion, in that enhanced US influence in North Korea might lead to a democratic unified Korean peninsula tilted toward the United States. The 2005 joint statement was an appeal to North Korea's desires for normalization in return for denuclearization, for the first time promulgating a set of commonly agreed principles in Northeast Asia. The US role in securing a peaceful Korean peninsula and in enabling an economically transformed Northeast Asia is critical, but it can succeed only to the extent that it fully reinforces North Korea's political and economic integration into the region. At the same time, the United States should seek ways to more actively participate as a partner in reaping the benefits of Northeast Asian economic integration, by playing the role of economic and political counterweight to China's rising influence. In this context, China-centered economic interdependence is unlikely to provide the political rationale for a marginalized US role; rather, it may motivate US allies to more deeply and broadly enmesh the United States in Northeast Asian affairs.

Notes

1. See Anne Wu, "What China Whispers to North Korea," *Washington Quarterly* 28, no. 2 (Spring 2005): 35–48.
2. See David Shambaugh, "China and the Korean Peninsula: Playing for the Long Term," *Washington Quarterly* 26, no. 2 (Spring 2003): 43–56.
3. Regarding the enormous amount of aid China gave to North Korea, former Chinese minister of economy and trade Li Lanqing is reported to have complained, "The DPRK's stomach is a rubber stomach." Satoshi Tomisaka, ed., *Taikitachosen Chugoku Kimitsu Fairu,* in Japanese ("China's Secret File on Relations with North Korea"), September 15, 2007, accessed at http://www.opensource.gov, doc. no. JPP20070919026005\3.
4. See Bonnie S. Glaser and Wang Liang, "North Korea: The Beginning of a China-U.S. Partnership?" *Washington Quarterly* 31, no. 3 (Fall 2008): 165–180.
5. Zhang Liangui, "Re-understanding the Six-Party Talks on the Korean Nuclear Issue," *Shijie Zhishi,* in Chinese, October 16, 2005, accessed at http://www.opensource.gov, doc. no. CPP20051028329001.

Appendix A: China–North Korea High-Level Bureaucratic Meetings, 1992–2006

1992, 1993
• No interaction.

1994
• A North Korean military delegation headed by Vice Marshal Choe Kwang, army chief of general staff, visits China.

1995
• June—Chinese vice foreign minister Tang Jiaxuan visits North Korea.

1996
• May—North Korean vice premier Hong Song Nam meets with Chinese vice premier Li Lanquing in China.

1997, 1998
• No interaction.

1999
• June—A North Korean delegation led by Kim Yong Nam, chairman of the Supreme People's Assembly Presidium, meets with Chinese president Jiang Zemin and Chinese National People's Congress Standing Committee chairman Li Peng.
• October—Chinese foreign minister Tang Jiaxuan visits Pyongyang.

2000
• March—North Korean Central Defense Commission chairman Kim Jong Il visits the Chinese embassy in Pyongyang.

• May—Kim Jong Il meets with Chinese president Jiang Zemin in Beijing.
• October—Chinese defense minister Chi Haotian meets with Kim Jong Il in Pyongyang.

2001
• January—North Korean Central Defense Commission chairman Kim Jong Il meets with Chinese president Jiang Zemin in Beijing.
• September—Jiang Zemin meets with Kim Jong Il in Pyongyang.

2002
• March—North Korean foreign minister Kim Yong Il visits China.
• May—North Korean Central Defense Commission chairman Kim Jong Il meets with Jia Qinglin, member of the Chinese Communist Party Politburo and secretary of the party's Beijing committees, in Pyongyang.

2003
• January—North Korean Supreme People's Assembly chairman Choe Thae Bok attends the Asian Parliamentary Association for Peace Executive Council conference in Beijing and meets with Chinese National People's Congress Standing Committee chairman Li Peng.
• March—Chinese former state councilor Qian Qichen secretly visits North Korea in Ryangang province and meets with North Korean Central Defense Commission chairman Kim Jong Il.
• April—Chinese president Hu Jintao meets with North Korean Central Defense Commission first vice chairman General Jo Myong Rok in Beijing.
• April—Jo Myong Rok meets with Chinese president Hu Jintao in Beijing.
• July—Kim Jong Il meets with Chinese vice foreign minister Dai Bingguo in Pyongyang.
• August—Chinese People's Liberation Army general political director and Chinese Communist Party Central Committee secretariat member Xu Caihou leads a Chinese delegation to Pyongyang for meetings that include Jo Myong Rok in preparation for the six-party talks. Photos are taken with Kim Jong Il.
• October—Kim Jong Il meets with Chinese National People's Congress Standing Committee chairman Wu Bangguo in Pyongyang. The two chairmen "agree in principle to continue to hold six-party talks."

2004
• March—Chinese foreign minister Li Zhaoxing travels to Pyongyang to meet with senior North Korean leaders, including Central Defense Commission chairman Kim Jong Il.
• April—Kim Jong Il visits China.

- September—Kim Jong Il meets in Pyongyang with a senior party delegation from China led by Chinese Communist Party Standing Committee member Li Changchun.
- October—North Korean prime minister Kim Yong Nam meets with Chinese leaders in Beijing and Tianjian to discuss ways to expand Sino–North Korean cooperation and friendship.
- November—Chinese foreign minister Li Zhaoxing and vice foreign minister Wu Dawei meet North Korean deputy foreign minister Kim Yong Il in Beijing to discuss Sino–North Korean cooperation between the six-party talks and the nuclear issue.

2005

- February—Chinese Communist Party International Liaison Department head Wang Jiarui meets with North Korean Central Defense Commission chairman Kim Jong Il and other top North Korean officials in Pyongyang to discuss the North Korean nuclear standoff and North Korean reluctance to return to the six-party talks. He delivers a letter from President Hu Jintao on China's policy objectives.
- March—North Korean prime minister Pak Bong Ju embarks on a week-long visit to China at the invitation of Chinese counterpart Wen Jiabao.
- April—North Korean vice foreign minister Kang Sok Ju leads a delegation to Beijing to discuss Pyongyang's possible return to the six-party talks regarding its nuclear weapons program.
- July—Chinese state councilor Tang Jiaxuan visits Pyongyang as a special envoy of Chinese president Hu Jintao and meets with Kim Jong Il.
- October—Chinese vice premier Wu Yi visits Pyongyang to join celebrations of the sixtieth anniversary of the Korean Workers Party, meets with Kim Jong Il, and participates in ceremonies marking the opening of the Tae'an glass factory, a Sino–North Korean joint venture.
- October—Chinese president Hu Jintao makes a state visit to Pyongyang, meets with Kim Jong Il, signs an accord on economic and technical cooperation, and visits the Tae'an glass factory.
- December—Chinese premier Wen Jiabao affirms China's policy of developing friendly and cooperative Sino–North Korean relations during a meeting with a North Korean delegation led by Cabinet Vice Premier Ro Tu Chol in Beijing. During the meeting, Ro and Chinese counterpart Zeng Paiyan sign an agreement on joint development of offshore oil wells.

2006

- January—North Korean Central Defense Commission chairman Kim Jong Il makes a secret week-long visit to China, accompanied by every member of the Chinese Communist Party Politburo and follows the route taken by Deng Xiaoping during the latter's famous "southern tour" of 1992.

Appendix B: China–South Korea High-Level Bureaucratic Meetings, 1992–2006

1992
- April—South Korean foreign minister Lee Sang Ock meets with Chinese counterpart Qian Qichen in Beijing.
- September—South Korean president Roh Tae Woo visits China and meets with Chinese president Yang Shangkun, Chinese Communist Party secretary-general Jiang Zemin, and Chinese prime minister Li Peng. Roh's visit marks the first visit to China by a South Korean president.

1993
- April—South Korean foreign minister Han Sung Joo meets with Chinese counterpart Qian Qichen in Bangkok.
- May—Han Sung Joo meets with Qian Qichen in Seoul.
- July—Han Sung Joo meets with Qian Qichen in Bangkok.
- September—Han Sung Joo meets with Qian Qichen at the United Nations.
- October—Han Sung Joo meets with Qian Qichen in Beijing.
- November—Han Sung Joo meets with Qian Qichen in Seattle.
- November—South Korean president Kim Young Sam meets with Chinese president Jiang Zemin at the Asia Pacific Economic Cooperation summit in Seattle.

1994
- March—South Korean president Kim Young Sam meets with Chinese president Jiang Zemin in Beijing.
- June—South Korean foreign minister Han Sung Joo meets with Chinese counterpart Qian Qichen in Beijing.
- October—Chinese premier Li Peng meets with Kim Young Sam in Seoul, marking the first visit to Seoul by a Chinese premier.

1995

• November—Chinese president Jiang Zemin meets with South Korean president Kim Young Sam, marking the first state visit by a Chinese president.

1996

• February—South Korean foreign minister Gong Ro Myung meets with Chinese counterpart Qian Qichen in Bangkok.
• February—Gong Ro Myung meets with Qian Qichen in Beijing.
• March—South Korean president Kim Young Sam meets with Chinese prime minister Li Peng at the Asia-Europe Meeting in Bangkok.
• July—Kim Young Sam meets with Li Peng at the Asia-Europe Meeting in Jakarta.
• July—Gong Ro Myung meets with Qian Qichen at the Association of Southeast Asian Nations ministerial meeting in Jakarta.
• September—Kim Young Sam meets with Li Peng at the Asia-Europe Meeting in New York.

1997

• February—South Korean National Assembly speaker Kim Soo Han visits Beijing.
• February—South Korean foreign minister Yoo Chong Ha meets with Chinese counterpart Qian Qichen in Singapore.
• May—Yoo Chong Ha meets with Qian Qichen in China.
• July—Yoo Chong Ha meets with Qian Qichen in Kuala Lampur.
• August—South Korean finance minister Kang Kyung Shik visits China.

1998

• November—South Korean president Kim Dae Jung visits China.
• December—Kim Dae Jung attends the Association of Southeast Asian Nations "Plus Three" conference and meets with Chinese prime minister Zhu Rongji.

1999

• March—South Korean foreign minister Hong Soon Young meets with Chinese counterpart Tang Jiaxuan in Berlin.
• May—Hong Soon Young meets with Tang Jiaxuan in the United States.
• July—Hong Soon Young asks Tang Jiaxuan, at a meeting prior to the Association of Southeast Asian Nations Regional Forum in Singapore, to help deter North Korea from test-launching another missile.
• July—South Korean president Kim Dae Jung meets with Chinese president Jiang Zemin on the sidelines of the Association of Southeast Asian Nations "Plus Three" conference in Singapore.

• August—South Korean defense minister Cho Song Tae meets with Chinese counterpart Chi Haotian in Beijing and calls for China to play a bridging role between North and South Korea by helping to persuade North Korea to abandon its missile launch program.

• September—Kim Dae Jung meets with Jiang Zemin on the sidelines of the Asia Pacific Economic Cooperation meeting in Auckland.

• November—Kim Dae Jung attends the Association of Southeast Asian Nations "Plus Three" conference in Manila; meets with Japanese prime minister Keizo Obuchi and Chinese prime minister Zhu Rongji on economic issues.

• December—Chinese foreign minister Tang Jiaxuan visits Seoul for consultations with South Korean officials, including Foreign Minister Hong Soon Young.

2000

• January—Chinese defense minister Chi Haotian visits South Korea, marking the first official visit to Seoul by a Chinese defense chief since the Korean War.

• April—South Korean foreign minister Lee Joung Binn meets with Chinese counterpart Tang Jiaxuan in China.

• June—Chinese Communist Party Politburo member Huang Ju visits South Korea.

• October—Chinese Premier Zhu Rongji visits Seoul and attends the Asia-Europe Meeting.

• November—South Korean president Kim Dae Jung and Chinese president Jiang Zemin hold summit talks on the sidelines of the Asia Pacific Economic Cooperation meeting in Brunei.

2001

• May—Chinese National People's Congress Standing Committee chairman Li Peng visits South Korea.

• June—South Korean prime minister Lee Han Dong visits China to discuss strengthening economic ties and new developments in inter-Korean relations.

• July—South Korean foreign minister Han Seung Soo and Chinese counterpart Tang Jiaxuan meet on the sidelines of the Association of Southeast Asian Nations Regional Forum in Hanoi and agree that Seoul and Beijing should exert joint criticism to pressure Tokyo into revising its controversial history textbooks.

2002

• January—South Korean National Assembly speaker Lee Man Sup meets with Chinese leaders in Beijing to discuss the situation on the Korean peninsula and the status of Sino–South Korean relations.

- March—South Korean foreign minister Choi Sung Hong meets in Beijing with Chinese foreign minister Tang Jiaxuan to brief him on the purpose of a planned April 3–5 trip to Pyongyang by Lim Dong Won, President Kim Dae Jung's special envoy, and to discuss disputes over China's policy toward North Korean defectors hiding in China.
- June—Choi Sung Hong and Tang Jiaxuan hold talks on the North Korean defectors issue on the sidelines of the Asia Cooperation Dialogue in Cha-am, Thailand.
- August—Tang Jiaxuan visits South Korea.

2003
- February—Chinese vice premier Qian Qichen meets with members of South Korean president-elect Roh Moo Hyun's team, and states the importance of a stable Korean peninsula.
- April—South Korean foreign minister Yoon Young Kwan meets with Chinese foreign minister Li Zhaoxing in Beijing. The two ministers agree to cooperate in establishing a multilateral dialogue, which is to include North Korea, to resolve nuclear tensions on the peninsula.
- June—Yoon Young Kwan and Li Zhaoxing discuss the North Korean nuclear issue on the sidelines of the Association of Southeast Asian Nations Regional Forum in Phnom Penh.
- July—South Korean president Roh Moo Hyun meets with Chinese president Hu Jintao and other senior Chinese leaders in Beijing.
- August—Li Zhaoxing visits Seoul to brief Yoon Young Kwan on preparations for the six-party dialogue in Beijing.
- September—Chinese National People's Congress Standing Committee chairman Wu Bangguo visits South Korea at the invitation of National Assembly speaker Park Swan Yong and meets with President Roh Moo Hyun.
- September—South Korean national security adviser Ra Jong Il visits China for consultations on the North Korean nuclear issue and regional security matters.
- October—Chinese premier Wen Jiabao meets with Roh Moo Hyun at the "Ten Plus Three" summit in Indonesia.
- October—Chinese president Hu Jintao meets with Roh Moo Hyun at the Asia Pacific Economic Cooperation "Economic Leaders" meeting in Bangkok.

2004
- March—South Korean foreign minister Ban Ki Moon meets with Chinese counterpart Li Zhaoxing in Beijing to discuss progress in dealing with the North Korean nuclear crisis.

- August—Ban Ki Moon visits China.
- August—Chinese People's Political Consultative Conference chairman Jia Qinglin arrives in Seoul for consultations marking the rapid expansion of Sino–South Korean economic relations.
- November—South Korean president Roh Moo Hyun meets with Chinese president Hu Jintao at the Asia Pacific Economic Cooperation meeting in Santiago to discuss ways to reconvene the six-party talks as quickly as possible.
- November—Chinese prime minister Wen Jiabao, South Korean president Roh Moo Hyun, and Japanese prime minister Junchiro Koizumi meet on the sidelines of the Association of Southeast Asian Nations "Plus Three" conference in Vientiane, Laos, release a joint action strategy for trilateral coordination to promote stability and development in Northeast Asia.
- December—South Korean National Security Council Standing Committee chairman Chung Dong Young, a special envoy of President Roh Moo Hyun, visits China and meets with National People's Congress chairman Wu Bangguo, State Councilor Tang Jiaxuan, and Foreign Minister Li Zhaoxing.

2005

- January—Chinese premier Wen Jiabao meets with South Korean prime minister Lee Hae Chan on the margins of a special Association of Southeast Asian Nations "Economic Leaders" meeting in Jakarta.
- March—South Korean defense minister Yoon Kwang Ung visits China to meet with Chinese counterparts and tours major Chinese military facilities.
- May—South Korean foreign minister Ban Ki Moon and Chinese foreign minister Li Zhaoxing, on the sidelines of the Asia-Europe Meeting in Kyoto, express concern about the exchange of invective between the United States and North Korea and its implications for resumption of the six-party talks.
- May—Chinese president Hu Jintao and South Korean president Roh Moo Hyun meet in Moscow on the sidelines of the sixtieth-anniversary commemoration of the end of World War II.
- June—South Korean prime minister Lee Hae Chan meets with Chinese counterpart Wen Jiabao during a three-day visit to Beijing and signs a memorandum of understanding on cooperative development of cutting-edge technology, including nano-technology.
- August—Ban Ki Moon meets with Li Zhaoxing in Beijing on the status of the six-party talks prior to visiting Washington, DC.
- September—Li Zhaoxing and Ban Ki Moon meet on the sidelines of the UN General Assembly meeting in New York.

- September—Chinese National People's Congress chairman Wu Bangguo meets with South Korean National Assembly speaker Kim Won Ki on the margins of the Second World Conference of Speakers of Parliaments, in New York.
- October—Chinese vice foreign minister Li Bin visits Seoul to brief South Korean counterpart Song Min Soon on Chinese president Hu Jintao's visit to North Korea and to discuss the anticipated fifth round of six-party talks.
- November—Hu Jintao makes a state visit to South Korea.
- November—Roh Moo Hyun hosts Asia Pacific Economic Cooperation leaders in Pusan.
- December—Roh Moo Hyun meets Wen Jiabao on the sidelines of the East Asian Summit in Kuala Lumpur.

2006

- January—South Korean National Assembly speaker Kim Won Ki visits China and meets with Chinese president Hu Jintao, Communist Party chairman Jia Qinglin, and National People's Congress chairman Wu Bangguo.
- April—Chinese defense minister General Cao Gangchuan makes an official visit to South Korea.
- June—South Korean foreign minister Ban Ki Moon meets with counterpart Li Zhaoxing in China.
- September—Chinese premier Wen Jiabao meets with South Korean president Roh Moo Hyun during the sixth Asia-Europe Meeting, in Helsinki.
- October—Roh Moo Hyun makes a working visit to China, meeting with Hu Jintao and other senior Chinese leaders.
- November—Hu Jintao meets with Roh Moo Hyun during the fourteenth Asia Pacific Economic Cooperation "Economic Leaders" meeting, in Hanoi.

Bibliography

Ahn Joong-young. "Economic Relations Between Korea and China." *Korean Journal of International Studies* 29, no. 1 (Spring–Summer 2002): 61–81.

Cha, Victor D. "Engaging China: Seoul-Beijing Détente and Korean Security." *Survival* 41, no. 1 (Spring 1999): 73–98.

Chen Jian. *China's Road to the Korean War: The Making of the Sino-American Confrontation.* New York: Columbia University Press, 1996.

Chen Xiangming. *As Borders Bend: Transnational Spaces on the Pacific Rim.* Lanham, MD: Rowman and Littlefield, 2005.

Cheong Young-rok. "Impact of China on South Korea's Economy." In *Dynamic Forces on the Korean Peninsula: Strategic and Economic Implications.* Joint U.S.-Korea Economic Studies no. 17. Washington, DC: Korea Economic Institute of America, 2007, pp. 61–82.

Chung Jae Ho. *Between Ally and Partner: Korea-China Relations and the United States.* New York: Columbia University Press, 2006.

Copeland, Dale C. "Economic Interdependence and War: A Theory of Trade Expectations." *International Security* 20, no. 4 (Spring 1996): 5–41.

Cossa, Ralph A., and Jane Khanna. "East Asia: Economic Interdependence and Regional Security." *International Affairs* 73, no. 2 (April 1997): 219–234.

Cotton, James. "China and Tumen River Cooperation: Jilin's Coastal Development Strategy." *Asian Survey* 36, no. 11 (November 1996): 1086–1101.

Dittmer, Lowell. "The Strategic Triangle: An Elementary Game-Theoretical Analysis." *World Politics* 33, no. 4 (July 1981): 485–515.

Eberstadt, Nicholas. *The North Korean Economy: Between Crisis and Catastrophe.* New Brunswick, NJ: Transaction, 2007.

Flake, L. Gordon, and Scott Snyder, eds. *Paved with Good Intentions: The NGO Experience in North Korea.* Westport, CT: Praeger, 2003.

Funabashi, Yoichi. *The Peninsula Question: A Chronicle of the Second North Korean Nuclear Crisis.* Washington, DC: Brookings Institution, 2007.

Garrett, Banning, and Bonnie Glaser. "Looking Across the Yalu: Chinese Assessments of North Korea." *Asian Survey* 35, no. 6 (June 1995): 528–545.

Gill, Bates. *Rising Star: China's New Security Diplomacy.* Washington, DC: Brookings Institution, 2007.

Goldstein, Avery. "The Future of U.S.-China Relations and the Korean Peninsula." *Asian Perspective* 26, no. 3 (2002): 111–129.

Gowa, Joanne. "Bipolarity, Multipolarity, and Free Trade." *American Political Science Review* 83, no. 4 (December 1989): 1245–1256.

Gowa, Joanne, and Edward D. Mansfield. "Power Politics and International Trade." *American Political Science Review* 87, no. 2 (June 1993): 408–420.

Gries, Peter Hayes. "The Koguryo Controversy, National Identity, and Sino-Korean Relations Today." *East Asia* 22, no. 4 (Winter 2005): 3–17.

Gurtov, Mel. "Fragile Partnership: The United States and China." Paper presented at the conference "Dynamics of Northeast Asia and the Korean Peninsula." Seoul, May 27–28, 1999.

Haggard, Stephan, and Marcus Noland. *Famine in North Korea: Markets, Aid, and Reform.* New York: Columbia University Press, 2007.

Ikenberry, John G., and Michael Mastanduno, eds. *International Relations Theory and the Asia Pacific.* New York: Columbia University Press, 2003.

Jia Hao and Zhuang Qubing. "China's Policy Toward the Korean Peninsula." *Asian Survey* 32, no. 12 (December 1992): 1137–1156.

Kim, Samuel S. "China's Conflict-Management Approach to the Nuclear Standoff on the Korean Peninsula." *Asian Perspective* 30, no. 1 (2006): 5–38.

———. "China's New Role in the Nuclear Confrontation." *Asian Perspective* 28, no. 4 (2004): 147–184.

———. "The Dialectics of China's North Korea Policy in a Changing Post–Cold War World." *Asian Perspective* 18, no. 2 (Fall–Winter 1994): 5–36.

———. *North Korean Foreign Relations in the Post–Cold War World.* Carlisle, PA: Strategic Studies Institute, April 2007.

Kim Byungsoo. "The Effect of Social Structural Factors on Foreign Market Entry." Unpublished dissertation, Stanford University, 2005.

Kim Jang Kwon. "Beyond Borders—Local Initiatives of Korea, Japan, and China Towards East Asian Economic Cooperation." Modified version of paper submitted to the Fifth Northeast Asia Economic Forum, Niigata, Japan, pp. 195–212.

Kim Jangho. "Back to the Basics: Multilateral Security Cooperation in Northeast Asia and the Neorealist Paradigm." *Korean Journal of International Relations* 45, no. 5 (2005): 37–56.

Kim Jong Kil. "Economic Relation Between Korea and China: Implications of Korean Economic Crisis for China." *Southeast Asia Studies* 8 (1999): 249–285.

Kim Jung Min. "Dissolution of Korean Minority Families in China: Socio-Demographic Changes in the Yanbian Korean Autonomous Prefecture." In

Study on Women and Family Life, vol. 9. Seoul: Myongji University Institute of Women and Family Life, pp. 67–87.

Kurlantzik, Joshua. *Charm Offensive.* New Haven: Yale University Press, 2007.

Lampton, David M., ed. *The Making of Chinese Foreign and Security Policy in the Era of Reform.* Stanford: Stanford University Press, 2001.

Lee Chae-jin. *China and Korea: Dynamic Relations.* Stanford: Hoover Institution, 1996.

Lee Doowon. "Economic Developments of Korea and China: Focusing on Role of FDI." *Journal of Economic Research* 8 (2003): 71–102.

Lee Jung-yoon and Jean-Paul Rodrigue. "Trade Reorientation and Its Effects on Regional Port Systems: The Korea-China Link Along the Yellow Sea Rim." *Growth and Change* 37, no. 4 (December 2006): 597–619.

Liberman, Peter. "Trading with the Enemy: Security and Relative Economic Gains." *International Security* 21, no. 1 (Summer 1996): 147–175.

Mansfield, Edward D., and Brian M. Pollins. "The Study of Interdependence and Conflict: Recent Advances, Open Questions, and Directions for Future Research." *Journal of Conflict Resolution* 45, no. 6 (December 2001): 834–859.

McMillan, Susan S. "Interdependence and Conflict." *Mershon International Studies Review* 41, no. 1 (May 1997): 33–58.

Medeiros, Evan. "Strategic Hedging and the Future of Asia-Pacific Stability." *Washington Quarterly* 29, no. 1 (Winter 2006): 145–167.

Moltz, James K., ed. *The North Korean Nuclear Program: Security, Strategy, and New Perspectives from Russia.* New York: Routledge, 1999.

Oh Kongdan and Ralph Hassig. *North Korea Through the Looking Glass.* Washington, DC: Brookings Institution, 2000.

Pollack, Jonathan D. *Korea: The East Asian Pivot.* Newport, RI: Naval War College Press, 2005.

Pollins, Brian M. "Does Trade Still Follow the Flag?" *American Political Science Review* 83, no. 2 (June 1989): 465–480.

Qian Qichen. *Waijiao Shiji* [Ten Stories of China's Diplomacy]. Beijing: Shijie Zhishi Chubanshe, 2003.

Rosecrance, Richard. *The Rise of the Trading State: Commerce and Conquest in the Modern World.* New York: Basic, 1986.

Roy, Denny. "Hegemon on the Horizon? China's Threat to East Asian Security." *International Security* 19, no. 1 (Summer 1994): 149–168.

Rozman, Gilbert. *Northeast Asia's Stunted Regionalism: Bilateral Distrust in the Shadow of Globalization.* London: Cambridge University Press, 2004.

Scobell, Andrew. "North Korea's Strategic Intentions." Carlisle, PA: Strategic Studies Institute, July 2005.

Shambaugh, David. "China and the Korean Peninsula: Playing for the Long Term." *Washington Quarterly* 26, no. 2 (Spring 2003): 43–56.

Shambaugh, David, ed., *Power Shift: China and Asia's New Dynamics.* Berkeley: University of California Press, 2006.

Snyder, Scott. *North Korea's Decline and China's Strategic Dilemmas: Report on a June 1997 Research Trip to Beijing, Shenyang, Yanji, and Changchun.* Washington, DC: US Institute of Peace, October 1997.

———. "Six Party Talks: 'Action for Action' and the Formalization of Regional Security Cooperation in Northeast Asia." *International Journal of Korean Unification Studies* 16, no. 1 (2007): 1–24.

So, Alvin S. "South-North Reconciliation and Prospects for North Korea–China Relations." *Asian Perspective* 25, no. 2 (2001): 49–71.

Suh Dae-sook. *Kim Il Sung: The North Korean Leader.* New York: Columbia University Press, 1988.

Sutter, Robert G. *China's Rise in Asia: Promises and Perils.* London: Rowman and Littlefield, 2005.

van Ness, Peter. "Competing Hegemons." *China Journal* no. 36 (July 1996): 125–128.

Wang Fei-ling. "Stability with Uncertainties: U.S.-China Relations and the Korean Peninsula." *Pacific Focus* 20, no. 1 (Spring 2005): 93–134.

Wu, Anne. "What China Whispers to North Korea." *Washington Quarterly* 28, no. 2 (Spring 2005): 35–48.

Wu Baiyi. "The Chinese Security Concept and its Historical Evolution." *Journal of Contemporary China* 10, no. 27 (2001): 275–283.

Yi Xiaoming. "Dynamics of China's South Korea Policy: Assertive Nationalism, Beijing's Changing Strategic Evaluation of the United States, and the North Korea Factor." *Asian Perspective* 24, no. 1 (2000): 71–102.

Yong Deng. *China Rising: Power and Motivation in Chinese Foreign Policy.* London: Rowman and Littlefield, 2004.

Yong Deng and Thomas G. Moore. "China Views Globalization: Toward a New Great-Power Politics?" *Washington Quarterly* 27, no. 3 (Fall 2004): 117–136.

Zhang Liangui. "Coping With a Nuclear North Korea." *China Security* (Autumn 2006): 2–18.

Zhang Xiaoming. "China and Inter-Korean Relations." *Asian Perspective* 26, no. 3 (2002): 131–144.

———. "The Korean Peninsula and China's National Security: Past, Present, and Future." *Asian Perspective* 22, no. 3 (1998): 259–272.

Zhao Quansheng. "China on the Korea Peace and Unification Process." *Pacific Focus* 17, no. 2 (Fall 2002): 117–144.

———. "Moving Toward a Co-Management Approach: China's Policy Toward North Korea and Taiwan." *Asian Perspective* 30, no. 1 (2006): 39–78.

Zheng Bijian. "China's 'Peaceful Rise' to Great-Power Status." *Foreign Affairs* (September–October 2005): 18.

Zhong Yang. "Reunification in Divided Korea and China: A Comparative Study." *Pacific Focus* 7, no. 2 (Fall 1993): 109–129.

Index

Agreement on Reconciliation, Nonaggression, and Exchanges, and Cooperation (Basic Agreement), 31, 32
Albright, Madeleine, 123
Alliances: bilateral, 11; implications of China's economic development for, 2; security, 2, 5, 13; termination of, 5
American Resolution Trust Corporation, 57
Antihegemonism, 208–210
Asia-Europe Meeting (ASEM) (2000), 90
Asia Pacific Economic Cooperation (APEC), 28, 30, 36, 39, 93
Asia Pacific Peace Committee, 122
Aso, Taro, 186
Australia: economic relations with China, 3

Banco Delta Asia, 172, 173
Bangladesh: investment from China in, 116
Ban Ki Moon, 222, 223, 224
Beijing Asian Games (1990), 30
Beijing Motor Show (2006), 74
Bush, George W., 148, 150, 151, 172, 200, 208

Cambodia, 116
Cao Gangchuan, 224
Capital: inflows, 56; investment, 62; markets, 57; shortages, 56, 129

Central Defense Commission, North Korea, 124
Chen Shui Bian, 104
Chi Haotian, 123, 216, 221
China: attempts to move from "special" to "normal" relations with North Korea, 203–204; attempts to show North Korea benefits of economic reform, 157–158; bilateral trade with South Korea, 2, 5; central planning in, 132n6; commitment to recognize sovereignty of North Korea, 145; competition with South Korea in international markets, 48, 49, 62–64, 70, 71–73, 74–76, 77; concerns over separatism by minority ethnic groups, 96; conflict with Japan, 6, 24; conflict with North Korea, 89; cross-border relationships with North Korea, 113; cross-recognition issue, 35, 36; desire for reunification with Taiwan, 28; development assistance from, 7, 9, 14, 112, 126; development strategies, 24; diplomatic brokering role with South Korea, United States and Japan, 110; diplomatic normalization of relations with South Korea, 1, 11, 23–44, 30–34; economic and political relations with North Korea, 109–132; and economic burden of North Korea, 2, 9, 13, 14, 111, 113, 114, 115, 119, 120, 121, 124, 125, 126,

128, 132, 144, 201–203; economic growth in, 1; economic interdependence with South Korea, 6; economic leverage of, 124–127, 157–158, 201–203; economic liberalization in, 84; economic reform in, 2, 6–9, 27; economic relations with Australia, 3; economic relations with South Korea, 1, 2, 15, 47–79; emphasis on formal policy of equidistance between Koreas, 34, 42–44, 84, 85–89; expansion of political influence by, 1; expansion of trade and investment with North Korea, 97, 98; export processing zones in, 53; five principles of peaceful coexistence, 138, 142, 144; focus on regional stability, 118–121; food assistance to North Korea, 119, 120; foreign policy in, 6–9, 138, 141, 142; foreign students in, 2; geo-strategic ties with North Korea, 30; globalization and, 6–9; as gravitational center of East Asia, 12; historical interest in Korean peninsula, 6; identification of South Korea as model for economic development, 54; ideological ties with North Korea, 1, 2, 23–28, 142; implications of economic relations with South Korea for Northeast Asian security, 199–214; increased production capacity in, 63; internalization of border areas policy, 96; investment in neighboring states, 116; investment in North Korea, 116, 117; investment in South Korea, 12, 48, 60, 60*tab,* 71–73; limits of influence over North Korea, 36, 37, 201–203; low labor costs in, 50, 51, 55, 56, 70; managing relations with both Koreas, 141–149; managing nuclear issue with North Korea, 34, 36, 86, 117–118, 124, 125, 143, 147, 148, 149–157, 174–176; marginalization of relations with North Korea, 138; military capacity, 3; motivation for normalization of relations with South Korea, 37–38; nationalism in, 94; need for peaceful regional environment, 142–143; need

to ensure stability in North Korea, 127–130; negative image of products from, 68, 69; normalization of diplomatic relations with Japan, 27; Northeast Asian history project, 94–97; North Korean attempts to leverage economic dependency and, 130–132; North Korean defiance of, 2; objections to North Korean nuclear testing, 12; objections to US–South Korea alliance, 102–103; one China policy, 84, 85; one-Korea policy in Cold War, 24–28; opening of relations with United States, 27; phases of development of political relations with South Korea, 84–93; policy dilemmas for future of North Korea, 137–158; policy of soft coercion toward North Korea, 14, 15; policy shift from equidistance to stability, 118–121; political alienation from North Korea, 4; political challenges in Sino–South Korean relationship, 64–76, 83–106; political impact of rise of, 9–13; political influence in East Asia, 3; political relations with South Korea since normalization, 84–93; primary interests and needs for future, 140–141; provincial-level relations with North Korea, 113; public opinion on Japan in, 185, 186; recovery of relations with North Korea, 121–124; regional stability interests, 85–89; regional strategy of, 141; rejection of sanction approaches to North Korea, 14, 15; relations with United States, 141; reserves of US dollars, 116; resolution of border disputes by, 8, 9; rising regional role of, 140–141; rivalry with Japan over Korean peninsula, 183–196; special economic zones in, 50, 53, 125; state-owned enterprise structure in, 54; strategy toward North Korea, 174–176; Strike Hard campaign against refugees in, 100; and Taiwan, 103–104; three-point economic cooperation policy with North Korea, 126–127; and Tibet, 103–104; as tourist destination, 2; trade with

North Korea, 41*tab,* 111, 112*tab,* 115, 116; trade with South Korea, 41*tab,* 47–48, 49*tab,* 59; tries to change friendship prices to market prices in North Korea, 33, 42, 111, 114; two-Korea policy of, 16, 23–44; UN membership, 35; view of North Korea as hedge against instability, 204–205; views of economic future of North Korea, 127–130; in World Trade Organization, 48, 55, 58–62, 67, 91. *See also* Sino–North Korean relationship; Sino–South Korean relationship

China Council for the Promotion of International Trade (CCPIT), 30

China Minmetals Corporation, 127

China National Overseas Oil Corporation (CNOOC), 61, 71

Choe Kwang, 215

Choe Thae Bok, 216

Choi Sung Hong, 222

Cho Song Tae, 221

Chun Doo Hwan, 32

Chung Dong Young, 223

Clinton, William J., 88, 117, 119, 211

Cold War: Chinese one-Korea policy in, 24–28; collapse of Soviet Union and, 1, 30; new, 189–191; trade and investment patterns since, 5

Conflict: China/Japan, 24; economic interdependence and, 11, 40–42; Japan/Russia, 24; labor-management, 61, 71, 72; likelihood of, 11; management, 83; military, 10, 151, 183; relationship to trade, 11; theory of trade expectations and, 40–42

Cooperation: comprehensive, 141; economic, 1, 37, 38, 144; industrial, 92; inter-Korean, 195; multilateral, 7, 38, 89–91, 143; political, 11, 15, 41, 48, 85; projects, 54; regional, 3, 85; security, 11, 143

Crawford Consensus, 150

Currency: devaluation, 56; nonconvertible, 57

Currency crisis, 55

Da Bingguo, 216

Daewoo Shipbuilding, 74

Dalai Lama, 104

Delto Banco Asia, 122

Democratic People's Republic of Korea (DPRK). *See* North Korea

Deng Xiaoping, 27, 28, 33, 37, 42, 43, 118, 119, 120, 123, 153, 213, 217

Development: assistance, 7, 112; of cross-border markets, 10; economic, 8, 64, 91, 138, 139, 141; equitable, 64; export-led, 1, 25, 54; loans, 54; overseas strategy, 9; regional, 141; regional stability and, 8; sustained, 140; technology, 63

Diplomacy: balanced, 141; "behind the scenes," 130; coercive, 171, 172; competitive, 123; hijack, 29; international, 155; maxi-mini, 30; mediation, 148; modern-state, 183; normalization and, 11, 23–44; open, 187; shuttle, 143, 147, 151, 152, 210; sports, 29, 30; torpedo, 29

East Asia: China as gravitational center of, 12; Chinese political influence in, 3; concept of nation-state in, 183; financial crisis in, 7; historical rivalries in, 6

Economic: assistance, 25; central planning, 24; collapse, 13; complementarities, 55; cooperation, 1, 37, 38, 125, 126, 144; dependency, 4, 7, 74–76; development, 64, 91, 138, 139, 141; exchange, 10; integration, 5, 14, 76–79; leverage, 3, 4, 48, 97, 109, 124–127, 157–158, 175, 201–203; policy, 10; protectionism, 61; reform, 2, 6–9, 14, 24, 27, 33, 127, 129, 143, 157–158; sanctions, 37; stabilization, 124, 126, 139; stagnation, 61; tensions, 62; transformative engagement strategies, 12

Economic interdependence, 4–6, 6–9; for attainment of political leverage, 13; as centripetal force, 7; and China's relations with Korean peninsula, 13–15, 201–206; comparison of opportunities against political costs, 34; contribution to peace and, 13; debates over, 9–13; effects on political relations, 104–106; and fears of economic

dependency, 15, 62–64; and future prospects for trade, 11; implications for US–South Korea alliance, 207–214; influence on political goals, 4; keeping the peace and, 11; likelihood of conflict and, 40–42; military conflict and, 10; opportunities for political cooperation in, 48; political and security issues with, 76–79; political influence and, 9–13; and political vulnerability, 48; reduction of likelihood of conflict and, 8; regional stability and, 13; security cooperation and, 195; strategic implications of, 74–76; as tool for constraining United States, 8
Economy: domestic, 62; market, 144, 203; planned, 203; political, 10, 48
Environmental issues, 92
Export-Import Bank of Korea, 58, 71

Five principles of peaceful coexistence, 138, 142, 144

Gando Treaty (1909), 96
Garlic wars, 65–67
Globalization: China and, 6–9; creation of domestic constituencies for international trade and, 48; political/security benefits from; seen as inevitable, 140; transformation of great-power politics and, 8
Gong Ro Myung, 220
Gorbachev, Mikhail, 32
Great Leap Forward, 26, 119, 120
Great West Development project, 92

Hall, Bobby, 118
Han Seung Soo, 221
Han Sung Joo, 86, 219
Hegemonism, 208–210; constraining, 8; of United States, 8, 147, 150
Hong Kong, 30, 33, 34, 58; indirect trade through, 42; as newly industrializing economy, 54
Hong Song Nam, 114, 215
Hong Soon Young, 220, 221
Huang Ju, 221
Hu Jintao, 85, 91, 124, 126, 141, 152, 153, 216, 217, 222, 223, 224

Human rights, 99, 108*n26*, 145
Hwang Jang Yop, 89, 98, 119, 120, 121
Hyundai Motors, 70, 73, 74, 122

India: strategic relationship with United States, 3
Indonesia: financial crisis in, 57; US attempts to strengthen ties with, 3
Industrial espionage, 73–74, 77
Industrialization: export-led, 5; South Korean, 1
Institute of Disarmament and Peace (North Korea), 31
Interaction, triangular: coalition formation and, 165; dynamics of, 165–168; "ménage à trois," 165; relevance of concept, 168–170; "romantic triangle," 165, 166, 168, 179; "stable marriage," 165, 166; strategic alignments and, 165; as vehicle for addressing regional security issues, 165
Interaction, triangular (China, United States, Soviet Union), 165
Interaction, triangular (South Korea, China, North Korea): attempts by North Korea to leverage economic dependency, 130–132; "China threat" and, 62–64; Chinese economic leverage in, 124–127, 157–158; Chinese investment in South Korea and, 71–73; Chinese relations with North Korea and, 109–132; Chinese transition from equidistance policy, 85–89, 118–121; competition for influence over North Korea in, 97–98; economic dependency *vs.* economic interdependence, 74–76; economic relations, 47–79; emerging political challenges in, 83–106; financial crisis and, 55–58; industrial espionage in, 73–74; inter-Korean reconciliation in, 89–91; managing Chinese policy toward North Korea, 141–149; multilateral cooperation and, 89–91; nuclear crisis and, 117–118, 149–157, 170–178; political challenges of economic relations, 64–76; political implications of economic integration,

76–79; refugee issues, 98–102; regional role for China, 140–141; regional stability and, 89–91; role of United States in, 102–103; security issues, 76–79; Sino–South Korean relationship in, 47–79; South Korean dependency and, 62–64; strategic policy dilemmas in, 137–158; trade disputes, 67–69; views of North Korea's economic future in, 127–130

Interaction, triangular (South Korea, China, United States), 163–180; competition between South Korea and United States in, 169; incentives for cooperation in, 167; nuclear crisis and, 164, 167, 169, 170–178; possible replacement of role of United States in, 166; relevance in consideration of North Korean issues, 164; relevance of, 166; as "romantic triangle" example, 168–170; security issues, 163–180

Interaction, triangular (South Korea, Japan, United States), 191–193

Interaction, triangular (United States, China, Japan), 165, 167, 169

Interaction, triangular (United States, China, Taiwan), 165

Interaction, triangular (United States, China, Vietnam), 165

International Atomic Energy Association (IAEA), 86, 150

International Crisis Group, 112

International Monetary Fund (IMF), 56

Investment: capital, 9, 62; diversification of, 15; expansion, 7; flows, 58, 59; foreign direct, 2, 48, 50, 58, 59, 65, 70; global, 58, 116; growth of, 12; infrastructure, 64; in labor-intensive sectors, 50, 51; manufacturing, 50; overseas, 60; overseas direct, 71, 116; as "pass through" for goods, 52, 54; policy, 70; politically directed, 126; post Cold War patterns, 5

Iraq War, 192

Japan: alliance with United States, 3, 88; conflict with China, 6, 24; conflict with Russia, 24; control of Korean peninsula, 25; cross-recognition issue, 35, 36; defeat in World War II, 25; divergence in South Korean and Chinese approaches to, 185; economic ties with North Korea, 14; historical interest in Korean peninsula, 6; imperialistic legacy of, 88; investment in China and United States, 59; Meiji Restoration in, 6; military buildup in, 194; normalization of diplomatic relations with China, 27; public opinion on China in, 186; relations with North Korea, 110, 130; relations with South Korea, 88, 96; rivalry with China over Korean peninsula, 183–196; as traditional security country, 198$n19$

Jiang Zemin, 54, 85, 88, 90, 91, 116, 123, 124, 131, 149, 150, 184, 185, 215, 216, 219, 220, 221

Jia Qinglin, 216, 223, 224

Jo Myong Rok, 216

Kang Sok Ju, 217

Kim Dae Jung, 13, 56, 84, 89, 90, 91, 122, 153, 166, 168, 188, 195, 220, 221, 222

Kim Dok Hong, 89, 119, 120

Kim Il Sung, 14, 23, 24, 25, 26, 27, 28, 35, 36, 86, 87, 110, 118, 120, 213

Kim Jong Il, 14, 57, 86, 116, 118, 122, 123, 124, 126, 129, 146, 152, 153, 174, 178, 216, 217

Kim Kye Gwan, 146, 210

Kim Soo Han, 220

Kim Won Ki, 224

Kim Young Nam, 121, 122, 215, 217

Kim Young Sam, 54, 84, 85, 87, 88, 104, 119, 120, 184, 189, 211, 219, 220

Kissinger, Henry, 27

Koguryo dispute, 83, 85, 92, 94–97, 207

Koizumi, Junichiro, 186, 192, 223

Korea-China Friendship Association, 76

Korean Asset Management Corporation (KAMCO), 57

Korea Institute for International Economic Policy (KIEP), 76

Korea International Trade Association (KITA), 63, 67

Korean National Intelligence Service, 74

Korean Overseas International
Cooperation Agency (KOICA),
54
Korean peninsula: autonomous Yanbian
region in, 95, 97; and China's rising
regional role, 140–141; Chinese
objectives toward, 14; Chosun
dynasty on, 6, 24; controlled by
Japan, 25; denuclearization of, 147;
goal of stability on, 137; historical
ties to China, 6; implications of
reunification for Sino-Japanese
rivalry, 193–195; inter-Korean
summits on, 122; Japanese
influences on, 6; nuclear crisis and,
149–157; perceptions of Chinese
heavy-handedness on, 146;
reunification on, 84, 88, 89–91, 103,
193–195, 212–213; Sino-Japanese
rivalry and, 183–196; US military
on, 11
Korean Peninsula Energy Development
Organization (KEDO), 86, 115, 118,
150
Korea Trade-Investment Promotion
Agency (KOTRA), 76
Korea Trade Promotion Corporation,
30
Korean War, 24, 25, 27

Laos: development assistance to, 9
Lee Hae Chan, 223
Lee Han Dong, 221
Lee Hee Beom, 63
Lee Joung Binn, 221
Lee Man Sup, 221
Lee Myung Bak, 85, 102, 164, 168, 175,
178
Lee Sang Ock, 39, 219
Liaoning SG Automotive, 74
Liberalization: currency, 55, 57;
economic, 84; financial, 48, 56, 57,
58; market, 58, 67; trade, 67
Li Bin, 224
Li Changchun, 217
Li Hung Chang, 183
Li Lanquing, 215
Lim Dong Won, 222
Li Peng, 35, 114, 215, 216, 219, 220,
221
Li Zhaoxing, 216, 217, 222, 223, 224

Malaysia: US attempts to strengthen ties
with, 3
Manchuria, 95
Mao Zedong, 23, 24, 25, 118, 169
Markets: access to, 49, 73; bond, 56,
80$n14$; capital, 57; competition for,
206; competition in, 63; consumer,
70; cross-border, 10; diversification
in, 77; domestic, 58, 59, 61, 63, 65,
70, 71; equity, 56, 80$n14$;
international, 54, 62, 63, 66, 70, 77;
open, 10; preferential access to, 25;
third-country, 12, 58, 60, 62, 206
Meiji Restoration, 6
Military Armistice Commission, 118,
167
Moon Chung-in, 187
Multipolarization, 7
Murtaugh, Philip, 72
Myanmar: development assistance to, 9;
investment from China in, 116

Nationalism, 188; Chinese, 94;
emotional, 188; ethnic, 95; South
Korean, 3, 94
Neutral Nations Supervisory
Commission (NNSC), 118
Nixon, Richard, 27
Nongovernmental organizations, 101
Northeast Asia: China's political
influence in, 1
North Korea: adventurism of, 29;
attempts to leverage economic
dependency, 130–132; autarkic
economic policies in, 27; central
planning in, 27; Chinese economic
leverage on, 124–127; Chinese
policy of soft coercion toward, 14,
15; Chinese strategy toward,
174–176; command economy in,
203; competition over between South
Korea and China, 97, 98; conflict
with China, 89; continuous
deterioration in, 139; crisis
escalation tactics of, 14; cross-border
relationships with China, 113; cross-
recognition issue, 35, 36; danger of
instability from collapse of state in,
120; defiance of China by, 2;
development assistance to, 9, 13;
dissatisfaction with economic

dependence on China, 12; domestic politics in, 25; economic and political relations with China, 109–132; economic dependence on China, 2, 9, 13, 14, 111, 113, 114, 115, 119, 120, 121, 124, 125, 126, 128, 132, 144, 201–203; economic reform in, 127, 129, 143; economic stagnation in, 44; economic ties with Japan, 14; evicted of nuclear inspectors, 86, 150; as failed state, 144, 145, 156; failure to pay for goods from China, 113, 127; famine in, 84, 99, 100, 114, 115, 119; fear of instability in, 14; feelings of betrayal of socialist ideals by China, 2; flow of refugees from, 13, 92, 98–102, 119, 152, 156; food crisis in, 9; geo-strategic ties with China, 30; gross national product, 110–111, 111ltab; as hedge against instability for China, 204–205; high-level interactions with China, 87*fig,* 123, 131*fig,* 215–217; ideological ties with China, 1, 2, 23–28, 142; infrastructure projects in, 125; isolation of, 139, 141, 143, 144; levels of change in, 154; market economy in, 203; market-oriented economy attempts in, 122, 123; "military-first politics" in: 139-140; nuclear program in, 12, 14, 34, 36, 85, 86, 92, 116, 117–118, 124, 125, 149–157; participation in nuclear talks, 88, 89; playing China and Soviet Union against each other, 25, 27; policy dilemmas for future of, 137–158; political alienation from China, 4; political weakness of, 84, 88, 141, 145; preservation of independence from China and, 13; provincial-level relations with China, 113; recovery of relations with China, 121–124; refugee flows from, 9, 13, 84, 87; regime survival in, 13, 109, 156; rejection of cooperation by, 143; relations with Japan, 110, 130; relations with United States, 110; restricted access to Chinese banking system, 14; sanctions against, 155, 172; seeking to draw United States into dialogue, 117–118; shock of collapse of Soviet Union in, 31, 110; South Korean strategy toward, 176–178; strategic realignment in, 213–214; tension with United States, 150; three-point economic cooperation policy with China, 126–127; trade with China, 41*tab,* 111, 112*tab,* 115, 116; trade with South Korea, 111, 112*tab*; treaties of friendship with Soviet Union/China, 27; "two meals a day" campaign in, 119; uncooperative behavior by, 139, 154–157; US strategy toward, 171–174; UN membership, 35; unwillingness to pursue reform, 44. *See also* Sino–North Korean relationship

North Korea Freedom Coalition, 108*n26*

Nuclear Nonproliferation Treaty (NPT), 37, 86, 150

Obuchi, Keizo, 185

Olympic Games: Beijing (2008), 92, 104, 209; Seoul (1988), 29

Operation East Sea, 39

Organization for Economic Cooperation and Development (OECD), 185

Pak Bong Ju, 217

Parhae kingdom dispute, 92, 96

Park Chi Won, 122

Park Chung Hee, 25, 27, 28, 64, 80*n14,* 95

Park Swan Yong, 222

People's Republic of China (PRC). *See* China

Policy: economic, 10; investment, 70; one-Korea, 24–28

Political: constituencies, 10; cooperation, 11, 15, 41, 48, 85; economy, 10; instability, 13, 87, 109, 112, 145; leverage, 14; multipolarization, 8; stabilization, 124

Power: national, 140; regional, 7, 38; state, 10

Production sectors: automobiles, 59, 60, 61, 63, 65, 73; communications, 59; computers, 60; electronics, 59; heavy industry, 60; intermediate goods, 59,

60; mobile phones, 61, 63; petrochemical, 67; semiconductors, 63, 73; shipbuilding, 63, 74; steel, 67, 73; telecommunications, 60

Qian Qichen, 28, 35, 36, 37, 39, 86, 216, 219, 220, 222
Qing Dynasty, 6

Reagan, Ronald, 31
Reform: economic, 2, 6–9, 14, 24, 27, 33, 127, 129, 143, 157–158; land, 24
Refugees: exploitation of, 101; friction over handling of, 98–102; media coverage of, 100–101; from North Korea, 9, 13, 84, 98–102, 152, 156; trafficking in, 100
Regional: cooperation, 3, 85, 141, 144; development, 141; economic strategy, 143; institutions, 89; integration, 91; multilateralism, 141; polarization, 189–191; power, 7, 38; responsibility, 142; rivalry, 212–213; security, 3, 6, 139; stability, 3, 8, 9, 13, 84, 85–91, 103, 110, 116, 138, 139, 141, 142–143, 164, 173, 189, 199, 200; views of third-party roles, 3
Republic of Korea (ROK). *See* South Korea
Roh Moo Hyun, 13, 85, 91, 92, 103, 166, 186, 187, 188, 191, 195, 207, 222, 223, 224
Roh Tae Woo, 30, 32, 36, 38, 39, 40, 43, 219
Ro Tu Chol, 217
Russia: conflict with Japan, 24; historical interest in Korean peninsula, 6
Russo-Japanese War (1904), 6

Samsung Heavy Industries, 74
Security: alliances, 2, 5, 13; confidence building in, 31; cooperation, 11, 143, 195; energy, 116; enhancement, 7; externalities, 4–6; multilateral, 11; Northeast Asian, 199–214; policy, 3; regional, 3, 6, 139
Seoul Asian Games (1986), 29
Separatism, 96, 97
Shanghai, 53, 59, 122

Shanghai Automotive Investment Corporation (SAIC), 60, 71–73
Shanghai Cooperation Organization (SCO), 8
Shanghai Exposition (2010), 92
Shevardnadze, Eduard, 32, 36
Shin Kanemaru, 32
Sin Ch'ae Ho, 95
Singapore, 33; investment in China, 59; as newly industrializing economy, 54; US attempts to strengthen ties with, 3
Sino-Japanese War (1894), 6, 183
Sino–North Korean relationship, 109–132; Chinese management of North Korean policy, 141–149; conflicts in, 89; defense ties, 123; economic and political relations, 109–132; economic future of North Korea in, 127–130; effect of China's diplomatic normalization with South Korea on, 109, 111, 114; equidistance policy in, 42–44, 84, 85–89, 118–121; food crisis, 84, 99, 100, 114, 115, 119; ideological ties in, 1, 2, 23–28; importance of petroleum in, 114, 115, 115*tab*; links between economic assistance and improved political relations, 121–124; multiple channels of communication in, 113; North Korea attempts to leverage economic dependency in, 130–132; nuclear crisis and, 12, 14, 34, 36, 85, 86, 88, 89, 92, 116, 117–118, 124, 125; policy dilemmas for future, 137–158; recovery of, 121–124; refugees and, 9, 13, 84, 87, 92, 98–102, 119; regional stability policy in, 118–121; role of Chinese economic leverage in, 124–127; strains in, 117–118; trade in, 111, 112*tab*, 113, 115, 116
Sino–South Korean relationship: absence of Soviet Union as critical factor in, 31; addressing unresolved political issues, 93–104; border issues in, 94–97; "China Threat" in, 62–64; competition for influence over North Korea in, 97–98; crises leading to closer ties, 29; diplomatic

normalization, 1, 11, 23–44; economic, 1, 2, 6, 15, 37, 38, 47–79; economic dependency issues in, 62–64; economic honeymoon period, 49–55; economic revitalization in, 58–62; effects of, 40–42; effects of political issues on economic relations, 104–106; factors in normalization of relations, 30–34; financial crisis and, 55–58; future economic prospects, 104–106; historical, 6; initial Chinese drift toward South Korea, 28–30; investment, 12, 30, 50, 58–62, 71–73; overseas training contracts in, 61; political and security issues with economic integration, 76–79; political challenges of economic relations in, 64–76, 83–106; political relations since normalization, 84–93; since normalization, 48–64; "technology leakage" in, 73–74; trade, 2, 5, 30, 34, 40–42, 47, 49*tab,* 58–62; US role in, 102–103

Smuggling, 113, 172

Song Ho Gyong, 118, 122

South Korea: alliance with United States, 102–103, 164, 188; avoidance of regional polarization by, 189–191; bilateral trade with China, 2, 5; chaebols in, 48, 56, 57; "China fever" in, 55, 58, 77; "China lobby" in, 48; choice between United States and China, 164, 165; competition with China for influence over North Korea, 97, 98; concerns about Chinese influence in North Korea, 146; concerns about economic dependence on China, 49, 64–76; concerns about political challenges of economic relations with China, 64–76; diplomatic normalization of relations with China, 1, 11, 23–44; diplomatic relations with Taiwan, 35; discomfort over reemergence of Sino-Japanese rivalry, 183–186; economic dependence on China as issue, 205–206; economic relations with China, 1, 2, 14, 15, 47–79; export-led development in, 1; financial crisis in, 48, 55–58;

financial reform in, 56; financial vulnerability in, 56; foreign policy orientation, 208–210; free trade agreement with United States, 13, 48, 75; high-level interactions with China, 87*fig,* 219–223; hollowing out of domestic economy in, 65, 69–71; illiberal leadership in, 25; implications of economic relations with China for Northeast Asian security, 199–214; industrial espionage against, 73–74; industrialization in, 1; inter-Korean reconciliation policy, 85, 88, 89–91; investment in China, 2, 12, 48, 50, 50*tab,* 51, 52*tab;* investment in United States, 48; military authoritarian regime in, 32, 54; motives for diplomatic normalization with China, 38–40; National Agricultural Cooperative Federation, 65; nationalism in, 3, 94, 188; need for tilt toward strong ally by, 3; nongovernmental organizations in, 101; Nordpolitik policy in, 32, 38, 43; normalization of diplomatic relations with Soviet Union, 32, 38; and North Korean defectors, 99; "peace and prosperity" policy in, 85; policy toward North Korea, 84, 87, 89–91; political challenges in Sino–South Korean relationship, 64–76, 83–106; political liberalization in, 32; political relations with China since normalization, 84–93; preferential access to US markets for, 25; preservation of balancing role between Japan and China, 186–189, 190, 197*n9;* preservation of independence from China and, 13; public opinion on importance of United States *vs.* China as partners, 94, 95; relations with Japan, 88, 96; role with larger regional powers, 187; security alliance with United States, 2, 3, 15; security cooperation and, 195; security needs, 164, 165; strategy toward North Korea, 176–178; Sunshine Policy in, 89, 90; and Taiwan, 103–104; and Tibet,

103–104; trade with China, 41*tab,* 47–48, 49*tab,* 59; trade with North Korea, 111, 112*tab*; US economic assistance to, 25; UN membership, 34, 35; willingness to dispense with Taiwan, 38, 39. *See also* Sino–South Korean relationship
Ssangyong Motors, 60, 61, 71–73
State(s): dependent, 41; failed, 7, 144, 145; power, 10; regional, 141; weak, 7
Strategic flexibility question, 3, 190, 192, 193

Tae'an Friendship Glass Factory, 126, 127, 217
Taft-Katsura Memorandum, 6
Taiwan, 30, 33, 43, 169; Chinese desire for reunification with, 28; diplomatic isolation of, 37, 38, 39; diplomatic relations with South Korea, 35; economic engagement strategies in, 12; investment in China, 59; marginalization of, 35, 103–104; as newly industrializing economy, 54; US interventions and, 3
Takeshima Island, 186, 192
Tang Jiaxuan, 118, 121, 215, 217, 220, 221, 222
Tariffs, 65
Technology: access to, 61; communication, 61; development, 63; environmental, 92; gap, 205; higher-value-added, 77; information, 60, 61; "leakage," 73–74; proprietary, 65, 74, 77; stolen, 73, 74; theft, 77; and theft of intellectual property, 65; transfer, 65, 70, 74, 206
Thailand: financial crisis in, 57; North Korean refugee flows through, 101
Theories: ideological, 129; international political economy, 48; international relations, 9, 10, 12; liberal, 10, 11; neoliberal, 10; realist, 10, 11; of trade expectations, 11, 40
Tiananmen Square incident, 29, 32
Tianma Auto, 74
Tibet, 103–104
Tourism, 2
Trade: between adversaries, 4; balances, 53, 53*tab,* 54, 57, 63, 113; barter, 26;

bilateral, 2, 12, 25, 30, 42, 49, 59, 67, 114, 116, 124, 128; border, 113, 125; cross-border, 26, 144, 203; deficits, 53; dependence, 10; as determining factor in political relations, 11; with developing states, 7; disputes, 66, 67–69; diversification, 15, 78; dumping in, 62, 67–69; expansion, 7; expectations, 11, 40–42; flows, 54; "follows the flag," 11; free, 5, 13, 48, 67, 75; future, 16, 24, 40; future prospects for, 11; global, 116; growth, 58; indirect, 42; inter-Asian, 3; liberalization, 67; market-based, 110, 114, 115; patterns, 7; post Cold War patterns, 5; reinforcement of relations between allies, 4; relationship to conflict, 11; unfair practices in, 77; unrecorded, 113
Treaty of Portsmouth, 6
Trilateral Coordination and Oversight Group (TCOG), 196

Unilateralism, 208
United Nations: Economic and Social Committee of the Asia Pacific, 39; membership issues, 34–37; resolutions condemning North Korea, 151, 173; Security Council, 37; World Heritage locations, 92
United Nations Command, 167
United Nations High Commissioner for Refugees (UNHCR), 99, 100, 145
United States: alliance with Japan, 3, 88; alliance with South Korea, 102–103, 164, 188; bilateral trade with South Korea, 5; cross-recognition issue, 35, 36; diminishing role on Korean peninsula, 122; enhanced position for Japanese alliance, 191–193; focus on cooperation with China, 200; free trade agreement with South Korea, 13, 48, 75; "hedging" against rise of China, 3; hegemonism of, 8, 147, 150; implications of Chinese policies for, 210–212; investment in China, 59; and nuclear crisis in North Korea, 118, 149–157; opening of

relations with China, 27; preferential access to markets for South Korea, 25; pressure for withdrawal of troops from South Korea, 147; regional role of, 11; relations with North Korea, 110, 118; response to North Korean pursuit of strategic realignment, 213–214; role in Sino–South Korean relationship, 102–103; security alliance with South Korea, 2, 3, 15; security policy in Asia, 3; strategic relationship with India, 3; strategy toward North Korea, 171–174; "Super 301" legislation, 37; and Taiwan, 3; tension with North Korea, 150
Unocal Corporation, 61, 71
US Trade Representative, 37

Vietnam: North Korean refugee flows through, 101; US attempts to strengthen ties with, 3

Wang Guangya, 8
Wang Jiarui, 152, 217
Wang Yi, 152
Wen Jiabao, 76, 217, 222, 223, 224
World Trade Organization (WTO), 48, 55, 58–62, 65, 67, 68, 91
Wu Bangguo, 222, 224
Wu Dawei, 217
Wu Yi, 126, 217

Xu Bo, 103, 104
Xu Caihou, 216

Yang Shangkun, 36, 123, 219
Yasukuni shrine, 186, 192
Yoo Chong Ha, 220
Yoon Kwang Ung, 223
Yoon Young Kwan, 222

Zeng Paiyan, 217
Zhu Rongji, 90, 121, 168, 220, 221

About the Book

With China now South Korea's largest trading partner and destination for foreign investment and tourism, what are the implications for politics and security in East Asia?

In *China's Rise and the Two Koreas,* Scott Snyder explores the transformation of the Sino–South Korean relationship since the early 1990s, assessing the strategic significance of recent developments in China's relationship with both North and South Korea as well as the likely consequences of those developments for US and Japanese influence in the region. His meticulous study lends important context to critical debates regarding China's foreign policy, Northeast Asian security, and international relations more broadly.

Scott Snyder is senior associate in both the International Relations Program of the Asia Foundation and the Pacific Forum CSIS. He is author of *Negotiating on the Edge: North Korean Negotiating Behavior* and coeditor (with L. Gordon Flake) of *Paved with Good Intentions: The NGO Experience in North Korea.*